Winning With the Dutch

ROBERT BELLIN

B. T. Batsford Ltd, *London*

First published 1990

© Robert Bellin 1990

ISBN 0 7134 5760 0

A CIP catalogue record for this book is available from the British Library

Typeset by Lasertext, Manchester
and printed in Great Britain by
Dotesios (Printers) Ltd,
Trowbridge, Wilts
for the publishers,
B. T. Batsford Ltd,
4 Fitzhardinge Street,
London W1H 0AH

A BATSFORD CHESS BOOK
Adviser: R. D. Keene GM, OBE
Technical Editor: Ian Kingston

Contents

Introduction

Welcome to the very special world of the Dutch Defence! This most versatile of defences to 1 d4 boasts several positive features: it is forcing (White cannot prevent you playing your defence, as is the case with, say, the Nimzo-Indian); it rules out radical strategic simplification (as occurs, for example, in the Queen's Gambit Declined when White plays the Exchange Variation); and it does not permit early major material simplification (which happens in standard lines of the popular King's Indian and Grünfeld Defences).

So how on earth is it that even now the Dutch Defence is something of a secret? The reason has its origin in the nineteenth century, when the massively influential world champion Wilhelm Steinitz ('the founder of modern chess') dogmatically dismissed the Dutch after a couple of crushing victories over Zukertort in the 1872 title match. His pedagogical pre-eminence was such as to eclipse the fact, for example, that the no less legendary Paul Morphy had regularly used the Dutch with success. The result was that the defence went under a cloud for generations.

The process of rehabilitation began in the 1920s, spearheaded by World Champions Alekhine and Botvinnik, and gradually continued until the point was reached in the 1951 World Championship match where it was employed by both players. Despite this zenith, the Dutch was subsequently once again overshadowed throughout the sixties and seventies, this time by exciting developments in the other major defences. Now at long last it seems that the Dutch's time has come as more and more top players have become aware of its creative and combative potential. The resurgence of interest during the eighties has sown a seed which will surely develop as we go into the last decade of the twentieth century.

This book summarizes the current state of all the major variations of the Dutch Defence and, in addition to its purely didactic aims, is intended to provide a useful and reliable basis for competitive preparation right across the spectrum from club to international level. The annotated illustrative games on which each chapter is based, including classics from the turn of the century as well as modern masterpieces, have been selected for their exceptional instructive value regarding typical plans, stratagems and tactics. Those who are new to the Dutch would be best advised first of all to simply play through the games without worrying too much about the detailed opening notes. This will enable the reader to find quickly which variation most appeals and obtain a basic 'feel' for it before proceeding to a more technical examination of its theoretical nuances.

One of the great advantages of playing the Dutch is that it is really several different defences in one: not only are there the three major variations—the Leningrad, Ilyin-Zhenevsky and Stonewall— but also other interesting lines such as the Hort–Antoshin, the hybrid Alekhine, and the Dutch Indian. Of these, the (mainly tact-ical) Leningrad and (mainly positional) Stonewall are currently the most popular and successful.

This book is selective in that poor lines for Black have generally been omitted (although, of course, not all of them, as it is as essential to know what is bad and does not work as to know what is good and does), but the assessments and opinions given are intended to be objective. In addition to presenting a distillation of current knowledge of the Dutch I have also sprinkled a few totally new suggestions here and there which the brave reader may care to try out.

It is my hope that those who work through this book diligently will acquire the information and understanding necessary to be able to step out successfully on the creative and very rewarding path of 'Winning With the Dutch'.

Acknowledgements

My thanks are due to Bob Wade for providing the friendliest of research facilities and to Clive Cubitt for his painstaking proof-reading.

1 Leningrad Main Line: 7 ... c6

The Leningrad Variation is characterized by the fianchetto of Black's KB which produces a curious kind of Dutch/King's Indian hybrid. The fact that Black has left his e-pawn unmoved makes communication between the wings more difficult, but on the other hand keeps his central structure very sound. Since it is virtually obligatory sooner or later to play ... d6, Black always has to keep an eye on the sensitive e6 square. In general, White will concentrate his attention on the centre and the queenside whilst Black will monitor the centre and develop counterplay on one or both flanks. Not surprisingly, the resulting middlegames are often extremely complex, both strategically and tactically. Battle may often be conducted on several fronts simultaneously and sometimes the whole board can be ablaze with action. All in all, then, the Leningrad is tailor-made for the adventurous player seeking challenge and excitement.

The introductory moves are as follows:

1	d4	f5
2	g3	♘f6
3	♗g2	g6
4	♘f3	♗g7
5	0–0	0–0
6	c4	d6
7	♘c3	c6 (1)

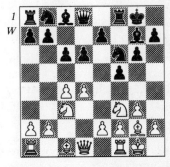

The basic idea of this move is to free the square c7 for the queen from where it can support the advance ... e7–e5. In addition, it controls d5, blunts the action of White's KB on the long diagonal

1

and creates the option of exerting direct pressure on the queenside by ... ♕b6 or, occasionally, ... ♕a5. As there is no immediate threat, White's range of response is very wide, although only the immediate advance of the d-pawn is generally thought to offer White chances of an opening advantage. Before considering the main move in detail we briefly note some alternatives:

(a) 8 ♖e1 ♘e4 9 ♕d3 ♘xc3 10 bc e5 11 e4 ♕a5 12 ♗g5 (thus far Holmov–Bannik, USSR Ch. 1962) 12 ... d5! 13 cd fe 14 ♕xe4 cd 15 ♕c2 e4 =.

(b) 8 b3 a5 9 ♗b2 ♘a6 10 ♕c2 ♕c7 11 ♖ad1 e5 12 c5 (Pachman–Gerusel, Mannheim 1975) 12 ... e4 13 cd ♕xd6 14 ♘e5 ♘b4 15 ♕b1 ♗e6 with a promising position for Black.

(c) 8 ♕c2 ♕c7 (8 ... ♔h8 is a useful alternative, e.g. 9 ♗g5 ♗e6 10 b3 ♘bd7 11 ♖ad1 d5 12 ♘e5 ♘e4 = Belyavsky–Yusupov, Reykjavik 1988) 9 e4 fe 10 ♘xe4 ♗f5 (or 10 ... ♘xe4 ♕xe4 ♗f5 12 ♕h4 e5 13 de de 14 ♗h6 ♘a6 15 ♖ad1 ♖ae8 with balanced chances; Gofstein–Bikhovsky, USSR 1977) 11 ♘h4 ♘xe4 12 ♗xe4 e6 13 ♗e3 ♘d7 14 ♘xf5 ef 15 ♗g2 ♘f6 16 ♖ab1 and a draw was agreed in Starck–Liebert, E. German Ch. 1962.

8   d5

Experience has shown this to be White's most effective approach. The positive aspects comprise ruling out the formation of a mobile black e- and f-pawn duo (thanks to the possibility of capturing *en passant*), exerting pressure on c6 and particularly the weakened e6, gaining space and providing an efficacious post for the knight at d4. The quid pro quo for these gains is Black's increased control of the dark squares, particularly c5, and the opening of the long diagonal for his KB.

The strategic problems confronting Black have been tackled in various ways over the years but only two approaches have stood the test of time and these will be examined via the introductory moves 8 ... ♗d7 and 8 ... e5. The best of the rest, 8 ... ♕a5, caused considerable havoc amongst White players until the discovery of 9 ♘d4 ♕c5 10 ♗g5! (with the point 10 ... ♕xc4? 11 dc bc 12 ♗xf6 ♗xf6 13 ♘xc6! ±±) following which the line rapidly vanished from international competition.

Ribli–Mestel
London 1986

1 d4 f5 2 g3 ♘f6 3 ♗g2 g6 4 ♘f3 ♗g7 5 0-0 0-0 6 c4 d6 7 ♘c3 c6 8 d5

8   ...   ♗d7 *(2)*

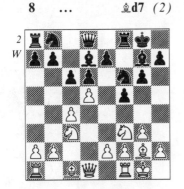

Although comparatively little explored, the indications are that this is a sound treatment with potential for further development. The main idea of the variation is to renounce ... e7–e5 in favour of a containment strategy in the centre coupled with action on the queen's wing. There are marked similarities with the 7 ... ♕e8 variation, the major difference being that here the queen is usually deployed directly into the action via ... ♕b6.

9   ♖b1

Awarded an exclamation mark by Ribli himself, this deferment of ♘d4 has the effect of deterring ... ♕b6 (on account of ♗e3) and enables White to get by without playing e3 (see note (b) below). It seems that the rook move does indeed have a legitimate claim to being the most precise.

Other tries:

(a) 9 ♕c2? (9 ♕b3 ♕b6 10 dc ♕xb3 11 ab ♘xc6= S. Webb–Larsen, London 1973) 9 ... ♘a6 10 a3 cd 11 cd ♖c8 12 ♘d4 ♘c5 13 ♖d1 ♘fe4 14 ♘xe4 fe! and with ... ♗a4 in the air White is in dire straits.

(b) 9 c5!? (although crude, this tactical lunge should not be treated lightly) 9 ... dc 10 ♘e5 and now not 10 ... ♗e8? 11 ♕b3 ♕b6 12 dc+ ♕xb3 13 cb! but 10 ... ♔h8 defusing such possibilities after which Larsen has opined that 'Black may be in good shape'.

(c) 9 ♘d4 ♕b6 (simultaneously reinforcing c6 and priming tactical discoveries on the ♘d4 by, for example, ... ♘e4) 10 e3 ♘a6 11 b3 (after 11 ♖b1 a game Palatnik–Gulko, Kiev 1973, went 11 ... ♘c5 12 b4 ♘ce4 13 ♘a4 ♕c7 14 f3 ♘g5 15 e4 ♘f7 16 ♘e6 ♗xe6 17 fe ♘e5 18 ef gf 19 ♕c2±; failing an improvement on this, 11 ... ♘c7 comes into consideration, e.g. 12 dc bc 13 b4 e5 with complex play) 11 ... ♘c5 12 ♗b2 a5 13 ♖b1 (the position is now the same as the column with the exception that Ribli substituted ♕d2 for e3; it is noteworthy that in this game Black plays the idea recommended by Ribli) 13 ... ♕a6! 14 a4?! (smothers Black's projected counterplay with a timely ... a4 but at the high cost of accepting considerable queen's wing vulnerability) 14 ... ♕b6! 15 ♖e1 ♖ae8 16 ♘ce2 cd 17 cd ♖c8 (Black displays an admirable flexibility of thinking) 18 ♘c3 ♘fe4! (suddenly, Black is on top) 19 ♘cb5 ♘a6 20 ♗f1 ♘b4 21 ♗c4 ♖c5! 22 ♘e2 ♗xb2 23 ♖xb2 ♖fc8∓ 24 ♘bc3 ♖xc4! 25 bc ♖xc4 26 ♘a2 ♕c5 27 ♘xb4 ab 28 h4 ♘c3?! (tempting, but it allows White unnecessary counterchances; 28 ... ♕a5! 29 ♕d3 b3! 30 ♖d1 ♖b4 with ... ♗xa4 and ... ♘c5 to follow was a surer method of turning the screw) 29 ♘xc3 bc 30 ♖xb7 ♗xa4 31 ♕d3? (misses the opportunity to muddy the waters by 31 ♕a1! with the possibility of creating threats against the enemy king) 31 ... c2 32 ♖c1 ♔f7 ∓∓ 33 h5 ♖c3 34 hg+ hg 35 ♕d2 ♕a3? (the wrong way; correct was 35 ... ♕c4 when the threat of ... ♖d3 forces White into the hopeless ending following 36 ♖b2 ♖d3 37 ♖bxc2 ♗xc2 38 ♕xc2 ♕xd5) 36 ♖a7! ♕xc1+? (Black would have retained real winning chances by 36 ... ♖d3 ♕xc2 ♗xc2 38 ♖xa3 ♖xa3 39 ♖xc2 ♖d3, but now with precise play White escapes with a draw) 37 ♕xc1 ♖d3 38 ♔g2! ♖d1 39 ♕a3 c1(♕) 40 ♕xa4 ♖g1+ 41 ♔f3 g5 42 ♖a8 ♕d1+ 43 ♕xd1 ♖xd1 44 ♖a5 g4+ 45 ♔e2 ♖b1 46 e4 ½-½ Spiridonov–Akesson, Polanica Zdroj 1981.

	9	...	♘a6
	10	b3	♘c5

	11	♗b2	a5
	12	♕d2	♕b6
	13	♘d4 *(3)*	

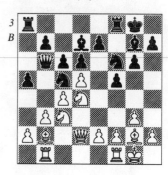

Both sides have deployed their forces harmoniously and a rich middlegame is in the offing. Many more practical trials are needed before any worthwhile assessment can be made but there seems no *a priori* reason for the resources of Black's position not to be adequate to meet whatever demands White makes upon them.

Our present example carried on as follows: 13 ... ♖ad8?! (Black's plan of centralising the rooks fails to accomplish anything; clearly, this is the point to look for an improvement—Ribli noted the possibility of 13 ... ♕a6 intending ... a4) 14 ♖fd1 ♖fe8 15 e3 e5 16 de ♗xe6 (the weak a-pawn would prove a liability after 16 ... ♘xe6 17 ♘a4!) 17 ♘xe6 ♖xe6 18 ♘a4! ♘xa4 19 ba (White has accurately assessed the open lines and diagonals for his pieces to be more important than the structural weakness incurred) 19 ... ♕a6 (or 19 ... ♕c7 20 ♗d4) 20 ♗d4 ♘e4? (allowing a surprising and decisive liquidation; 20 ... ♖d7 was mandatory and would have enabled Black to put up a stiff defence with good chances of resisting White's pressure) 21 ♗xe4 ♖xe4 22 ♗xg7 ♔xg7 23 c5! (cleverly creating a deadly passed pawn) 23 ... ♖d7 (23 ... d5 24 ♖b6 followed by 25 ♕b2+ and 26 ♖xb7 is also hopeless) 24 cd ♖xa4 25 ♕c3+ ♔h6 26 ♕f6 ♕e2 27 ♕e6 ♖xa2 28 ♖f1 ♖g7 29 ♖be1! 1–0.

Uhlmann–Vaiser
Szirak 1985

1 d4 f5 2 g3 ♘f6 3 ♗g2 g6 4 ♘f3 ♗g7 5 0-0 0-0 6 c4 d6 7 ♘c3 c6 8 d5

8 ... e5

Long established as the most popular choice here, this move constitutes Black's most consequent and challenging response to White's advance of the d-pawn.

9 de

A logical capture which procures White the better pawn structure. Alternatives forfeit any real prospects of obtaining an opening advantage:

(a) 9 dc bc 10 b3 is an unimpressive suggestion of Simagin's after which 10 ... e4! leaves Black with a centre whose dynamic potential at least balances its vulnerability.

(b) 9 e4 cd (9 ... c5 is also fully playable) 10 cd ♘a6 11 ef (11 ♗g5? h6 12 ♗xf6 ♕xf6 13 ef gf left Black with all the play in Tsvetkov–Kotkov, Bulgaria–RSFSR 1957) 11 ... gf 12 ♘h4 gives a complicated position with chances for both sides.

9 ... ♗xe6 (4)

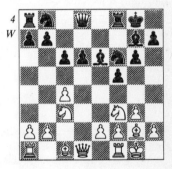

A position of major importance in the theory of the Leningrad variation.

Both pawn configurations have now been broadly established and because of their contrasting characteristics they are of crucial importance in determining the respective strategies to be adopted. From the static point of view, White's structure is clearly superior as it is compact and without weakness whereas Black's is not only generally loose but also suffers from a particular defect in the vulnerable d-pawn on a half-open file. Consequently, Black must make the most of the dynamic potential of his position deriving from his good central control and kingside attacking chances (the positive concomitant of Black's unruly pawn structure) plus free and active development.

The battle lines, then, are clear: White will pressurize the d-pawn and seek simplification in order to highlight the intrinsic weakness of Black's pawns, while Black will endeavour to generate sufficient piece activity to offset his structural inferiority.

10 b3

Experience has shown that only two methods of defending the c-pawn leave White any real prospects of fighting for an advantage from the opening—10 b3 and 10 ♕d3—which we shall examine in detail in the context of complete games. It is worth noting some alternatives for the light they shed on how Black's pieces can co-operate in non-critical situations:

(a) 10 ♘g5? (a baseless offer) 10 ... ♗xc4 11 b3 ♗f7 12 ♗a3 ♘e8 13 ♘xf7 ♖xf7 14 ♖c1 ♘a6 15 h4 ♘c7 16 e4 f4 and Black is well placed with a pawn to the good; Ribli–Sax, Hungarian Ch. 1971.

(b) 10 ♘d2 ♘bd7 (this rare but effective placement of the knight points up the inadequacy of Whi-

te's retreat) 11 ♕c2 ♘b6 12 ♘a4 (better 12 b3 d5 although Black's position is still promising) 12 ... ♘xa4 13 ♕xa4 ♕e7 14 ♕c2 (the queen is misplaced) 14 ... d5 15 cd ♘xd5 16 a3 ♖ad8 17 ♘c4 f4! and with development completed and a strong central position Black advantageously begins to attack on the king's flank; Etruk–Holmov, TU Spartakiad 1965.

(c) 10 ♗f4 (misguided since Black is now relieved of the major weakness in his position) 10 ... ♗xc4 11 ♗xd6 ♖e8 12 ♘e5 ♗e6 13 ♕d3 ♘bd7 14 ♘xd7 ♘xd7 (14 ... ♕xd7 also comes into consideration) 15 ♖fd1 ♕f6 16 f4! ♖ad8 17 ♗c7 ♖c8 18 ♗d6 with an invitation to repetition suiting the nature of the position; Aronson–Hasin, Moscow 1956.

10 ... ♘a6 *(5)*

Black wisely prefers development to material grabbing by 10 ... ♘e4 which gives White a choice of advantageous continuations, e.g. 11 ♘xe4 ♗xa1 (the irresolute 11 ... fe was fittingly punished in Kjarner–Etruk, Parnu 1967, by 12 ♘d4 ♗f7 13 ♗xe4! ♕e7 14 ♗g2 c5 15 ♘c2 ♗xa1 16 ♘xa1 ♘c6 17 ♘c2 (a typical position in which White's control of the vital a1–h8 artery into the heart of Black's king's position and iron grip on the centre outweigh the slight material deficit) 17 ... h5 18 ♗b2

♔h7 19 ♕d2 a5 20 a4 ♘b4 21 ♘e1! (heading for another weakened dark square in the vicinity of the enemy king—g5) 21 ... ♖ad8 22 ♘f3 d5 (at last a vestige of counterplay, but it arrives too late) 23 ♘g5+ ♔g8 24 cd ♘xd5 25 ♘e4 ♗e8 26 ♖d1 ♗c6 27 ♕h6 ♘f4 (a despairing lunge which mercifully cuts short Black's agony) 28 ♕h8+ ♔f7 29 ♕g7+ ♔e8 30 ♖xd8+ 1–0. On 30 ... ♔xd8 31 ♕xe7+ ♔xe7 32 gf White exchanges into an easily won ending, whilst 30 ... ♕xd8 31 ♕e5+ leaves Black with no satisfactory answer.) 12 ♕xd6 (12 ♗g5 ♕c7 13 ♕xd6 is also good as is the more complicated 12 ♘fg5!? ♕d7 13 ♘xd6 ♖d8 14 ♗f4 of Plaskett–Vincent, 1983) 12 ... ♕xd6 13 ♘xd6 ♗c8 (13 ... b6 14 ♗g5 ♗f6 15 ♗xf6 ♖xf6 16 ♘e8 ♖f7 17 ♘g5 ♖e7 18 ♘xe6++ Malich) 14 ♗g5 ♗f6 15 ♗xf6 ♖xf6 16 ♘xc8 ♘a6 17 ♘e7+ ♔f8 18 ♘xc6 bc 19 ♘e5± Syre–Pahtz, E. German Ch. 1975.

11 ♗f4

A relatively recent attempt to inject fresh problems into the position, probably born of lack of satisfaction with the prospects offered by the alternatives:

(a) 11 ♗a3? ♕a5! 12 ♕xd6? ♖fe8 13 ♗b2 ♘e4 14 ♘xe4 ♗xb2 15 ♘eg5 ♖ad8∓∓; this line of Taimanov's serves to illustrate

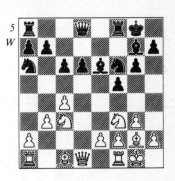

that Black's set-up is more than resilient enough to deal with crude attempts to over-run it.

(b) 11 ♗e3 ♕e7 12 ♖c1 ♘c5 13 ♗d4 ♗d7 (13 ... a5 gives Black a perfectly acceptable game) 14 ♕d2 ♘e6 15 ♗xf6 (thus far Vaganian–Knezevic, Leningrad 1977) 15 ... ♗xf6! 16 ♖fd1 ♘c5 is assessed as unclear by Makarychev; White's plan fails to impress.

(c) 11 ♘g5 ♗c8! 12 ♖b1 ♕e7 (12 ... ♘g4 may be more precise; Adorjan–Vaiser, Szirak 1985, continued 13 ♘a4 ♕e7 14 b4 ♘c7 15 b5 c5 16 ♗f4 and in this obscurely balanced position the gladiators agreed a draw) 13 ♕c2 h6 (the immediate 13 ... ♘c5? would allow 14 b4 with b5 to follow and advantage to White) 14 ♘f3 ♘c5 15 ♗a3 ♗e6 16 ♖bd1 ♖ad8 with fully satisfactory play for Black; Petrosian–Knezevic, Banja Luka 1979.

(d) 11 ♗b2 (certainly the most natural follow-up) 11 ... ♕e7 12

♕c2 d5 13 cd ♘b4! 14 ♕c1 ♘fxd5!
15 ♘a4 ♖ad8 and with his development completed and pieces
actively placed Black can look to
the future with confidence; Sche-
eren–V. Kovacevic, Thessaloniki
Ol. 1984.

11 ...   ♘h5!

Quite in the spirit of the Leningrad, Black parries the attack on
the d-pawn with a counterattack.

12   ♗d2

12 ♗g5 would be hazardous,
e.g. 12 ... ♕a5 13 ♘d4 ♕xc3 14
♘xe6 ♕xa1 15 ♕xa1 ♗xa1 16
♘xf8 ♗h8! 17 ♘e6 ♖e8 18 ♘f4
♘xf4 19 ♗xf4 ♖xe2 20 ♗xd6
♖xa2 and White is struggling (21
b4 ♖d2! or 21 ♖e1 ♗d4!).

12   ...   ♘c5
13   ♕c2   a5
14   ♖ad1   f4!? *(6)*

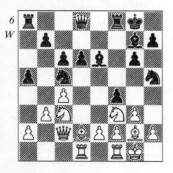

This belligerent thrust signals
the beginning of a mutually
difficult middlegame replete with
problems and prospects for both
sides. Our illustrative game con-

cluded as follows: 15 ♗c1 ♕e7
(15 ... ♗f5!) 16 ♘d4 ♗d7 17 a3
♖f7?! (the situation is too volatile
to permit this ideal doubling on
the f-file; the prophylactic 17 ...
♘e6 might be the best way of
drawing the sting from White's
intended b3–b4–b5, though 17 ...
♖ae8 is a natural and good
enough alternative) 18 b4 ab 19
ab ♘e6 20 ♘f3! g5 21 g4! (it was
necessary to prevent ... g4) 21 ...
♘f6 22 h3 h5?! (precipitate; 22 ...
♖d8 preparing succour for the
perennial weakling seems more in
tune with the needs of the position)
23 gh g4 (23 ... ♘xh5 24 ♘e4 ±)
24 hg ♘xg4 25 ♘e4 d5 (on 25 ...
♗e5 comes 26 ♕d3 ♖g7 27 h6!
♖g6 28 ♘xd6 ♘f8 29 c5 ♖ × h6
30 ♘f5± according to Uhlmann)
26 cd cd 27 ♘c5! (avoiding Black's
trappy idea 27 ♖xd5 ♗a4! 28
♕b1 ♗c6 29 ♖a5 ♖xa5 30 ba
♘d4 with good counterchances)
27 ... ♖c8 28 ♖xd5!? (fearlessly
ambitious!) 28 ... b6 29 ♖fd1 ♘f6
(the best try; 29 ... ♗e8 30 ♕g6!
is good for White and 29 ... bc 30
♖xd7 ♕xd7 31 ♖xd7 ♖xd7 32
♗h3 skewers Black's position) 30
♖e5 bc 31 ♘g5 f3? (in time trouble,
Black fails to find the amazing
saving grace pointed out by
Uhlmann: 31 ... cb! 32 ♕g6! ♘g4!
33 ♘xf7 ♕h4!! 34 ♘h6+! ♘xh6
35 ♖xe6 ♘g4 36 ♗b2 ♕xf2+
37 ♔h1 ♕h4+ with perpetual

check!) 32 ef! ♖ff8 33 ♖de1 cb 34 ♕g6 ♗e8 35 ♕b1 ♗xh5 36 ♖xe6 ♕c7 37 ♖e7 ♕c2 38 ♕xb4 ♗g6 39 ♘e6 ♖f7 40 ♖xf7 ♗xf7 41 ♘xg7 ♔xg7 42 ♗b2 (a deadly pin) 42 … ♖c4 43 ♕b8 ♕f5 44 ♖e4 ♔g6 45 ♕d6 ♗d5 46 ♗xf6 ♖c1+ 47 ♔h2 ♖c6 48 ♕g3+ 1–0. Hard fighting!

Yusupov–Barbero
Mendoze 1985

1 d4 f5 2 g3 ♘f6 3 ♗g2 g6 4 ♘f3 ♗g7 5 0-0 0-0 6 c4 d6 7 ♘c3 c6 8 d5 e5 9 de ♗xe6

10 ♕d3
This protection of the c-pawn with a developing move seems the most natural.

10 … ♘a6
Black does best to get on with his development as quickly as possible especially as it carries with it a threat to drive away the white queen and thereby win the c-pawn.

11 ♗f4 (7)

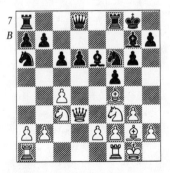

A logical continuation of the mobilization of White's forces which immediately brings pressure to bear on the weak spot in Black's camp.

We also note one poor and one important alternative:

(a) 11 ♘d4?! (it throws instructive light on the idiosyncratic nature of the Leningrad that this natural centralization is out of keeping with the needs of the position) 11 … ♗f7 12 b3 d5! 13 ♗a3 ♖e8 14 ♖fd1 dc 15 bc ♕a5 16 ♗d6 ♘c5 17 ♕c2 ♘ce4 18 ♘xe4 ♘xe4 and White's disadvantage is rapidly assuming decisive proportions; Grooten–Perez-Garcia, Wijk aan Zee II 1986.

(b) 11 ♘g5 (this hunting of the minor exchange demands precise handling by Black) 11 … ♗c8! (the most challenging response; it is not entirely out of the question to allow White to implement his strategy, e.g. 11 … ♕e7 12 ♗f4 ♖ad8 13 ♖ad1 ♘g4! 14 ♘xe6 ♕xe6 15 e4 ♘c5 16 ef gf 17 ♕c2 ♘e5 18 b3 ♕g6, Fridstein–Lutikov, Moscow 1958, and although White has the two bishops and much superior pawn structure, his position is to some extent all dressed up with nowhere to go, while Black has a pair of frisky knights champing at the bit to join in the general plan of harassing White's king) 12 ♗f4 (on 12 ♖d1 h6! 13 ♘f3, Black should eschew 13 ... ♗e6? 14 ♕xd6 ♕xd6 15 ♖xd6 ♗xc4 16 ♘e5 ♗f7 17 ♗xh6!± Ivkov–Sahovic, Zemun 1982, in favour of 13 ... ♘e4! 14 ♘xe4 fe 15 ♕xe4 ♗f5! 16 ♕h4 (or 16 ♕e3 ♘b4) 16 ... g5 17 ♕h5 ♕f6 with excellent compensation) 12 ... ♘h5! 13 ♖ad1 (it has long been established that 13 ♕xd6 ♘xf4 14 ♕xf4 h6 15 ♘f3 g5 gives Black sufficient play for the pawn, e.g. 16 ♕c1 ♗e6 17 ♖d1; thus far Simagin–Hasin, Moscow Ch. 1956, and now Simagin gives 17 ♗. ♕e7! 18 b3 ♖ad8 as best) 13 ... ♘xf4 14 gf h6 15 ♘f3 ♖f6 16 ♖d2 ♘c5 17 ♕c2 ♕e7 18 ♘d4 ♗d7 with chances for both sides in a difficult position; Garcia–Palermo–Ivkov, Havana 1986.

11 ...   ♘e4!?

Amongst the various options at Black's disposal at this point, this mettlesome attempt to seize the initiative makes the most favourable impression.

As a safety net, there is always the solid, if craven, antithesis to the text—11 ... ♘e8. But one senses that should such moves ever be required it would be better to switch variations.

12 ♘xe4   fe
13 ♕xe4   ♘c5 *(8)*

Black augments the cohesion of his forces with tempo gain. By contrast, the apparently more

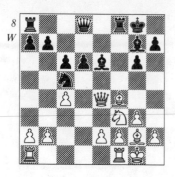

forceful 13 ... ♗f5 began a sequence ending in fatal organic dislocation in Vukic–Kaizauri, Skara 1980: 14 ♕e3 ♗xb2 (14 ... ♕b6!? is unclear according to Vukic) 15 ♖ad1 ♖e8 16 ♕d2 ♕f6 17 e3 ♗a3 (something is wrong when such moves are necessary) 18 ♘d4 ♗b4 (18 ... g5? 19 ♗xd6!) 19 ♕e2 ♗d7 20 h4 ♘c7 21 ♕b2! c5 22 ♕b3! a5 23 ♘c2 a4 24 ♕d3 ♗c3 25 ♗xd6 ♘a6 26 ♗xb7 ♖a7 27 ♗e5! 1–0. The scattered black forces are pitiful in their disarray; a drastic reminder of the indispensable need for harmony and coordination.

14 ♕e3

A necessary improvement on 14 ♕c2? after which 14 ... ♗f5 15 ♕d2 (15 ♕c1 intending to answer 15 ... ♘a4 by 16 b3 looks relatively best) 15 ... ♘e4 16 ♕e3 (16 ♕c1 is preferable although after 16 ... ♕b6 Black maintains strong pressure) 16 ... ♖e8 17 ♕a3 ♕b6 18 ♗c1 d5 gives powerful play for the pawn; Nordstrom–Niklasson,

Swedish Ch. 1974.

13 ...   ♗xc4

The animated middlegame we are about to embark upon is teeming with possibilities and clearly offers vast scope for new discoveries.

15   ♖ad1   ♖e8

Again, counterattack is the best policy since 15 ... ♗d5 16 ♘g5! brings Black into difficulties.

16   ♕c1   ♗xe2
17   ♖xd6   ♕a5

Of course not 17 ... ♕b6 18 ♗e3 ♖xe3 19 ♕xe3 ♗xf1 20 ♗xf1 and all White's pieces are poised for a concerted assault on the black king.

18   ♗d2   ♕b5
19   ♘d4   ♕d3 *(9)*

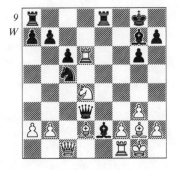

The combatants have traded blows with accuracy and imagination, creating a position of continuing complexity and approximately equal chances. In the game, White's tactic of continually adding fuel to the flames finally

paid off after 20 ♗e3!? (20 ♕xc5 simplifies into a level ending after 20 ... ♕xd2 21 ♘xe2 ♕xe2 22 ♕b4! ♕xb2 23 ♕xb2 ♗xb2 24 ♖b1) 20 ... ♘e4? (a pity that in the labyrinth of variations such as 20 ... ♖xe3? 21 fe ♗h6 22 ♘f5! Black loses his way; 20 ... ♗f8 21 ♕xc5 ♗xd6 22 ♕xd6 ♖xe3 23 fe ♗xf1 24 ♗xf1 ♕xe3+ was correct with good chances of holding the position) 21 ♖d7 c5 (the point of Black's play, exploiting the pin on the rook but there is a surprising riposte ...) 22 ♖xg7+? (... which White misses!; 22 ♖e1! cd 23 ♖xg7+! ♔xg7 24 ♗h6+! ♔f7 25 ♕f4+ ♘f6 26 ♗d5+! would have sewn matters up in spectacular style) 22 ... ♔xg7 23 ♘xe2 ♕xe2 24 ♖e1 ♕h5 25 ♗xe4 (in time trouble, White plays safe and transposes into a slightly favourable endgame in preference to the more accurate but less clearcut maintenance of pressure by 25 ♕c2) 25 ... ♖xe4 26 ♗h6+ ♔xh6 27 ♕xh6+ ♔xh6 28 ♖xe4 ♖g8 29 ♔f1 ♖g7 30 ♔e2 ♖d7 31 h4 ♔g7 32 ♖e5! b6 33 ♖e6 ♔f7 34 ♖c6 ♔e7 (34 ... ♖e7+!) 35 h5!± ♔f7?! (35 ... gh 36 ♖h6 ♔d8 was the simplest) 36 hg+ hg 37 f4 ♔g7 38 ♔e3 ♔f7 39 b3 ♔g7 40 ♔e4 ♔f7 41 ♔f3 (41 ♔e5!±) 41 ... ♖e7 42 ♔g4 ♖d7 43 ♔h4 ♖d2 44 ♖c7+ ♔f6 45 ♖xa7 b5? (45 ... ♔f5 had to be played) 46

♖c7 (46 ♖a5 was more precise) 46 ... c4 47 ♖c6+! ♔f5? (47 ... ♔f7 would have obliged White to play more delicately) 48 ♖c5+ ♔e6 49 ♖xb5 c3 50 ♖c5 c2 51 b4 g5+ 52 fg ♖d4+ 53 ♔h5 ♖xb4 54 ♖xc2 1–0.

2 Leningrad Main Line: 7 ... ♘c6

1	d4	f5
2	g3	♘f6
3	♗g2	g6
4	♘f3	♗g7
5	0-0	0-0
6	c4	d6
7	♘c3	♘c6 (10)

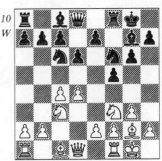

This provocative knight development simultaneously puts pressure on d4 and prepares ... e7–e5 and intentionally aims to goad White into the space-gaining but committal advance d4–d5 following which two entirely different types of game arise according to which way the knight jumps. It is generally agreed that this variation is Black's least soundly based option positionally—either the knight goes offside or the pawn structure becomes compromised—but it frequently leads to fearsome complications and it would clearly be premature to believe that the last word has yet been said.

Before proceeding with our examination of the major continuation 8 d5 we will briefly look at some alternatives:

(a) 8 ♕c2 e5 9 de de 10 ♖d1 ♗d7! 11 ♗e3 (not 11 ♘d5? e4! 12 ♘xf6+ ♗xf6 13 ♘e1 ♘d4 14 ♕d2 ♗a4! 15 b3 ♗xb3! and White has lost material; Bertok–Ghitescu, Reggio Emilia 1968/69) 11 ... e4! 12 ♘d4 ♘g4 13 ♘xc6 (after 13 ♘e6? ♘xe3 14 fe ♗xe6 15 ♖xd8 ♖axd8 16 ♘d5 ♘e5! the queen proved no match for Black's well coordinated pieces in Peev–Nikolaevsky, Varna 1968) 13 ... ♘xe3 14 ♕c1 ♕e8 15 ♕xe3 ♗xc6 and Black may look to the future

13

with confidence thanks to his bishop pair and cramping e-pawn.

(b) 8 b3 ♘e4 (the immediate 8 ... e5 has to reckon with 9 de de 10 ♗a3) 9 ♗b2 e5 10 de ♘xc3 11 ♗xc3 ♕e8! 12 ♕c2 de 13 ♕b2 ♕e7 14 ♖fd1 g5∓ 15 ♖d5? (the prospect of being buried under an avalanche of black pawns panics White into a faulty manoeuvre) 15 ... ♗e6 16 ♖b5? a6 17 ♖xe5 (17 ♖xb7 ♗c8∓ ∓) 17 ... ♘xe5 18 ♘xe5 c6 with a decisive material advantage;   Welsh–Alexander, Cheltenham 1954.

8   d5

Botvinnik–Matulovic
*USSR v Rest of the World
Belgrade 1970*

8   ...   ♘a5 (11)

With this sideways swipe at the c-pawn Black begins a plan which bears a close affinity to the Panno variation of the King's Indian Defence. The intention is to secure the wayward knight's position by ... c7–c5 and then proceed with ... a7–a6 and ... b7–b5 thus generating counterplay against c4 in particular and on the queen's flank in general. In addition, there sometimes arise possibilities of striking in the centre with ... e7–e5. As in the Panno, however, there is the perpetual problem that should Black's initiative dissipate without anything concrete being achieved then the errant knight may become a liability of decisive proportions.

9   ♘d2

This manoeuvre, known from the Panno, is probably White's most reliable method of damping down Black's activity. There are several playable alternatives:

(a) 9 b3 (an interesting exchange offer which clearly gives White strong positional compensation if accepted) 9 ... ♘e4 (9 ... c5 would be the sensible way to decline if preferred) 10 ♘xe4 ♗xa1 11 ♘eg5 c5 12 ♕e1 ♗g7 13 ♗d2 b6 14 e4 ♘b7 15 ef gf 16 ♕e2 with approximately balanced chances; Udovcic–Gufeld, Leningrad 1967.

(b) 9 ♕a4 c5 10 dc ♘xc6 (10 ... bc 11 ♘d4 c5! is interesting) 11 ♖d1 ♕a5 12 ♕xa5 ♘xa5 13 ♘d5 ♘xd5 14 cd ♗d7 with full equality; Vladimirov–Gastonyi, Leningrad v Budapest 1961.

(c) 9 ♕d3 c5 (parrying the

threatened 10 b4) 10 b3 (after 10 ♘g5 a6 11 e4 b5 12 cb ab 13 ♘xb5 fe 14 ♘xe4 ♘xe4 15 ♗xe4 ♗a6 16 a4 c4, Dely–Gufeld, Debrecen 1970, or 10 ♗d2 a6 11 ♖ac1 ♖b8 12 b3 b5!, Paldan–Pedersen, Danish corr. Ch. 1973–4, Black succeeds in stirring up adequate counterplay) 10 ... a6 11 ♗b2 ♖b8 12 ♖ae1 b5 13 ♗a1 bc 14 bc ♖b4 (the immediate 14 ... ♘g4!? merits investigation) 15 ♘d2 ♘g4 16 a3 ♖b8 (16 ... ♘e5 17 ♕c2 ♖xc4!? is quite a reasonable exchange sacrifice) 17 ♕c2 ♗d7 18 e3 ♘e5 19 ♘e2 ♕e8 20 ♖b1 ♗a4 21 ♕a2 ♕d8 22 f4! and having beaten off Black's initiative in instructive fashion White is on the way to gaining the upper hand; Nikolac–Bertok, Yugoslavia 1969.

9 ...   c5
10   a3!

Indirectly preventing ... e7–e5 which against other moves is generally Black's best method of creating counterplay as the following examples show:

(a) 10 b3? ♘xd5! 11 ♗xd5+ e6 12 ♘db1 ed 13 ♕xd5+ ♔h8 14 ♗f4 ♖e8 15 ♗xd6 ♗e6 and White is in trouble, e.g. 16 ♕d3 ♕b6 or 16 ♕xc5? b6 17 ♕a3 ♗xc4.

(b) 10 ♖b1 e5! 11 de ♗xe6 12 b3 d5 13 ♗a3 (steering for equality with 13 cd is the prudent

course) 13 ... ♖c8 14 ♘a4 b6 15 b4 cb 16 ♗xb4 dc with excellent compensation for the sacrificed material; Pinter–Bjelajac, Pernik 1978.

(c) 10 ♕c2 e5! 11 a3 (11 de ♗xe6 12 ♖d1 ♕e7 13 b3 ♘c6 leaves Black actively placed, e.g. 14 ♗b2 ♘d4 15 ♕d3 f4! 16 gf ♗f5 17 e4 ♗e6! and the coming ... ♘f6-h5xf4 gives a strong attack; J. Piket–M. Gurevich, Lucerne 1989) 11 ... b6 12 b4 ♘b7 13 ♗b2 ♕e7 14 ♖ae1 ♘d8 15 e3 ♘f7 and having usefully redeployed the problem knight Black's prospects are fully satisfactory; Vaganian–Tal, USSR 1970.

10   ...   ♗d7
11   ♕c2

Avoiding the trap 11 b4? cb 12 ab ♘xc4! 13 ♘xc4 ♕c7! after which Black regains his material and assumes the initiative, e.g. 14 ♕b3 ♖fc8 15 ♘a5 ♕xc3 16 ♕xc3 ♖xc3 17 ♘xb7 ♖b3 and White is in difficulties.

11   ...   ♕c7

Once again preventing b2–b4 by utilizing the sensitivity of c4.

12   b3   a6

The central advance 12 ... e5 leaves White an indisputable positional advantage after 13 de ♗xe6 14 ♗b2 and so Black is forced to fall back on the alternative wing demonstration plan. It appears, however, that here too

White can maintain the upper hand.

13   ♗b2   b5 *(12)*

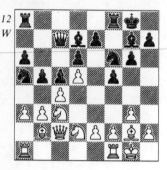

14   ♘d1!

Although at first sight Black's position looks active enough, this subtle retreat begins a sophisticated plan, first employed by Botvinnik in the analogous Panno King's Indian position in a celebrated game versus Geller in 1952, which brilliantly highlights the deficiencies of Black's set-up. In essence, the idea is to post the bishop at c3 simultaneously surveying the hobbled horse in Black's camp and clearing a path for the tour ♘d1–b2–d3–f4 by its more fleet of foot white counterpart. Once a white knight establishes itself on f4 the weakness of e6 may become a real problem for Black.

14   ...   bc
Can Black improve hereabouts?

15   bc   ♖ab8
16   ♗c3   ♘g4

Black seeks to relieve the pressure by means of exchanges. While this may indeed be the best policy, the defender must beware of dropping his guard as forces are reduced because White's advantage is of a particularly insidious and persistent nature as the present game well shows.

17   ♗xg7   ♔xg7
18   ♕c3+

The queen takes over on the key c3 square menacing both flanks simultaneously.

18   ...   ♔g8
19   ♘b2!   ♖b7
20   ♘d3   ♖fb8
21   ♖ab1!

Appreciating that as the rooks disappear so too do Black's chances of counterplay. Moreover, the exchanges accentuates the superior activity and coordination of White's minor pieces.

21   ...   ♖xb1
22   ♖xb1   ♖xb1+
23   ♘xb1   ♕b6
24   ♘d2   ♘f6 *(13)*

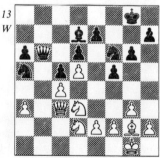

While to the inexpert eye it may appear that an amicable handshake is just around the corner, in fact the real fighting is just about to begin! Space considerations do not permit us to follow the further vicissitudes in too great detail (especially since White unfortunately strays from the consistent course quite soon) but hopefully this will not prevent the reader from drawing the unavoidable if unpalatable conclusion that those wishing to play 8 ... ♘a5 must either come armed with a big improvement or be prepared for a long and arduous defensive task. Still, at the end of it there may be a half point waiting, even against a world champion! 25 h3! ♔f7 26 ♔h2 ♘b7 27 e4 fe 28 ♘xe4 ♘d8 29 ♘g5+ (29 ♘f4! would have set Black greater problems; as it is, he is freed from having to defend the ♘f6 and this permits him to regroup) 29 ... ♔e8! 30 ♘f4 ♘f7 31 ♘fe6 ♘xg5 (with the exchange of the problem QN Black's defensive prospects improve enormously) 32 ♘xg5 ♕b1! 33 ♗e4 ♕a2! 34 ♔g2 ♗f5 35 ♗xf5 gf 36 ♕d3 h6 37 ♘e6 ♘e4 38 ♕f3 ♕xc4 (38 ... ♘f6!) 39 ♕h5+ ♔d7 40 ♕xf5 ♘f6 41 ♘xc5+ ♔e8 42 ♕g6+ ♔d8 43 ♘e6+ ♔d7 44 ♘f4 ♘xd5 45 ♕xh6 (45 ♕f5+ ♔c6 46 ♕xd5+ ♕xd5 47 ♘xd5 ♔xd5 48 ♔f3 ♔e5 should be

drawn) 45 ... ♕e4+ 46 ♔h2 ♕e1 47 ♘d3 ♕c3 48 ♕g6 ♕xa3 49 h4 (49 g4 ♕c3 50 g5 was a stronger but riskier winning attempt) 49 ... ♕c3 50 h5 ♕f6 51 ♕g4+ e6 52 ♕a4+ ♔e7 53 ♕xa6 ♕f3? (53 ... ♕f5 collecting the h-pawn was correct) 54 ♕a7+ ♔d8 55 ♕h7 ♘f6 56 ♕h8+ ♔d7 57 ♕g7+ ♔c6 58 h6 ♘g4+ 59 ♔g1 ♕d1+ 60 ♔g2 ♕e2 61 ♔h3? (61 ♕c3+ ♔d7 62 ♕d4 ♘xh6 63 ♕g7+ ♔c6 64 ♕xh6 ♕xd3 65 ♕xe6 would have preserved winning chances) 61 ... ♘xh6 62 ♕xh6 ♕xd3 63 ♕xe6 ♕f1+ ½–½.

Ribli–Barber
Lugano 1985

1 d4 f5 2 g3 ♘f6 3 ♗g2 g6 4 ♘f3 ♗g7 5 0-0 0-0 6 c4 d6 7 ♘c3 ♘c6 8 d5

8   ...   ♘e5

Although current fashion in the Leningrad has focused attention on ... c6 systems (and 7 ... ♕e8 in particular) at the expense of 7 ... ♘c6, aficionados of uncompromising play ensure that the knight move still appears from time to time albeit almost invariably in the form of this centralizing variation. The basic point at issue is whether the assortment of tactical and attacking chances Black acquires after White captures the knight (presently considered the main continuation) are sufficient to off-set the positional drawbacks. The last word on this question has yet to be said despite the recent trend of games going in White's favour: any system capable of dealing Karpov one of the most crushing defeats of his career must have rather a lot going for it.

9   ♘xe5

The critical response, but there are also two worthwhile alternatives:

(a) 9 ♘d2 (of course not 9 b3? ♘e4 and Black wins material) 9 ... c6! 10 h3 (against 10 b3 I recommend 10 ... cd 11 cd ♘h5! intending 12 ♗b2 f4 with active play on the king's wing) 10 ... ♕b6 11 ♘a4 ♕c7 with a promising position for Black; Taimanov–Vinogradov, Leningrad Ch. 1946.

(b) 9 ♕b3 is only just beginning to be explored and deserves respect, as witness the following defensive fiasco: 9 ... ♘ed7 10 ♗e3 ♘c5 11 ♗xc5 (in *ECO* this capture is mentioned in a note and evaluated with a laconic '=', quite erroneously, as we shall see) 11 ... dc 12 ♘g5! ♖b8 13 ♕a3 a6 14 ♕xc5 b6 15 ♕b4 h6 16 ♘f3 b5 17 ♘e5 1–0 Seirawan–Pellant, 1983. The best antidote to this is 9 ... ♘xf3+! 10 ef (or 10 ♗xf3 ♘d7 11 ♗e3 ♘c5 and the removal of a pair of knights makes it far less attractive for White to capture on

c5, failing which Black's position is fully satisfactory) 10 ... e5 11 de ♗xe6 12 ♖e1 ♕d7 13 f4 c6 14 ♗e3 ♕f7 15 ♕a3 ♗xc4 (15 ... ♖fd8!?) with a very healthy equality for Black; Pilnik–Tartakower, Paris 1954/55.

9   ...   de *(14)*

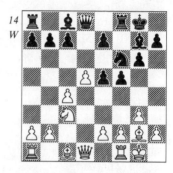

14
W

The modified pawn structure delineates the respective spheres of action: for White, the centre and queenside; for Black, the centre and kingside.

10   ♕b3

A multi-purpose and sensible move which puts pressure on b7, sets up a *vis-à-vis* along the important a2–g8 diagonal, and prepares to bring a rook to the d-file. Apart from the centrally consolidating 10 e4, the other tenth moves hardly encompass the same breadth or depth of efficacy although one or two of them nevertheless pose Black some delicate problems which, perhaps, have not yet entirely been solved:

(a) 10 f4? e4∓ 11 ♗e3 ♘g4 12 ♗d4 e5 13 ♗c5 b6! 14 ♗xf8 ♕xf8 (Vinogradov) with more than adequate compensation for the (probably temporary) sacrifice of material.

(b) 10 ♖e1?! e4 is fine for Black.

(c) 10 ♕c2 permits untroubled liquidation of Black's structural weakness by 10 ... e6.

(d) 10 ♗g5?! ♘d7! leaves the bishop flailing.

(e) 10 c5!? e4 (10 ... e6 looks safer) 11 ♕b3 ♔h8 12 ♖d1 ♕d7?! (artificial to say the least) 13 ♗e3 c6 14 f3 cd 15 ♘xd5 ♘xd5 16 fe fe 17 ♖xd5± on account of the superior pawn structure and queenside pressure; Cramling–G. Flear, 1983.

(f) 10 b3!? e4 11 ♗a3! ♖f7 (11 ... ♘g4!?) 12 f3! ef 13 ef f4 14 ♖c1 with a clearly more harmonious position for White; Dlugy–Gallego, World Jr. Ch. Sharjah 1985.

10 ... e6
Ribli assesses 10 ... ♔h8 11 ♖d1 as ±, but it may be worthwhile further investigating the plan of leaving the centre pawns untouched, e.g. 10 ... h6 11 ♖d1 ♔h8 12 c5 g5 13 ♗d2 e4 14 ♗e1 a6 15 ♕a3 ♕e8 16 b4 ♗d7 17 ♕b3 ♘g4 with good kingside attacking prospects for Black; Siekansky–Hawelko, Polish Ch. 1989.

11 ♖d1 ed
If this seems too risky then the playable 11 ... ♕e7 is available, e.g. 12 ♗g5 (± Ribli) h6 13 ♗xf6 ♗xf6 14 e4 (thus far Schmid–Menvielle, Tel Aviv Ol. 1964) and now *ECO* recommends 14 ... ♖b8 with an evaluation of equality. Clearly, there remains much to be properly worked out here.

12 ♘xd5 c6
13 ♗g5!?
A startling new idea. Older analyses had only considered the attacking attempt 13 c5 which fails after 13 ... cd 14 ♗xd5+ ♘xd5 15 ♖xd5 ♕e8! as White has no useful discovered check.

13 ... cd
The offer cannot be declined because after 13 ... ♕a5 White plays 14 ♘e7+ followed by capturing on c8 and then b7 with advantage.

14 ♗xd5+ ♔h8
15 ♗xb7 *(15)*

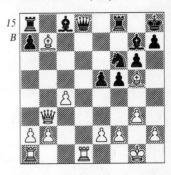

The point of White's combination is now revealed: to bring about an approximate, heterogeneous balance of queen and pawns versus rook and two minor pieces. Such positions are notoriously resistant to generalization and necessitate concrete appraisal, and here lies the nub of White's discovery—that the black pieces are lacking in coordination and a useful plan whereas White's pawns can be rapidly mobilized and made into a real threat.

15   ...   ♕xd1+

Perhaps Black can improve at this juncture. It's true that 15 ... ♗d7 is unplayable on account of 16 ♗xa8 ♕xa8 17 ♗xf6 ♗xf6 18 ♖xd7, but 15 ... ♖b8 immediately enables the a-pawn to be saved, e.g. 16 ♖xd8 ♖xd8 17 ♖d1 ♖g8! (not 17 ... ♖xd1? 18 ♕xd1 ♗xb7 19 ♗xf6 ♗xf6 20 ♕d6±+) 18 ♕a3 ♖xb7 with conspicuously better chances than in the game.

16   ♖xd1   ♖b8
17   ♕a3   ♗xb7

17 ... ♖xb7? 18 ♗xf6 wins for White.

18   ♗xf6   ♗xf6
19   ♕xa7

With the capture of a third pawn the situation has clarified in White's favour. Although there would still be considerable technical difficulties to overcome against the most stubborn defence, the game illustrates well just how difficult it is to manage the maximum resistance in practice:

19 ... ♗a8 20 b3 ♖bd8 21 ♖xd8 ♖xd8 22 f3 e4 (22 ... ♔g8 was mandatory) 23 ♕f7! ♗d4+ 24 ♔g2 ef+ 25 ef ♗g7 26 ♕e7 ♖f8 (on 26 ... ♖d2+ 27 ♔f1 ♗c6, 28 ♕c7! wins material) 27 b4 (once the pawns start rolling there is no hope) 27 ... h5 28 b5 ♔g8 29 b6 ♗f6 30 ♕e6+ ♔g7 31 c5 ♖d8 32 c6 ♖d2+ 33 ♔f1 f4 34 b7 1–0.

Karpov–Jacobsen
*USSR v Scandinavia, junior
match 1968*

1 d4 f5 2 g3 ♘f6 3 ♗g2 g6 4 ♘f3 ♗g7 5 0-0 0-0 6 c4 d6 7 ♘c3 ♘c6 8 d5 ♘e5 9 ♘xe5 de
   10   e4 *(16)*

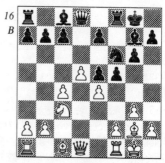

This central advance both fixes Black's front e-pawn (and thereby deadens the KB) and provides White with a means of opening up the position at an opportune moment. It has long been considered the best continuation despite its tendency to produce formidable complications.

10   ...   f4

This bold thrust nails Black's colours to the mast and commits him to an all out assault on the enemy king. Although present day interest has focused almost exclusively on this uncompromising attacking line, there does exist a quieter alternative which certainly deserves mentioning and that is 10 ... e6. There are two main ways for White to meet this central challenge:

(a) 11 ♕b3 ed (should Black suddenly experience a change of heart and a craving for complications, then 11 ... f4 is still available with the usual unclear consequences) 12 cd ♔h8 (12 ... ♘e8 13 ef gf 14 d6+ is promising for White) 13 ♗e3 f4!? (the staid 13 ... ♘e8 brought Black a draw in Tartakower–Alexander, Hastings 1953/54) 14 ♗c5 ♖e8 15 ♖fd1 b6 16 ♗a3 ♗g4 17 f3 ♗d7 18 gf ♘h5 19 ♘e2 ef when Black is not without chances on the kingside to offset White's undoubted central supremacy; Uhlmann–Espig, E. Germany 1972.

(b) 11 ef ef (the untested 11 ... gf has its points) 12 ♗e3 (Gheorghiu's bald 12 ♕b3± has yet to be confirmed in practice) 12 ... e4?! (looks premature here; *ECO* has suggested 12 ... ♘g4 13 ♗c5 ♖e8) 13 ♗d4 ♖e8 14 ♖e1

b6 15 f3± and the game opens up to White's advantage; Collins–Sherwin, New York 1952.

11   b3

The right idea but insufficiently energetically executed—the bishop needs to be fianchettoed in order to find worthwhile development, but equally the queen requires an active station and therefore 11 b4 (reserving b3 for the queen) has become the major continuation. We shall examine that move in the context of the next game and note the other eleventh turn possibilities here:

(a) 11 gf ef (11 ... ♘h5!? 12 f5 ♘f4 also gives compensation for the pawn) 12 ♗xf4 (12 e5 leads to strange positions tending in Black's favour, e.g. 12 ... ♘g4 13 e6 ♘e5 14 ♕b3 f3 15 ♗h3 b6! with ... ♗a6 in the air) 12 ... ♘xe4! 13 ♗g3 (or 13 ♘e2 ♘d6! with balanced prospects) 13 ... ♘xg3 14 hg e6 and Black has overcome his opening problems; Hodakowsky–Hübner, Aibling 1965.

(b) 11 c5 g5 12 ♕b3?! ♔h8 13 ♘b5?! (having blocked his b-pawn White has difficulty forming a plan) 13 ... c6 14 ♘c3 ♕e8 15 ♕d1 ♗d7 16 b4 ♖d8 17 ♗b2 ♘g4∓ Black has completed his development and is ready to proceed with the kingside attack; a perfect example of how Black should build up the position when left undisturbed; Wells–Hansen, World Jr. Ch. Kiljava 1984.

(c) 11 f3?! (pusillanimous prophylaxis) 11 ... c6! 12 dc ♕b6+ 13 ♔h1 bc (keeping control of the important d5 square) 14 b3 g5 15 ♗a3 ♔f7! 16 gf gf 17 ♘a4 ♕c7 18 ♕e1 ♖g8 and Black can be well satisfied with his share of the chances in a difficult position for both sides; Hjartarson–Plaskett, Hastings 1985/86.

| 11 | ... | g5 |
| 12 | f3 | |

White is concerned at the possibility of the g-pawn advancing even further.

| 12 | ... | ♕d6 |
| 13 | g4 | h5 *(17)* |

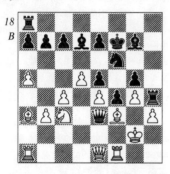

A sight to gladden every Leningrad player's heart! One glance suffices to show that White's strategy has failed miserably and allowed Black to create a deadly kingside attack. The further course of the game is extremely instruc-

tive: 14 h3 hg 15 fg (acquiescing to the opening of the h-file would be tantamount to resignation) 15 ... ♗d7 16 a4 ♕b6+ 17 ♔h2 ♔f7 18 ♗f3 ♖h8 19 ♔g2 ♖h4 20 a5 ♕c5 21 ♗a3 ♕e3 22 ♕e1 *(18)*

A sight to gladden every Leningrad player's heart!

22 ... ♗xg4! (having this up his sleeve was the reason Black allowed the queen to be driven into the enemy camp with its exchange apparently inevitable— excellent calculation!) 23 hg (23 ♗xg4 ♘xg4) 23 ... ♘xg4 24 ♖h1 ♖xh1 25 ♕xe3 ♘xe3+ 26 ♔xh1 g4 (despite the reduction in forces, White is still in trouble due to the powerful connected passed pawns) 27 ♗e2 f3 28 ♗c5 (not 28 ♗d1? f2 and ... ♖h8 mate will follow) 28 ... ♗h6 29 ♖e1 b6 30 ♗xf3 (or 30 ♗xe3 ♗xe3 31 ♗xf3 ♖h8+ 32 ♔g2 gf+ 33 ♔xf3 ♗d2–+) 30 ... bc 31 ♗d1 ♔g6 32 ♘b5 ♗f4 33 ♖xe3 (if 33 ♔g1 then 33 ... g3 followed by ... ♖h8– h2 etc.) 33 ... ♗xe3 34 ♘xc7

♖h8+ 35 ♔g2 ♖h4 36 a6 ♗f4
37 ♔g1 g3 38 ♗f3 ♖h2 39 ♗g2
♔f7 40 ♔f1 ♖h6 41 ♔e2 ♖b6
0–1.

C. Hansen–J. Kristiansen
Esbjerg 1984

**1 d4 f5 2 g3 ♘f6 3 ♗g2 g6 4 ♘f3
♗g7 5 0-0 0-0 6 c4 d6 7 ♘c3 ♘c6
8 d5 ♘e5 9 ♘xe5 de 10 e4 f4**

11   b4   g5

With the centre locked, both
sides pursue their respective flank
initiatives with great energy. It
would be quite wrong for Black
to meddle with the centre, e.g. 11
... e6 12 ♗b2 ed 13 ed ♗f5 14
♖e1 and with the inevitable arrival
of the knight at e4, Black will find
himself at a significant positional
disadvantage.

12   ♖e1

A somewhat enigmatic move,
not exactly forced, which passively
vacates f1 for the bishop in the
event of a ... g4 ... f3 pawn storm,
and actively observes the e3 square
(see the note to White's fifteenth
in Farago–Poutiainen below).

12   ...   a6

A necessary preparation for the
transfer of the queen to the kingside, simply preventing ♘b5. An
untested alternative plan is 12 ...
g4 13 c5 f3 14 ♗f1 h5, though
such an approach lacks flexibility.

13   ♗b2   ♛e8 *(19)*

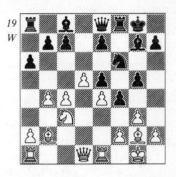

An attractive, rich position of
clearly drawn battle lines which
should have no trouble attracting
supporters for both sides. Practical experience so far is extremely
limited, and many more tests will
be required before a trustworthy
judgement can be advanced.

14   c5

Optimally priming White's position for various breakthroughs.
An earlier game, Farago–Poutiainen, Budapest 1975, went 14 ♖c1
♘g4 15 ♖c2? (looks natural
enough but lands White in dire
straits; 15 f3 was subsequently pro-
posed as an improvement, the idea
being 15 ... ♘e3 16 ♖xe3! fe 17
g4! with superb positional compensation for the material deficit,
but Black can also improve with
15 ... ♛h5! with obscure play) 15
... ♛h5 16 h3 f3! 17 ♗xf3 (White
suddenly finds himself between
Scylla and Charybdis: 17 hg
♗xg4 18 ♗f1 ♖f6 would be fatal)
17 ... ♛xh3 18 ♛d3 ♘xf2! 19 ♖xf2

(19 ♔xf2 ♕h2+ 20 ♔e3 ♖xf3+
21 ♔xf3 g4+ 22 ♔e3 ♗h6
mate!)   19   ...   ♕xg3+
20 ♔f1 ♗h3+ 21 ♔e2 g4 0–1.
A very instructive miniature,
played with panache.

14   ...   ♗d7?!

With the laudable aim of developing the queen's rook, but unfortunately White can throw a tactical spanner in the works by 15 c6!
bc 16 dc ♗xc6 17 ♘d5 when the
soft underbelly of Black's position
has been dangerously exposed. In
fact, in the game this opportunity
to seize the initiative was missed,
and the proceedings took an
entirely different course, albeit one
still full of points of interest and
instruction.

Presumably, 14 ... ♘g4 must
still come into consideration, and
Kristiansen himself has noted 14
... ♕f7 as an improvement.

15   ♖c1   ♖d8
16   a4   ♕f7

Threatening to unleash the black
forces by ... ♘g4.

17   gf!

An economical way of cutting
dead Black's f-file pretensions.

17   ...   ef?

Black has spotted an amazing
idea which seduces him into this
inferior capture. After the obvious
17 ... gf, there would be real prospects of creating play along the
g-file, but as it is Black's dreams
of attack fade away before they
get going: 18 e5! ♘xd5! 19 ♗xd5
e6 20 ♗e4! (after the natural-
looking 20 ♗f3 comes 20 ... ♗c6
21 ♕e2 ♖d2!! and Black wins!) 20
... f3 21 ♔h1 ♕h5 22 ♖e3 ♖f4
23 ♗xf3 ♖xf3? (the last chance
was 23 ... g4) 24 ♖xf3 g4 25 ♘e4!
(with this fine defensive move all
Black's tactics are foiled and
White assumes the initiative) 25
... gf 26 ♕d4! ♕h4 27 ♖d1 ♖f8
28 ♖g1 ♖f4 29 ♕xd7 ♖g4 30
♕xe6+ 1–0.

3 Leningrad Main Line: 7 ... ♕e8

1	d4	f5
2	g3	♘f6
3	♗g2	g6
4	♘f3	♗g7
5	0-0	0-0
6	c4	d6
7	♘c3	♕e8 *(20)*

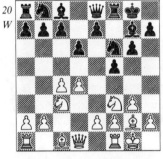

It seems strange now to think that it wasn't really until the 1980s that this typical Classical Dutch move was transplanted to the Leningrad and worked up into a coherent system. From e8 the queen supports the advance ... e7–e5 and also helps prepare, in conjunction with the QB, to contest the centre by ... c7–c6.

Occasionally the queen also finds useful employment on f7 putting pressure down the f-file and attacking the c-pawn, and from time to time we will see the queen deployed at g6 or h5 after the advance ... h6 and ... g5.

8 d5

The familiar method of preventing ... e5 and probably best. At any rate the alternatives do not look particularly threatening to Black, e.g.:

(a) 8 e4 fe 9 ♘g5 ♘c6 10 ♗e3 ♗g4 11 ♕d2 ♕d7 and Black's active development assures him a satisfactory game; Afifi–Yusupov, Tunis 1985.

(b) 8 ♖e1 ♕f7 (of course not 8 ... ♘e4 immediately because of 9 ♘xe4 fe 10 ♘g5± ±) 9 b3 ♘e4 10 ♗b2 ♘c6 11 ♖c1 h6 12 ♖f1 (in order to threaten capturing on e4; 12 d5 ♘b4 would leave a2 tactically vulnerable) 12 ... ♘xc3 13 ♗xc3 e5 with full equality; Gavrikov–Malanyuk, USSR Ch. 1986.

25

(c) 8 ♘d5 ♘xd5 9 cd ♛b5 10 ♘e1 (Black has a fine game after 10 ♛b3 ♛xb3 11 ab c6 12 ♗g5 ♖e8 13 ♖fc1 e6 14 de ♗xe6; Zukhovitsky–Mih. Zeitlin, USSR 1986) 10 ... ♘a6 (10 ... a5!?) 11 e3 ♗d7 12 ♘d3 c5 13 dc ♗xc6 14 ♗xc6 bc 15 ♛b3+ ♖f7 16 ♛xb5 cb 17 ♗d2 e5= Balashov–Malanyuk, USSR. Ch. 1986.

(d) 8 ♛b3 ♘a6 9 ♗g5 c5 10 ♗xf6 ♗xf6 11 ♖ad1 ♗g7 and after this prophylaxis against e2–e4 (which would now be answered by f5–f4) prospects are balanced thanks to Black's possession of the two bishops; Lerner–Malanyuk, USSR Ch. 1986.

(e) 8 b3 (a useful waiting move hoping to show that Black's threatened advance of the e-pawn is actually loosening and opens the position prematurely) 8 ... ♘a6 (this standard treatment is the most solid; 8 ... e5 9 de de 10 e4! ♘c6 11 ♘d5! has indeed been shown to favour White) 9 ♗b2 (9 ♗a3 c6 10 ♛d3 ♖b8 11 e4 fe 12 ♘xe4 ♗f5 13 ♘xf6+ ♗xf6 14 ♛e3 b5 gives a dynamic balance; Kishnyev–Bukhman, Budapest 1989) 9 ... ♗d7 10 d5 c6 11 ♖c1 h6 12 e3 ♖c8 13 ♘d4 ♛f7 with a typically rich position for both sides; Kasparov–Malanyuk, USSR Ch. 1988.

8   ...   ♘a6

The most effective method of developing the queenside given that White's d-pawn advance ceded Black control of c5.

9   ♘d4

The most natural follow-up to the previous move, but there is also a case for trying to throw Black's plans out of gear by preparing a rapid advance of the b-pawn, e.g. 9 ♖b1 ♗d7 10 b4 (10 ♘d4 would transpose to Tukmakov–M. Gurevich below) 10 ... e5 11 de ♗xe6 12 ♘d4 ♗xc4 13 ♗xb7 ♖b8 14 ♗c6+ since White has simultaneously downgraded Black's pawn structure and turned the stranded a6 knight into a real liability; Ruka-vina–Cvitan, Yugoslav Ch. 1986. 9 ... c6 looks a sensible attempt at improvement.

9   ...   ♗d7 *(21)*

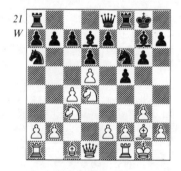

Necessary preparation for the advance of the c-pawn which forms an indispensable link in Black's counterplay.

Essentially, White must now

decide whether to concentrate operations in the centre or on the queenside, and accordingly our illustrative games will feature the continuations 10 e4 and 10 ♖b1.

In addition to these the following examples are also worth noting:

(a) 10 e3 c6 11 b3 (a game Gavrilov–M. Gurevich, USSR 1982, continued interestingly with 11 ♖b1 ♘c7 12 b4 cd 13 cd ♖c8 14 a4 ♘a8 15 ♕b3 and Black is uncomfortably cramped; 11 ... ♖b8 looks more precise) 11 ... ♘c7 12 ♗b2 c5 13 ♘de2 (as the game goes, White gets into difficulties over the weakness of c4 and so 13 ♘f3 with a later re-routing to d2 was preferable) 13 ... b5 14 ♕c2 ♖b8 (Black has a pleasant initiative while White has nothing to do) 15 ♖ac1 (exacerbates the problems of the position; either 15 ♖ab1 or 15 cb should have been played) 15 ... bc 16 bc ♘g4! 17 ♗a1 ♘e5 18 ♘d1 ♗a4 19 ♕d2 ♘xc4! and Black has won a sound pawn in very instructive fashion; Belyavsky–Malanyuk, USSR Ch. 1983.

(b) 10 b3 (this move has much in common with 10 ♖b1 but here White chooses to forgo b4 options in favour of a different placement of the rook) 10 ... c6 11 ♗b2 ♘c7 12 ♖c1 (12 ♕d2 merits attention, e.g. 12 ... c5 13 ♘f3 a6 14 ♖ae1

b5 15 ♕d3 ♖b8 16 ♗a1 h6 17 ♘d2 ♘g4 18 e3± since the sting has been taken from Black's counterplay and White is ready to push through in the centre; P. Stefanov–Marasescu, Romanian Ch. 1983. Perhaps Black should prefer 13 ... ♖b8 and possibly dispense with ... a6 altogether.) 12 ... ♖b8 13 ♕d2 c5 14 ♘f3 a6 (Kremenetsky considers 14 ... b5 15 cb ♘xb5 16 ♘xb5 ♖xb5 17 ♗xf6 ♗xf6 18 ♕c2 intending ♘f3–d2–c4 to be ±, but this is hard to credit given the open nature of the position and Black's bishops) 15 ♕c2 b5 16 ♘d2 e5!? 17 de ♗xe6 18 ♗a1 (18 e4? would allow the characteristic and instructive tactical blow 18 ... bc 19 bc fe 20 ♘cxe4 ♖xb2!) 18 ... ♕e7 19 e4 f4! (a typical sidestepping response to White's tortuously prepared central advance) 20 ♘d5 (of course not 20 gf? ♘h5 when the black squares around White's king are irreparably weakened) 20 ... ♘fxd5 21 cd ♗d7 22 ♗xg7 ♕xg7 23 ♘f3 ♗g4 and with transition to a classic good knight versus bad bishop position imminent Black's winning chances are good; F. Lengyel–Kremenetsky, Satu-Mare 1983.

R. Hernandez–Chernin
Cienfuegos 1981

1 d4 f5 2 g3 ♘f6 3 ♗g2 g6 4 ♘f3

♗g7 5 0-0 0-0 6 c4 d6 7 ♘c3 ♕e8
8 d5 ♘a6 9 ♘d4 ♗d7

10   e4

Such rustic applications of the pedagogues' panacea for dealing with the Dutch—play e4—rarely prove really threatening as long as they are met precisely. Generally speaking, White does better to promote strategical complexity rather than clarify matters with an early showing of his hand. Nevertheless, any logical opening up of the centre is always an acid test of Black's defensive resources and needs careful handling.

10   ...   ♘xe4

Of course Black can just as well capture with the pawn as long as transposition to the column is effected by exchanging knights as well; failure to do so leads to grave problems for Black, as shown by Ivkov–Bischoff, Thessaloniki Open 1984: 10 ... fe 11 ♘xe4 c5? 12 ♘e6 ♗xe6 13 de ♘c7 14 ♘xf6+ ♗xf6 15 ♕e2 ♖b8 16 a4 ♘a6 17 h4! and with h5 to come, Black's fragile kingside defences will soon be ripped apart.

11   ♘xe4   fe
12   ♗xe4   (22)

An important *tabiya* for the 7 ... ♕e8 variation, containing an interesting mixture of structural and dynamic pros and cons for both sides. White's advanced d-

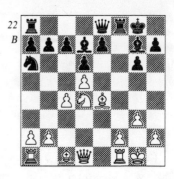

pawn assures him a spatial advantage and he is without structural weakness, his pieces can develop freely and the half-open e-file beckons for major piece operations; the pride and joy of his position at the moment is the beautifully centralized knight which is particularly happy to be keeping e6 under surveillance. By comparison, Black is cramped and suffers from a problem e-pawn, none too sturdy kingside and the e6 weakness in the heart of his position. To offset these static deficiencies, Black has active pieces and useful lines to operate along in the half open f-file and h8–a1 diagonal as well as prospects of creating play in the centre and/or on the queenside by appropriate pawn pushes.

12   ...   c6

This appears to be Black's most reliable continuation judging from the evidence so far. The alternatives:

(a) 12 ... c5?! 13 dc? (13 ♘e6! looks unpleasant for Black; cf. Ivkov–Bischoff, note to Black's tenth above) 13 ... bc 14 ♖b1 ♖c8 15 ♗e3 ♕f7 16 ♕e2 e5 17 ♘b3 ♘c7 18 ♗g2 d5 with promising dynamic possibilities for Black in a complex position; Schmidt–Grigorov, Prague 1985.

(b) 12 ... ♘c5 13 ♗g2 a5 14 ♗g5 ♕f7 15 ♕d2 ♗xd4 16 ♕xd4 e5 17 ♕c3 with a clear positional superiority for White thanks to the bishop pair; Van der Sterren–Belyavsky, Wijk aan Zee 1984.

13   ♗e3

Not 13 dc? bc transposing to Schmidt–Grigorov above.

13   ...   ♘c7
14   ♕d2   c5!

Now that ♘e6 is no longer possible Black is happy to stabilize the centre so as to launch a flank initiative.

15   ♘e2   b5
16   cb   ♗f5!

Forcing White to retreat since exchanging would irretrievably weaken the d-pawn.

17   ♗g2   ♕xb5 *(23)*

Yet another demonstration of the versatility of the e8 placement of the black queen! It is interesting to observe how Black has usurped the initiative despite White having apparently played only natural and sensible looking moves. Note that White has failed to develop

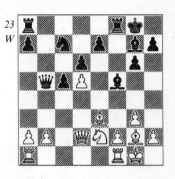

23
W

any play at all against Black's sensitive e6 and e7 points whereas Black has both isolated White's d-pawn and created a target of the b-pawn by opening up the b-file.

18   ♘c3   ♕d3

Proceeding in instructive safety-first style denying the opponent any chance of attacking on the kingside.

19   ♖fd1   ♕xd2
20   ♖xd2   h6

Preventing counterplay against the e-pawn by ♗g5 and rooks to the e-file. Now White is reduced to passive defence while Black can gradually apply the pressure with every chance of a positive outcome as indeed was the case in the game: 21 ♖c1 ♖ab8 22 ♗f1 ♗d7 23 ♗c4 ♖b4 24 b3 ♖fb8 25 a3? (precipitates the end, although continued passivity would have to contend with the undermining advance of Black's a-pawn; White ought to have gone fishing in muddy waters by 25 ♘e4 with

sacrificial possibilities on c5) 25 ...
♖xb3! (a typical and instructive
exchange offer to batter down the
defensive wall) 26 ♗xb3 ♖xb3 27
♘e2 a5 28 ♗d4 ♗f8! 29 ♖b2 a4
30 ♖xb3 ab 31 ♖b1 c4! 32 ♖c1
♘xd5 0–1. White is helpless
against the black pawns, e.g. 33
♘c3 (33 ♖xc4? ♗b5) 33 ... ♘xc3
34 ♗xc3 ♗b5 followed by ...
♗g7 and the blockade is broken.

Ryshkov–Zarubin
Leningrad 1983

**1 d4 f5 2 g3 ♘f6 3 ♗g2 g6 4 ♘f3
♗g7 5 0-0 0-0 6 c4 d6 7 ♘c3 ♕e8
8 d5 ♘a6 9 ♘d4 ♗d7**

10   ♖b1
A useful move side-stepping the
veiled attack from Black's KB and
introducing b4 options into the
position.
10   ...   c6
The only sensible continuation
at this juncture. One final warning
against ... c5 when it can be answered by ♘e6: 10 ... c5? 11 ♘e6
♗xe6 12 de ♕c8 13 ♘d5 ♘xd5
14 cd c4 15 ♗g5 ♖e8 16 e4 fe 17
♗xe4 ♕c5 18 ♗e3 ♕b4 19 ♕g4
♘c7 20 h4 (with this Black's fate
is irredeemably sealed) 20 ... ♖f8
21 h5 ♘e8 22 hg h6 23 ♕h4 ♘f6
24 ♗f3 ♘e8 25 ♗xh6 ♖xf3 26
♗xg7 ♔xg7 27 ♕h7+ 1–0
Burger–Dlugy, 1983.
11   b3

The immediate double step
advance of the b-pawn appears to
have tactical objections, e.g. 11
b4?! (or similarly 11 dc bc 12 b4?!
♘xb4 13 ♖xb4 c5 14 ♘d5 cb 15
♘c7 ♕c8 16 ♘xa8 ♘e4 17 ♗xe4
fe 18 ♗g5 ♖f7 19 ♘c2
♕xa8 20 ♘xb4 ♗h3∓ Kara-
sev–Cherepkov, Leningrad 1983/
84) 11 ... ♘xb4 12 ♖xb4 (perhaps
12 a3 is worth consideration) 12
... c5 13 ♖xb7 cd 14 ♘b5 ♕c8 15
♖c7 (or 15 ♖xa7 ♕xc4 16 ♖xa8
♖xa8 17 ♘d4 ♖xa2 18 e3 ♘e4±)
15 ... ♕b8 16 ♖c6 ♘e4! 17 ♗xe4
♗xc6! 18 dc fe and Black's
material advantage should be
decisive; Milut–Armas, Romanian
Ch.
11   ...   ♘c7 *(24)*

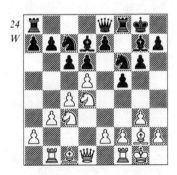

11 ... ♖b8 merits careful consideration here as it could quite
easily turn out to be the most
precise move. Cebalo–Jacimovic,
Pula 1985, continued 12 ♗b2 ♘c7
13 b4 (perhaps too forcing; 13 e3
would be normal) 13 ... e5! 14 de

♘xe6 15 e3 ♕f7 16 ♕b3 ♘xd4 17 ed and now instead of 17 ... b5 Black could either bring about a stable equality by 17 ... ♗e6 18 d5 cd 19 cd ♗d7 or try for more by 17 ... f4!?

12   ♗b2

This looks natural enough but it has the drawback of allowing Black to get on with his plan unhindered. Alternatives:

(a) 12 b4 (with the black knight's retreat the tactical problems have disappeared) 12 ... e5 13 de (both 13 ♘b3 cd 14 ♘xd5 ♘cxd5 15 ♗xd5+ ♘xd5 16 ♕xd5+ ♗e6 and 13 dc ed! 14 cd ♕xd7 15 ♘a4 ♘e4 16 ♗b2 b5 are in Black's favour) 13 ... ♘xe6 14 ♘b3 (better to support the knight by 14 e3) 14 ... ♘g4! 15 ♗b2 ♘e5 (Black has neatly highlighted the drawback of the b4 advance—the weakening of c4—and has achieved a perfectly viable position) 16 ♘d2 a5?! (rather than spurring White on with his plan he should make him think twice by playing 16 ... a6) 17 b5 ♘c5 18 bc bc 19 ♘a4! and White's position is the more purposeful; Tukmakov–M. Gurevich, USSR 1982.

(b) 12 e3 (creating an alternative retreat for the knight) 12 ... c5 13 ♘de2 b5 14 cb ♘xb5 15 ♘xb5 ♗xb5 16 ♗b2 ♕f7= 17 ♖e1 ♘e4 18 ♗xg7 ♕xg7 19 ♖c1 a5 20 ♘f4 ♗d7 21 ♕c2 ♘f6 22 ♕d3

♖fb8 23 ♘e6 ♗xe6 24 de ♖a7 25 ♖c4 ♕f8 26 e4 fe 27 ♗xe4 ♕e8 28 ♕d2 ½–½ Adorjan–Grigorov, Prague 1985.

(c) 12 dc bc 13 b4 e5 14 ♘b3 ♕e7, with chances for both sides in a complicated position, is a suggestion of Tukmakov's.

12   ...   c5

13   ♘f3

The knight is not well placed on c2, e.g. 13 ♘c2 ♖b8 (13 ... g5 intending play on the kingside comes into consideration) 14 e4 (the point of leaving the bishop's diagonal clear) 14 ... b5 15 e5?! (over-optimistic) 15 ... de 16 d6 ♘e6 17 ♘xb5 ♗xb5 18 de ♕xe7 19 cb (thus far Szilagyi–Armas, Tatabanya 1985) 19 ... ♘d4 20 a4 ♖fd8 and Black dominates the centre.

13   ...   ♖b8

14   ♘d2   b5

15   cb

White has decided to leave his e-pawn untouched for as long as possible and therefore has to deal with the threatened ... b4 in more radical fashion. Both 15 e3 and 15 e4 were alternatives worth attention with balanced chances.

15   ...   ♘xb5

16   ♘c4   g5

With the centre stable and some progress already made on the queenside Black now turns his attention to the opposite flank.

| 17 | ♘xb5 | ♗xb5 |
| 18 | ♕c2 | |

Erroneously egging Black on. Much safer was 18 e3 in order to be able to open the e-file in the event of Black still pushing on with ... f4.

| 18 | ... | **f4** (25) |

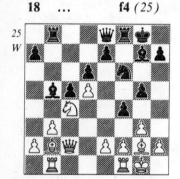

Black has made considerable progress and is clearly in the driving seat.

| 19 | **♕f5?** | |

Merely a waste of time.

19	...	h6
20	gf	♗d7
21	♕d3	gf
22	e4	

White pins his hopes on countering Black's kingside attacking chances by central action but this turns out to be misguided.

| 22 | ... | ♕h5 |
| 23 | f3 | ♗b5 |

Removing the sting from e5.

| 24 | e5 | de |
| 25 | ♖fe1 | **e4!** (26) |

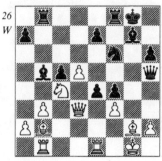

Black has neatly thwarted White's counterplay and now passes to decisive action on the kingside. The game concluded: 26 fe ♗xc4 27 bc (27 ♕xc4? f3 28 d6+ ♔h8 29 de f2+ 30 ♔xf2 ♘g4++ 31 ♔g3—31 ♔e2 ♘e5+ costs the queen—31 ... ♕xh2+! 32 ♔xg4 ♖f4 mate) 27...♘g4 28 ♕h3 ♕g5! 29 ♗xg7 ♕xg7 30 e5 ♖xb1 31 ♖xb1 ♘xe5 32 ♔h1 f3 33 ♗f1 ♖f6? (Black loses his way; simply 33 ... ♔h8 with 34 ... ♖g8 to follow would quickly wrap things up) 34 ♕c8+ ♔h7 35 ♗h3 ♕f8 36 ♕xc5 ♖f4 37 ♖b7 ♖xc4 38 ♕e3? (38 ♖xe7+! ♔h8 39 ♕e3! keeps matters unclear) 38 ... ♕f6 39 ♗f1 ♖h4 40 ♖xa7?? ♖xh2+ 0-1.

4 Leningrad: Miscellaneous Systems

In this chapter we review various White alternatives to the mainline sequence 1 d4 f5 2 g3 ♘f6 3 ♗g2 g6 4 ♘f3 ♗g7 5 0-0 0-0 6 c4 d6 7 ♘c3. Working backwards, we shall simply note our recommended responses where the deviations are no more than modifications of previously encountered plans, but those incorporating new strategic concepts will be examined in greater detail in the context of complete games.

Seventh move alternatives (after 6 ... d6 (27))

In addition to the classic knight development 7 ♘c3 White has also experimented with the following possibilities:

(a) 7 b3 This flexible move may comfortably be met by the standard 7 ... c6 with essentially similar play to the main line but of greater interest are the following continu-

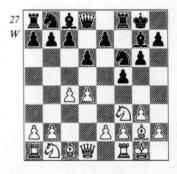

27
W

ations, attempting, in the first case, to exploit the lack of control of e4, and in the second the weakening of the a1–h8 diagonal: (i) 7 ... ♘e4 8 ♗b2 ♘d7 9 ♕c2 and now instead of 9 ... ♘df6 10 ♘bd2 e6 11 ♘e1 ♘xd2 12 ♕xd2 ♕e7 13 ♘d3± (Petrosian–Kaiszauri, Vilnius 1978) Black should prefer the immediate 9 ... e6, e.g. 10 ♘bd2 ♘xd2 11 ♕xd2 ♕e7 and he is poised to play the liberating ... e6–e5 when appropriate; (ii) 7 ... e5!? 8 de de 9 ♕c2 (evidently, the prospect of being pinned precludes

33

the capture on e5) 9 ... e4! 10 ♖d1
♕e7 11 ♘d4 c5 12 ♘b5 and now
not 12 ... ♘c6? 13 ♗f4± (Ban-
giev–Lutikov, USSR Navy Ch.
1970) but 12 ... a6! with fine prospects for Black.

(b) 7 b4 e5! 8 de de 9 ♗b2 e4
10 ♘d4 ♕e7 11 ♕b3 ♔h8 with
chances for both sides.

(c) 7 d5 By advancing in the
centre immediately White cuts out
Black's main line option of 7 ...
♘c6. The simplest response is 7 ...
♘a6 8 ♘d4 ♗d7 9 ♘c3 ♕e8
transposing to Chapter 3. Botvinnik has claimed that 10 ♘b3 leaves
the position slightly in White's
favour, but this contentious assessment has yet to be upheld in
practice. One additional example
of play: 10 ♖e1 ♘c5 11 ♕c2 c6 12
♘b3 ♘ce4! 13 ♘xe4 fe 14 ♗xe4
♕f7! (the veiled threat against f2
enables Black to regain his pawn
with advantage) 15 ♗e3 cd 16 cd
♖fc8 17 ♕d3 ♘xe4 18 ♕xe4 ♗f5
19 ♕h4 ♗xb2∓ Prakhov–Bert-
holdt, Bad Salzungen 1960.

Early b3 fianchetto
White may opt for a quick queenside fianchetto at almost any stage.
All Black's standard responses
remain valid but the most distinc-
tive counter features an intriguing
Leningrad/Stonewall hybrid.

Portisch–Smyslov
Portoroz 1971

**1 d4 f5 2 g3 ♘f6 3 ♗g2 g6 4 ♘f3
♗g7 5 b3 0-0 6 ♗b2 d5** *(28)*

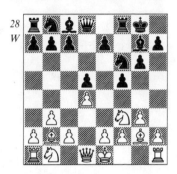

This bold advance signals a radical departure from the standard
Leningrad strategies. In place of
the usual quicksilver centre and
fleet-footed piece play, we have a
locked pawn front which slows
the mid-board battle considerably
and sees both sides jockeying for
optimum positioning behind their
own lines before engaging in hand
to hand combat. Comparison with
the standard Stonewall shows that
it is easier for Black to develop his
pieces in the Leningrad version
since in general there is less central
congestion and in particular
Black's QB, usually the problem
piece, finds useful deployment at
e6. One suspects that the Leningrad Stonewall could well prove
to be a major growth area in the
future development of the Dutch

Defence.

7	c4	c6
8	0-0	♗e6

With this immediate development Black declares himself unconcerned at the possible knight sally which White chooses to implement. The preparatory 8 ... ♔h8, enabling the bishop to drop back to g8 if attacked, is an alternative and equally valid approach.

9	♘g5	♗f7
10	♘c3	♕e8!

A key move in Black's plans; from f7 the queen will not only protect d5 but also maintain the pressure against c4 as will be seen.

11	♕d3	h6
12	♘xf7	♕xf7
13	f3	

A direct and natural-looking continuation which aims to open up the centre as rapidly as possible. Black's resources are also fully adequate to meet immediate play on the queen's wing, e.g. 13 cd cd 14 ♕b5 e6 15 ♘a4 ♘c6 16 ♘c5 ♘e4! with excellent central counterplay.

13	...	♘bd7
14	e4 *(29)*	

It appears that Black is in imminent danger of being rolled up in the centre, to his permanent spatial disadvantage, but there is a hidden weak spot in White's position which Black uncovers

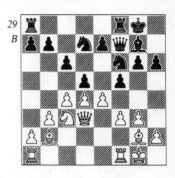

with considerable effect. Thus hindsight indicates that White should have played 14 cd ♘xd5! (not 14 ... cd 15 e4±) 15 ♘xd5 ♕xd5 with balanced chances according to Portisch.

14	...	dc!
15	bc	♘b6

Now all becomes clear; the weakness of the white c-pawn, and subsequently the c4 square, enables Black to seize the initiative and generate long-term pressure on the queenside.

16	c5	

16 d5 would be no better for then the other knight would swing into action on the e5 and c5 squares after 16 ... ♘fd7.

16	...	♘c4
17	♗c1	♖ad8
18	♖b1	♘d7!

Simultaneously increasing the pressure on the white centre and parrying the threat of 19 ♖xb7 on account of 19 ... ♘xc5.

19	d5	b5!

The knight has no intention of vacating its powerful outpost. If now 20 cb then the white d-pawn would come under attack after 20 ... ♘dxb6.

	20	dc	♘xc5
	21	♕c2	a6 *(30)*

White's proud-looking centre of the previous diagram has been shattered and it is merely a matter of time before the remnant straggler at c6 is ripe for the plucking. Rather than exit prosaically White attempts to muddy the waters with a pawn offer which at least allows him to dream of counterplay down the long diagonal. Black's play, however, is laser-accurate to the last, and it is the white king which becomes exposed: 22 f4 ♗xc3! 23 ♕xc3 ♘xe4 24 ♗xe4 fe 25 a4 ♕d5 26 ab ab 27 ♗b2 ♖f6 28 ♗a1 ♕c5+ 29 ♔h1 ♕xc6 30 ♖bd1 e3+ 31 ♔g1 ♖d2 32 ♖xd2 ed 33 ♕b3 ♖d6 34 ♕c3 e5! 35 ♖d1 (the attempt to keep the diagonal open

would meet with an elegant refutation: 35 fe d1♕ 35 ed ♕h1+! 37 ♔xh1 ♕xf1 mate) 35 ... ♕c5+ 36 ♔h1 ♕e3 37 fe ♖d3 0-1.

As an addendum to this fine game let us also note a more recent variation of the same theme which provides much interesting food for thought.   Yusupov–Malanyuk, USSR Ch. 1987: 1 d4 f5 2 g3 ♘f6 3 ♗g2 g6 4 b3 ♗g7 5 ♗b2 0-0 6 ♘f3 d6 7 0-0 c6 8 ♘bd2 ♔h8 9 c4 d5!? (electing for the Stonewall formation even at the cost of a tempo!) 10 ♘e5 ♗e6 11 ♘d3 ♘bd7 12 ♖c1 (Malanyuk gives 12 f3 ♕b6 13 e3 c5!? as unclear) 12 ... ♘e4 13 ♘f4 ♗f7 14 cd cd 15 f3 ♘d6 16 e3 (16 e4? ♕b6!) 16 ... ♕a5 17 ♘d3 (17 ♗c3 ♕b6 leaves the bishop misplaced) 17 ... ♖ac8 (Black has completed his development harmoniously and has no problems) 18 ♕e2 ♕a6 19 ♖fe1 ♖xc1 20 ♖xc1 ♖c8 21 ♖xc8 ♘xc8 22 a4 and now instead of 22 ... ♘d6 23 ♗f1 ♕c6 24 ♕d1 ♔g8 25 ♔f2 ♕c7 26 ♕c1 ♕xc1 27 ♘xc1 which left White a tiny edge which he worked hard to exploit before agreeing to a draw on move sixty, Malanyuk proposes 22 ... e5 23 de ♘xe5 24 ♗f1 ♘xd3 25 ♗xg7+ ♔xg7 26 ♕xd3 ♕xd3 27 ♗xd3 ♘e7 28 ♗b5 a6 29 ♗d7 ♔f6 as Black's surest path to the draw. That one of the foremost modern connoisseurs of the Leningrad should be ready to adopt the Stonewall formation a tempo down, yet nevertheless equalise without difficulty against a player of Yusupov's calibre, bodes well indeed for the future of the Leningrad Stonewall.

Sixth move alternatives
1 d4 f5 2 g3 ♘f6 3 ♗g2 g6 4 ♘f3 ♗g7 5 0-0 0-0 *(31)*

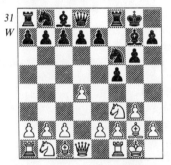

Some succinct suggestions for meeting the various offbeat alternatives to the natural 6 c4:

(a) 6 d5 is met most simply either by 6 ... c6 7 c4 d6 transposing to chapter 1 or 6 ... ♘a6 7 c4 d6 as in 7 d5 above.

(b) 6 c3 d6 (6 ... d5 is feasible) 7 ♕b3+ e6 8 ♘bd2 (Black is certainly happy to oblige with a Stonewall after 8 ♘g5 d5 since White will lose time) 8 .. a5 9 a4 ♘a6 10 ♖e1 ♘e4 with pleasant prospects for Black; Kavalek–Ciocaltea, Caracas 1970.

(c) 6 ♘c3 is best answered by 6 ... d5 with a favourable Stonewall

because the standard 6 ... d6 can leave Black facing tricky problems in the centre after either 7 ♖e1 or 7 ♕d3.

(d) 6 b3 — see Portisch–Smyslov above.

(e) 6 ♘bd2 d6 (apart from 6 ... d5 other experimental byways also beckon for those of an adventurous disposition, e.g. 6 ... c6 7 b3 a5 8 a4 ♘a6 or even 6 ... ♘a6 immediately) 7 c3 (7 ♖e1 ♘c6 8 e4 can be met either simply by 8 ... fe 9 ♘xe4 ♘xe4 10 ♖xe4 ♗f5! or more enterprisingly with 8 ... f4!? with complex play) 7 ... ♘c6 8 ♖e1 (other moves are no better, e.g. 8 ♕b3+ ♔h8 9 d5? ♘a5! 10 ♕a3 c5 with a favourable main line position, or 8 b4 a6 9 ♕b3+ e6 10 ♗b2 ♔h8 11 c4 e5! with balanced prospects) 8 ... e5 9 de ♘xe5!? (Black posits that the removal of this pair of knights will promote his attacking prospects; 9 ... de 10 e4 f4!? with unclear play also comes into consideration) 10 ♘xe5 de 11 e4 f4!? This typical pawn sacrifice gives Black plenty of chances. The game Kaplun–M. Gurevich, USSR 1983, illustrates the potential dangers to the white king: 12 ♘c4 (on 12 gf follows 12 ... ♘h5! and the weakness of the f4 square coupled with the vulnerability of the h2 and f2 points plus easy access of the black forces to the kingside all add up to an onerous defensive task for White) 12 ... fg 13 hg ♕e7 14 b3 ♖e8 15 ♗a3 ♕f7 16 ♕c2 a5 (a good move which sets up the possibility of a timely ... a4 initiative stealer) 17 ♘e3 ♗e6 18 ♖ed1 (the natural 18 ♖ad1 would land White in trouble after 18 ... a4) 18 ... ♗f8! (shrewdly trades the passive KB for its active counterpart and simultaneously gains the rooks access to the f-file) 19 ♗xf8 ♖xf8 20 ♖d2 h5 (whereas piece play alone would be unable to breach the defences the humble footsoldier can perform wonders, as we shall see) 21 c4 (attempting to pressurize the one weakspot in the black camp — the e-pawn) 21 ... ♘g4 22 ♘xg4 ♗xg4 23 ♖d5 ♕e7 24 ♕b2 ♖ae8 (inviting the rook to wander offside in search of booty) 25 ♖f1 c6! 26 ♖xa5 h4 27 b4 (hoping to get the rook back into play via a3) 27 ... ♖f7 28 f4? (28 f3 was mandatory when the struggle is still in progress whereas now Black clearly gains the upper hand) 28 ... h3! 29 ♗h1 (29 ♖xe5? hg∓∓ or 29 ♗f3 ♕d7!∓) 29 ... ef 30 gf ♖ef8 31 ♕d2 ♗e6 32 ♖f3 ♕h4 33 ♖g5 ♗g4! 34 ♕f2 h2+! (glorious and decisive self-immolation!; if now 35 ♔f1 then 35 ... ♕xg5 36 fg ♖xf3 wins) 35 ♕xh2 ♕xh2+ 36 ♔xh2 ♗xf3 37 ♗xf3 ♖xf4 38 ♗g2 ♔g7 39 a4 ♖f2 40 ♖c5 ♖c2 41 ♔g3 ♖c3+ 0–1.

Fifth move alternatives
1 d4 f5 2 g3 ♘f6 3 ♗g2 g6 4 ♘f3 ♗g7

There are no specially individualistic fifth moves available to White which will not transpose elsewhere, but it is worth noting the following instructive example: 5 ♘c3 0-0 6 h4?! c5 7 d5 d6 8 0-0 (stamps White's flank gesture as a sham) 8 ... ♘h5! (eyeing the weakened g3 and clearing the bishop's path) 9 e3 ♘d7 10 ♕e2 ♘e5 11 ♗d2 ♖b8 12 a4 a6 with the advantage over the entire board; note how White's only positive plan, playing e4, is ruled out on account of the extra strength lent the reply ... f4 by White's thoughtless sixth; Bobekov–Lutikov, Bulgaria v RSFSR 1958.

Karlsbad Variation: 1 d4 f5 2 g3 ♘f6 3 ♗g2 g6 4 ♘h3

First played back in the 1923 Karlsbad tournament, this variation still commands respect today. The rationale behind the knight's lateral development stems from the light square sensitivity in Black's formation, especially the almost invariable weakness of e6. By manoeuvring the KN to f4 White pressurizes this Achilles' heel in particular and the white squares in general, since the KB remains unblocked. Not infrequently, White augments his strategy by developing the queen to b3, simultaneously eyeing b7 and looking down the a2–g8 diagonal at e6. Black's counter strategy may well seek to utilize White's diminished control of e5 as well as a tempo-enhanced pawn advance on the kingside (... g5).

Sikhov–Korchnoi
USSR Student Team Ch.
Liningrad 1950

1 d4 f5 2 g3 ♘f6 3 ♗g2 g6 4 ♘h3
    4 ... ♗g7 (32)

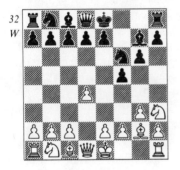

5 c4

There are some interesting alternatives to this standard approach:
(a) 5 d5!? attempting to restrict Black's options is an idea which has yet to be properly explored. One example: 5 ... d6!? 6 ♘f4 c5!? 7 h4 0-0 8 h5 ♕e8 9 hg hg 10 ♘d2 ♘a6 11 ♘f3 ♘e4 with chances for both sides in a sharp position, Solmundarsson–Padevsky,

Siegen Ol. 1970.
(b) 5 c3 c6! (anticipating the queen's development to b3, blocking the attack on b7 and preparing to oppose queens) 6 ♘d2 (in Toth–Knezevic, Italy 1973, a balanced and very difficult position arose after 6 a4 d6 7 ♕b3 e5 — 7 ... ♕b6 would be ineffective here on account of 8 ♕a2 — 8 de de 9 ♘a3 ♘a6 10 ♗e3 ♕e7 11 ♘c4 ♘d5) 6 ... d6 7 ♘f3 ♕c7 8 ♕b3 ♕b6 9 ♘f4 ♕xb3 10 ab ♘e4 11 ♘d3 ♗e6= Geller–Gufeld, Kislovodsk 1968.
(c) 5 0-0 0-0 6 ♘f4 e6!? (this method of circumventing White's usual strategy certainly deserves further investigation) 7 c4 d6 8 ♕b3 ♘a6 9 ♘c3 c6 10 ♖d1 ♕c7 (with a harmonious development behind his flexible pawn structure Black can be satisfied with his position) 11 e4?! (mis-timing the key central advance as Black shows in an instructive sequence) 11 ... fe 12 ♘xe4 ♘xe4 13 ♗xe4 e5! 14 de ♘c5 15 ♕e3 ♘xe4 16 ♕xe4 ♗xe5∓. Bereft of the protective KB White's king is prey to the black bishops on an open board; we have been following the exemplary miniature. P. Nikolic–Bjelajac, Novi Sad 1982, which concluded thus: 17 ♕e2 ♗f5 18 ♘d3 ♗d4! 19 ♗f4 ♖ae8 20 ♕d2 c5 21 ♘b4 ♗e4 22 ♘c2 ♗xb2 23 ♗xd6 ♕f7 24 ♖e1 ♗c3! neatly

refuting White's desperate attempts to distract the black pieces; White resigns.

5 ... 0-0
6 ♘c3 d6

Black proceeds in keeping with the main line strategy already outlined in Chapter 1. Once again 6 ... e6!? comes seriously into consideration (see P. Nikolic–Bjelajac above). Two further examples: 7 0-0 (7 ♘f4 followed by h4 is a sharp alternative) 7 ... d6 (7 ... ♕e7 lands Black in difficulties after the positional pawn sacrifice 8 d5 e5 9 d6! ♕xd6 10 ♕xd6 cd 11 ♘b5 and Black's mobilization is severely hampered, Taimanov–Liebert, Rostov 1961) 8 b3 c6 9 ♕c2 (9 ♗a3 can also be answered by 9 ... a5 but not 9 ... ♕a5?! 10 ♕c1 ♖d8 11 b4 when Black is cramped; Ree–Hübner, Wijk aan Zee 1975) 9 ... a5 10 ♗a3 ♘a6 11 ♖ad1 ♕c7 12 ♘f4 ♘b4 13 ♕b1 e5 and with the liberating ... e5 thrust Black secures equality; Averbakh–Gulko, USSR 1976.

Another logical response to White's system which has hardly been played at all yet is 6 ... ♘c6!?, e.g. 7 d5 ♘e5 8 b3 ♘f7 9 ♗b2 e5 10 de de 11 ♕xd8 ♖xd8 and Black has no difficulties; Osnos–Legky, Lvov 1984.

7 ♘f4

Alternatively:

(a) 7 0-0 is considered inexact because Black may reply 7 ... e5 8 de de 9 ♕xd8 ♖xd8 10 ♘d5 ♖d7! (necessary on account of the twin threat of capturing on c7 immediately and on b7 after 11 ♘e7+ and 12 ♘xc8) with good prospects of containing White's initiative according to theoretical works. Personally, I find Black's position here unappealing and would prefer 7 ... e6 or 7 ... c6.

(b) 7 d5 is generally held to be the most precise continuation as it prevents ... ♘c6 and enables ... e6/e5 to be captured (*en passant*). More importantly, it means that after 7 ... c6 8 0-0 e5 9 de Black cannot try 9 ... ♘a6 because of 10 ♗f4 and is thus compelled to play 9 ... ♗xe6 after which White has 10 ♕b3! ♕e7 11 ♘g5 ♗f7 (11 ... ♗c8 12 e4! ±) 12 ♘xf7 ♖xf7 13 ♗f4 ♘a6 14 ♖ad1 ♘e8 15 ♕a3 when Black is under fierce pressure; Ree–Rakic, Maribor 1980.

In the search for better defensive methods the following come strongly into consideration:

(b1) 7 ... ♘g4!? is an interesting suggestion of Dolmatov which has yet to be tested in practice.

(b2) 7 ... ♘a6!? 8 0-0 ♗d7 with similar play to Chapter 1, e.g. 9 ♖e1 c6 10 e4 fe 11 ♘xe4 ♘xe4 12 ♖xe4 ♘c5 with plenty of possibilities for Black in a roughly equal position.

(b3) 7 ... c6 8 0-0 ♗d7!? 9 ♕b3 (Dolmatov notes the very unclear variation 9 c5!? dc 10 ♕b3 ♕b6 11 dc+ ♕xb3 12 cb ♕b6 13 ba(♕) ♘c6 14 ♘a4 ♕b4) 9 ... ♕b6 10 ♗e3 ♕xb3 11 ab c5 12 ♘f4 ♘a6 13 ♘e6 ♖fc8 14 ♘xg7 ♔xg7 15 ♘a2? (it would have been better to play to open up the centre by 15 ♗d2 intending e4) 15 ... b5! 16 cb ♗xb5 17 ♘c3 ♘c7∓ White's doubled isolated b-pawns are a lasting liability; Zaichik–Dolmatov, Harkov 1985.

7	...	c6
8	d5	e5
9	de	♘a6!?

At the very least this is a superior move-order to the commonly played 9 ... ♕e7 after which White may choose to obtain the preferable position by the simple means of 10 ♖b1!? ♗xe6 (now 10 ... ♘a6 would be met by 11 b4 threatening 12 b5) 11 ♘xe6 ♕xe6 12 0-0 ♘a6 13 b3 with the bishop pair and sounder pawn structure; Legky–Machulsky, Tallin 1985.

10 ♗e3?!

This simplistic move, hoping to prevent ... ♘c5, meets with a vigorous rebuff. After the more natural 10 0-0 ♘c5 Harding notes 11 ♖e1 (11 b4 ♘ce4) 11 ... g5 12 ♘h3!? (12 ♘d3 ♘ce4) 12 ... h6 13 e4 ♗xe6 as adequate for Black (which it certainly is) and 13 ... ♘cxe4 as worth checking (which

it may be).

10	...	♕e7
11	0-0	g5!
12	♘d3	♘g4!
13	♗d2	♗xe6
14	b3	♘c5 (33)

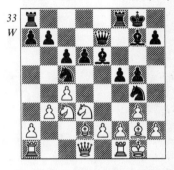

Black has energetically pushed back the white pieces and wrested the initiative. As the game proceeds we see Black convert his superior dynamism into a tangible queenside pawn majority whilst White's attempts to counter in the centre are contained by the bulwark knight on e5. A final effort to undermine the knight by removing its KB protection is crisply refuted by an exchange sacrifice. 15 h3 ♘e5 16 ♘xc5 dc 17 ♕c2 ♖ad8 18 ♖ad1 f4! 19 ♘e4 h6 20 ♗c3 ♖xd1 21 ♕xd1 b5! 22 cb cb 23 ♕a1 ♗f7 24 ♖d1 b4 25 ♗b2 c4 26 bc ♗xc4 27 ♖d2 ♔h8 28 ♘d6 ♗g8 29 ♗e4?! fg 30 fg ♕e6! 31 ♔g2 ♗h7 32 ♗xh7 ♔xh7 33 ♕b1+ ♔h8 34 e4? g4! 35 ♘f5 ♖xf5! 36 ef ♕c6+ 37 ♔g1

(37 ♔f2 ♕f3+ 38 ♔g1 ♕e3+ 39 ♖f2 ♘d3 would result in a lost king and pawn ending) 37 ... ♘f3+ 38 ♔f2 ♘xd2 39 ♗xg7+ ♔xg7 40 ♕xb4 ♕b6+ 41 ♕xb6 ab 42 hg ♘e4+ 43 ♔e3 ♘c3 44 ♔f4 ♔f6 0–1.

Fourth move alternatives
1 d4 f5 2 g3 ♘f6 3 ♗g2 g6 *(34)*

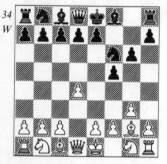

Other fourth moves pose no danger to Black:

(a) 4 ♘d2 ♘c6!? (reacting to the fact that the d-pawn is now undefended; 4 ... d5 is also eminently playable) 5 d5 (on 5 c3 Black may either revert to the trusty 5 ... d5 or experiment with 5 ... e5!? with the idea 6 ♗xc6 bc 7 de ♘g4 8 ♘df3 ♕e7 9 ♗f4 ♗g7 10 ♕d4 c5 11 ♕d5 ♖b8 when the threat of 12 ... ♗b7 puts White in a quandary) 5 ... ♘b4!? (an interesting departure from the usual ... ♘e5) 6 c4 (the original course taken by Szabo–Gheorghiu, Budapest 1970, clarified in Black's favour after 6 ♘c4 c6! 7 d6 b5! 8 ♗d2 bc 9 ♗xb4 ed 10 ♗xd6 ♗xd6 11 ♕xd6 ♕e7) 6 ... a5 7 a3 ♘a6 8 b4 ♗g7 9 ♖b1 0-0 10 ♘gf3 ab 11 ab c5!= Gheorghiu.

(b) 4 ♘c3 d5! 5 ♗g5 c6 and in comparison with similar variations arising from 2 ♗g5 White's KB is passively placed.

(c) 4 h4 is less outré than it appears at first sight, but not surprisingly fails to challenge Black's equanimity, e.g. 4 ... ♗g7 5 ♘h3 d6 6 d5 (6 c3 c6 is fine for Black, cf. 5 c3 in the Karlsbad Variation) 6 ... c6 7 c4 e5 8 de ♗xe6 9 ♘d2 ♕b6 10 0-0 0-0 11 ♘g5 ♖e8 and in this balanced position White's h4 advance begins to look superfluous; Olafsson–Alexander, Amsterdam Ol. 1954.

Systems with c4 and ♗g5
Systems where White combines ♗g5 with c4 are best implemented via the move order 1 d4 f5 2 c4 without fianchettoing then KB. That Black has an easy time of it when White plays ♗g5 in the context of a main line fianchetto is well illustrated by the game Usachi–Stein, Ukraine Ch. 1957, which went 1 d4 f5 2 c4 ♘f6 3 ♘c3 g6 4 g3 ♗g7 5 ♗g2 0-0 6 ♗g5 c6 7 ♕d2 d6 8 ♖d1 ♕c7 9 ♘f3 ♘bd7 10 0-0 (10 d5 meets with tactical problems after 10 ... ♘b6 11 b3 cd 12 cd ♘e4! 13 ♘xe4 fe

14 ♘d4 ♘xd5 15 ♗xe4 ♘c3 etc.)
10 ... e5 11 de de 12 ♗h6 ♗xh6
13 ♕xh6 e4 14 ♘d4 ♘e5 and
Black's advanced pawn chain and
well posted knights give him the
better position thanks to his kingside attacking chances.

Smyslov–Belyavsky
Sochi 1986
1 d4 f5 2 c4 ♘f6 3 ♘c3 g6

4 ♗g5 *(35)*

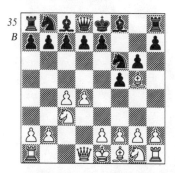

When White has ♗g5 in mind
he must play it straight away and
not preface it by ♘f3: 4 ♘f3 ♗g7
5 ♗g5 0-0 6 ♕d2?! (this is the real
culprit although other moves also
leave Black free to carry out his
basic plan unhindered, e.g. 6 ♕c2
d6 7 e3 c6 8 ♗e2 ♕a5 9
0-0 e5 and White certainly cannot
lay claim to any advantage; Baumbach–Babrikowsky, E. German
Ch. 1976) 6 ... ♘e4! 7 ♘xe4 fe 8
♘g1 b5! 9 e3 (9 cb a6 gives Black
control of the centre and open

lines while White's development
remains difficult to complete)
9 ... ♖f5! 10 ♗h4 bc 11 ♗xc4 +
d5 with a positional advantage
to Black; Kelecevic–Rajkovic,
Yugoslavia 1973.

4 ... ♗g7
5 ♕d2

Nor are other moves to be
feared:

(a) 5 ♗xf6 ♗xf6 6 e4 fe 7 ♘xe4
0-0 8 ♘f3 d6 9 ♗e2 ♗f5 10
♘xf6+ ef 11 0-0 c6= Sokolov–
Shahovic, Yugoslavia 1973.

(b) 5 e3 c5 6 ♗d3 d6 7 ♘f3
0-0 8 0-0 ♘c6 9 d5 ♘b4 10 a3
♘xd3 11 ♕xd3 ♘d7 12 ♗f4 h6
13 h3 a6 (with the more purposeful
piece coordination plus the latent
power of the bishop pair Black
has the superior prospects) 14 a4
b6 15 ♗g3 g5 16 ♖ab1 ♕e8 17
b4 ♕h5 18 ♘e2 (Black now carries
out an imaginative manoeuvre
designed to stifle any queenside
counterplay in order to be able to
concentrate on the king's wing
undistracted) 18 ... a5! 19 bc bc
20 ♘d2 ♘b8 21 f4 ♘a6 22 ♘f3
♘b4 and Black is firmly in control;
Lerner–Belyavsky, USSR, Ch.
1984.

5 ... c5!

This central challenge also has
the virtue of freeing the queen for
action. While Black should avoid
5 ... h6 6 ♗xf6 ♗xf6 7 e4 which
leaves him with a rickety kingside

in the face of a strong central preponderance, there may be a valid alternative in 5 ... ♘c6, e.g. 6 h4 (6 ♖d1 h6 7 ♗xf6 ♗xf6 8 ♘f3 d6 9 e4 e5 is equally satisfactory for Black) 6 ... h6 (not exactly forced) 7 ♗xf6 ♗xf6 8 e4!? (8 ♘f3 d6 9 e4 e5 10 de de 11 ♕xd8+ ♗xd8 could easily find White rueing the disappearance of his QB; Koblencs–Lutikov, Lativa v RSFSR 1955) 8 ... ♘xd4 9 ef ♘xf5 10 ♗d3 with attacking chances in return for the pawn.

6   dc

6 d5 is a serious alternative which awaits testing in practice but 6 ♘f3?, erroneously noted as good for White by Belyavsky and Mikhalchishin, is in fact a dreadful mistake on account of 6 ... ♘e4!

6   ...   ♘a6

6 ... ♕a5? 7 ♗xf6 ♗xf6 8 ♘d5 puts Black in trouble.

7   ♗h6

Proceeding with one of the central ideas of this system — the exchange of Black's potentially powerful KB. Another approach would be to develop and keep Black out of the key central squares: 7 ♘h3 ♘c5 8 f3 0-0 9 e3 d6 10 ♗e2, with a rich position which Belyavsky and Mikhalchishin contentiously assess as slightly in White's favour.

7   ...   ♗xh6

Black dismisses 7 ... 0-0 correctly reckoning that his king will be safer in the centre than on the kingside.

8   ♕xh6   ♘xc5
9   ♘h3

9 f3 ♕a5 10 0-0-0 b5 11 cb a6 12 e4 (Belyavsky and Mikhalchishin) would produce mutually difficult complications.

9   ...   ♕a5
10   0-0-0 *(36)*

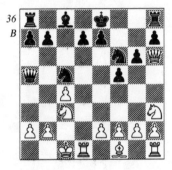

10   ...   b5!

In such positions material is of little consequence in the race to get to the king first.

11   ♘g5?

Too optimistic; consolidation by 11 cb a6 12 b6! ♕xb6 13 f3 ♖b8 14 ♕d2 0-0 15 e3 was in order.

11   ...   ♗b7!

Bringing d5 under control and thus avoiding variations such as 11 ... b4? 12 ♕g7 ♖f8 13 ♘d5 ♘xd5 14 ♘xh7 ♘e6 15 ♕xg6+ and wins.

12   ♕g7

There is no time to take the pawn, e.g. 12 cb ♘ce4 13 ♘cxe4 ♗xe4 14 ♘xe4 ♘xe4∓ Belyavsky and Mikhalchishin.

| 12 | ... | ♖f8 |
| 13 | ♘xh7 | |

Consistent but quite hopeless although the white position was beyond salvation anyway.

13	...	♘xh7
14	♕xh7	b4
15	♘d5	

Trying to gain time by the mate threat to organize his defences; 15 ♕xg6+ ♔d8 16 ♘d5 ♕xa2 wins easily for Black.

15	...	♗xd5
16	♖xd5	d6
17	♔b1	b3!

A decisive thrust just as White had seemed to have wriggled out.

| 18 | ab | ♖b8 |

With the entry of the rook the attack becomes irresistible.

19	♕xg6+	♔d7
20	♖xf5	♕e1+
21	♔a2	♘xb3
	0–1	

An impressive miniature against a former World Champion.

Other variations with c4 (1 d4 f5 2 c4 ♘f6)

None of these lines has any theoretical bite and are therefore rarely seen. Consequently, the examples presented here should be taken as just that since experience is as yet too limited to have hammered out any definitive paths.

(a) 3 g3 g6 4 ♗g2 ♗g7 5 ♘c3 0-0 (naturally, this opening sequence is flexible) 6 e3 d6 7 d5 (7 ♘ge2 e5 equalizes immediately) 7 ... e5 (of course, other methods familiar from the main lines are also applicable here) 8 de c6 9 ♘ge2 ♗xe6 10 b3 ♕c7 11 ♗b2 a5 12 ♕c2 ♘a6 and Black has an easy game; Vidmar jr.–Fuderer, Yugoslav Ch. 1951.

(b) 3 ♘f3 g6 4 e3 ♗g7 5 ♗e2 d6 6 0-0 ♘e4!? (utilizing White's lack of control of e4 to uncover the KB and support the vital ... e5 advance that way) 7 ♕c2 0-0 8 ♘bd2 ♘xd2 9 ♗xd2 e5 10 de de again with complete equality; Trifunovic–Grob, Zurich 1954.

| 3 | ♘c3 | g6 (37) |

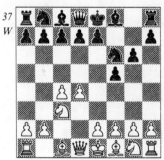

| 4 | ♘f3 | |

There have also been experiments with less natural continuations:

(a) 4 f3 (employed once by

Korchnoi, so not to be taken lightly) 4 ... ♗g7 5 e4 d6 (5 ... fe immediately looks preferable) 6 ♗d3 (6 e5!? requires a better response than 6 ... de 7 de ♕xd1+ 8 ♔xd1 ♘h5 9 f4 ♗e6 10 ♘f3± Korchnoi–Lombardy, Lone Pine 1979) 6 ... fe 7 fe?! (7 ♘xe4 appears necessary, but what comment is that on 4 f3?) 7 ... ♘c6 8 ♘f3 ♗g4 9 ♗e3 0-0 10 0-0 e5 11 d5 ♘d4 with a beautifully flowing positional advantage; Boros–Kusminich, USSR 1957.

(b) 4 e3 ♗g7 5 ♗e2 0-0 6 h4?! d6 7 h5 gh (an interesting decision, certainly not forced) 8 ♗xh5 e5 9 ♗e2 (thus far Hodos–Savon, USSR Ch. 1962) 9 ... c5! with chances and problems for both sides.

(c) 4 ♕c2 ♗g7 5 e4 fe 6 ♘xe4 0-0 shows clearly that brute implementation of the supposedly advantageous e4 advance can easily backfire and merely put White's development out of kilter.

4   ...   ♗g7

Now there are a number of contrasting plans available:

(a) 5 ♕c2 0-0 6 e4 fe 7 ♘xe4 ♘xe4 8 ♕xe4 d6 9 ♗e2 ♘c6 10 0-0 ♗f5 11 ♕h4 e5 12 ♗g5 ♕d7 with full equality; Nemet–Matulovic, Yugoslav Ch. 1972.

(b) 5 e3 0-0 6 b4!? (routine development cannot bring White any advantage, e.g. 6 ♗e2 d6 7

0-0 and now Black may choose according to taste between 7 ... c6 8 ♕c2 ♘a6 9 ♖d1 ♕e8 10 b3 e5= Larsen, or 7 ... ♘c6 8 d5 ♘e5 9 ♘d4 c5=; similarly, 6 ♗d3 d6 7 0-0 ♘c6 8 d5 ♘e5 also gives balanced play) 6 ... b6 7 ♕b3 c5 8 a3 e6 9 ♗e2 ♕e7 10 0-0 d6 11 ♗b2 ♘bd7 12 ♖ad1 ♘e8 and Black's flexible pawn structure and lack of weak points offset White's slight spatial edge in a mutually difficult position; Quinteros–Sax, Wijk aan Zee 1973.

(c) 5 ♗f4 d6 6 h4 (6 ♕b3 c6 or 6 ... e6 should both be perfectly adequate for Black) 6 ... ♘h5 (the most consequent riposte to White's provocative strategy) 7 e3 ♘d7 (after the natural 7 ... 0-0 White can bring tactical succour to his set-up by 8 c5!) 8 d5 ♘xf4 9 ef e5 10 de ♘c5 and this analysis by Vukovic leaves Black with excellent prospects.

The tacit prophylaxis of 2 ... ♘f6
There is a simple reason for preferring 2 ... ♘f6 to 2 ... g6: to avert the blitzkrieg attacks launched by 3 h4. These are dangerous for Black in all forms: 1 d4 f5 2 c4 g6 3 h4, or 2 ♘f3 g6 3 h4, or even 2 g3 g6 3 h4. Theory considers that White has at least sufficient compensation for the exchange offer which generally occurs on h5 (after a ... ♘f6, h5 ♘xh5, ♖xh5 gh

sequence) and in practice the defensive problems are extremely taxing.

Here is one warning example: 1 d4 f5 2 c4 g6 3 h4 ♘f6 4 h5 ♘xh5 5 ♖xh5 gh 6 e4 d6 (6 ... ♗g7 7 ♕xh5+ ♔f8 8 ♕xf5+ ♔g8 9 ♘f3 ♕f8 10 ♕h5 ♕f7 11 ♕h4 ♗f6 12 ♗g5± Polovdin) 7 ♕xh5+ ♔d7 8 ♕xf5+ e6 9 ♕h5 c6 (9 ... ♕f6 10 ♘f3±) 10 ♘c3 ♕e8 11 ♕h2!± ♔c7 12 ♗f4 ♘d7 13 ♘f3 b6 14 0-0-0 ♔b7 (14 ... ♗b7 15 ♔b1! enables the rook to go to c1 should it be required, and points up the long-term passivity of Black's position and his inability to undertake anything positive) 15 ♗xd6 ♘f6 16 ♗xf8 ♕xf8 17 ♘e5 ♗d7 18 d5 cd 19 ed ed 20 ♘xd7 ♘xd7 21 ♘b5 ♘c5 22 ♕c7+ ♔a6 23 cd ♔a5 24 b4+ ♔xb4 25 ♕g3! ♘a4 26 ♖d4+ ♔a5 27 ♕b3 ♖c8+ 28 ♔d1 1–0 Polovdin–Kovalev, USSR 1982.

5 Hort–Antoshin Variation

The Hort–Antoshin variation is a close relative of the Leningrad and transposition during the first few moves frequently occurs. Here, though, everything is subordinated to forcing through the ... e5 advance, natural development included, and consequently Black's strategy demands sophisticated positional insight and a well-developed sense of danger in order not to backfire.

We shall examine three games covering the main replies at White's disposal: first, where White avoids the kingside fianchetto, and then in turn the fianchetto both with and without c2–c4.

Antoshin–Hort
Moscow 1960

1	d4	f5
2	c4	♘f6
3	♘c3	d6
4	♘f3	c6 (38)

This last is the characteristic move of the variation; unchal-

38
W

lenged, Black's intention is to follow up with ... ♕c7 thus supporting the ... e7–e5 advance.

5   ♕c2

Proposing to cross Black's plans by advancing his own e-pawn first. Other possibilities:

(a) 5 e3 ♕c7 6 d5 (White cannot afford to be casual: 6 ♗d3 e5 7 e4 f4 concedes Black a significant spatial advantage on the kingside Etruk–Antoshin, USSR 1962) 6 ... e5 7 de ♗xe6 8 ♘d4 ♗d7 9 ♗d3 g6 10 b3 ♘a6 11 ♗b2 ♗g7 12 0-0 0-0 with a balanced position; Khouk–Hort, Leipzig Ol. 1960.

(b) 5 ♗g5 ♘bd7 6 e3 is best

48

met by 6 ... g6 and not 6 ... e5?! which facilitates an opening up of the position before Black is able to cope, e.g. 7 de de 8 ♕c2 e4 9 ♘d4 ♘e5 10 0-0-0 ♕e7 11 f3 ef 12 gf ♕f7 13 f4!± instructive play; Kotov–A. Zaitsev, Sochi 1967.

(c) 5 g3 will transpose to Gavrikov–Psakhis below.

| 5 | ... | ♘a6 |
| 6 | a3 | |

White would not be able to operate comfortably with threats of ... ♘b4 constantly in the air.

| 6 | ... | g6 |

Simultaneously promoting the development of both bishops.

7	e4	fe
8	♘xe4	♘xe4
9	♕xe4	♗f5
10	♕h4	

Hoping to exploit Black's weakened kingside. In Robatsch–Antoshin, Sochi 1974, White kept his queen centralized and a mutually difficult struggle developed after 10 ♕e3 ♗g7 11 ♗d2 0-0 12 ♗c3 ♘c7 13 ♗e2 b5 14 b3 a5 15 a4 b4 16 ♗b2 ♕d7.

| 10 | ... | ♗g7 |
| 11 | ♗e2 (39) | ♗f6 |

An ambitious move which considerably increases the tension. Fourteen years later Antoshin preferred to pursue equality through simplification: 11 ... e5!? 12 ♕xd8+ ♖xd8 13 ♗e3 ed 14 ♗xd4 ♔f7 15 ♗xg7 ♔xg7 16

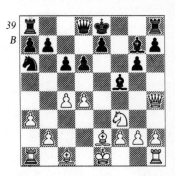

♘d4 ♘c5 17 0-0 d5 18 b4 ♘e6= Smyslov–Antoshin, Sochi 1974.

12	♕h6	c5
13	♗g5	♕a5+
14	♔f1	♗xg5
15	♘xg5	cd

Thus Black, temporarily at least, has an extra pawn but the position remains totally unclear and capable of going either way. It seems likely that White's following queen manoeuvre is not the best: 16 ♕g7 ♕e5 17 ♕f7+ ♔d7 18 ♘f3 ♕f4! (18 ... ♕e4 19 ♖d1 ♖af8 20 ♕g7 gives Black problems) 19 ♕d5 (since now 19 ♖d1 would fail against 19 ... d3!) 19 ... d3! 20 ♗xd3 (not 20 ♕xb7+? ♘c7 21 ♗d1 ♖hb8 22 ♗a4+ ♔d8 23 ♕c6 ♖b6 snaring the queen) 20 ... ♗xd3+ 21 ♕xd3 ♖hf8 22 ♖e1 ♖ac8 (Black is clearly on top) 23 b3 ♘c5 24 ♕e3 e5 25 ♘d2 ♘d3 26 ♕xf4 ♖xf4 27 ♖e2 ♖af8 28 f3 ♘c1 29 ♖e4? (collapses immediately; 29 ♖e3 would have hung on longer) 29 ... ♘xb3! 0–1.

Gavrikov–Psakhis
USSR Ch. 1985

1	d4	f5
2	g3	♘f6
3	♗g2	d6
4	c4	

The usual range of less orthodox methods is available:

(a) 4 ♘h3 c6 5 c4 ♕c7 (simply 5 ... e5 is also playable) 6 ♘c3 e5 7 0-0 ♗e7 and as White does not have the c4–c5 possibility as in the analogous main line Black is able to complete his kingside development satisfactorily.

(b) 4 ♘c3 ♘bd7 5 ♘h3 (5 e4 fe 6 ♘xe4 ♘xe4 7 ♗xe4 ♘f6 8 ♗g2 c6 and Black has no worries) 5 ... e5 6 0-0 ed 7 ♕xd4 ♗e7 8 b3 c6 9 ♗b2 d5 10 e3 0-0 with approximately equal chances in a rich position; R. Byrne–Gheorghiu, Varna Ol. 1962.

(c) 4 d5 e5!? 5 de ♘c6 6 ♘h3 ♗xe6 7 ♘g5 ♗g8 8 0-0 and in this entirely satisfactory position for Black several continuations deserve trying, e.g. 8 ... ♕d7 or 8 ... d5, but 8 ... h6? is mistaken since 9 ♘f3 ♕d7 10 ♘d4 harmonizes the white forces and leaves Black at some disadvantage; Kottnauer–Davie, Dundee 1967.

4	...	c6

4 ... e5 is not unthinkable but as yet there are no practical examples.

5	♘f3	

Somewhat more precise than developing the queen's knight first, since 5 ♘c3 gives Black the additional possibility of playing 5 ... e5!? immediately, when White's chances of gaining an advantage are minimal, e.g. 6 de (or 6 e4 ♕c7 7 ef ♗xf5 8 ♘f3 ♗e7 and Black is quite OK, Mikenas–Cherepkov, TU Ch. USSR 1971) 6 ... de 7 ♕xd8+ ♔xd8 8 ♘f3 e4 9 ♘g5 ♔e8 10 f3 h6 11 ♘h3 ef 12 ♗xf3 ♘bd7 13 ♘f4 ♘c5 14 b3 ♔f7 = Bannik–Antoshin, USSR Ch. 1957.

5	...	♕c7 (40)

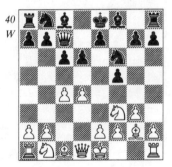

6	♘c3	

Alternatively:

(a) 6 0-0 e5 7 de de 8 ♕c2 (Romanishin–Antoshin, Cienfuegos 1977) 8 ... e4! is given as unclear by Botvinnik.

(b) 6 b3 e5 7 de de 8 ♗b2 ♘bd7 9 ♕c2 g6 10 ♘bd2 ♗h6!? 11 ♕c3 e4 with a mutually difficult position; Krause–Sydor, Dortmund 1976.

(c) 6 d5!? is a surprising gambit which gains time and opens up the position at the cost of an important central pawn. Practice indicates it deserves respect: 6 ... cd 7 cd ♘xd5 8 0-0 ♘f6 9 ♘c3 ♘c6 (one suspects Black could profitably seek an improvement here) 10 ♗g5 e6 11 ♖c1 (better than 11 ♗xf6 gf 12 ♘b5 ♕e7 13 ♖c1 d5 14 ♘fd4 a6 15 ♘xc6 bc 16 ♘d4 c5 17 ♘xf5 ♕d7! when the black infantry dominate the centre; Spassov–Jankov, Primorsko 1972) 11 ... ♗e7 12 ♘b5 ♕d7 13 ♗xf6 gf 14 ♘fd4 d5 15 ♘xe6! and Black is lost; Baranov–A. Zaitsev, ½-final TU Ch. USSR 1965.

6 ... e5
7 0-0

Other continuations promise little:

(a) 7 c5?! clarifies the centre to Black's advantage, e.g. 7 ... e4 8 cd ♗xd6 9 ♘g5 (or 9 ♘d2 ♗e6 10 e3 h5 11 ♘e2 h4 12 ♕c2 ♘a6 13 a3 ♕f7 with Black clearly in control; Opocensky–Antoshin, Leipzig 1965) 9 ... h6 10 ♘h3 ♘a6 11 a3 ♕f7 12 f3 ef 13 ♗xf3 ♗e6 14 ♗f4 ♖d8 15 0-0 ♘c5! and again Black is clearly on top; Golovko–Antoshin, USSR 1970.

(b) 7 e4 prematurely picks a tactical fight where Black's

resources are more than adequate: 7 ... fe 8 ♘g5 ♗g4 9 ♕b3 ed 10 ♘cxe4 ♘bd7 11 h3 ♘xe4 12 ♗xe4 ♘c5! 13 ♕c2 ♕e7! 14 0-0 ♗d7 15 ♗xh7 0-0-0 and Black soon broke through on the kingside; Hofmann–Nevole, corr. 1969/70.

(c) 7 de permits Black's KB to take an active part in the proceedings and thereby enhance his prospects of equalizing, e.g. 7 ... de 8 e4 (better than 8 0-0 ♗b4! 9 ♕c2 0-0 10 a3 ♗e7 11 e4 f4!? 12 gf ef 13 e5 ♘g4 with a typical sharp Dutch position where White's king is likely to be in the greater danger; Ignatiev–Chechelnitsky, Moscow 1964) 8 ... ♗b4! 9 ef (9 ♕b3 ♘a6 10 0-0 fe 11 ♘g5 ♗xc3 12 ♕xc3 ♗f5 is fine for Black; Karasev–Cherepkov, Leningrad Ch. 1974) 9 ... ♗xf5 10 ♕b3 ♘a6 11 0-0 and now instead of 11 ... 0-0-0?! which was shown to be good for White in Farago–Bokor, Hungarian Ch. 1967, after 12 ♗e3 ♗c5 13 ♗xc5 ♘xc5 14 ♕a3 ♘a6 15 ♘b5!, Black should prefer short castling, 11 ... 0-0, when the activity of his pieces goes a long way to offsetting the isolated pawn.

7 ... e4!

Experience has shown that this is Black's best try. It is instructive to note the drawbacks of the alternatives:

(a) 7 ... ♗e7 8 c5! (White could

also get the better of it with 8 de de 9 e4 obtaining an improved version of note c above) 8 ... e4 9 cd ♗xd6 10 ♘e5! ♗e6 (10 ... ♗xe5 11 de ♕xe5 12 ♗f4 gives White a strong initiative in return for the pawn) 11 f3 ♗xe5 12 de ♕xe5 13 fe fe 14 ♗f4 ♕c5+ 15 ♔h1 ♘bd7 16 ♖c1 ♕h5 17 ♕d6 and Black is in dire straits; Udovcic–Lombardy,   Zagreb 1969.

(b) 7 ... ♗e6 8 d5! ♗d7 9 e4 fe 10 ♘g5 ♗e7 11 ♘gxe4 ♘a6 (11 ... 0-0? 12 c5! is dreadful for Black; Kozma–Marsalek, Czechoslovakia 1962) 12 ♗e3 and with a spatial advantage, more active pieces, and firm control of the central blockading square, e4, White's positional superiority is indisputable.

Let us note that it is only here that we join our game properly as it actually arose via the move order 1 ♘f3 f5 2 g3 ♘f6 3 ♗g2 d6 4 d4 c6 5 0-0 ♕c7 6 c4 e5 7 ♘c3 e4. Such transpositions are a common occurrence.

8   ♘g5

This has supplanted 8 ♘e1 in contemporary praxis although the inadequacies of the retreat have yet to be shown over the board. The following is known: 8 ♘e1 ♗e7 9 f3 ef (attempting to hold the e4 point gets Black into trouble after 9 ... d5 10 cd cd 11 ♗f4) 10

ef (Korchnoi preferred to capture with the bishop: 10 ♗xf3 0-0 11 ♘g2 ♘bd7 12 ♗f4 ♖f7 13 b4 ♘f8 14 b5 ♘g6 15 bc bc but could claim no advantage in a complicated position;   Korchnoi–Antoshin, Moscow 1961; Antoshin analysed 13 c5 ♘f8 14 d5 — Black must always be alert to this sudden pawn rush — 14 ... ♘g6 15 cd ♗xd6 16 ♗xd6 ♕xd6 17 dc ♕c5+ 18 ♔h1 bc= as the weaknesses cancel out) 10 ... 0-0 11 ♘d3 ♗e6?! (simply 11 ... ♖e8 intending ... ♘bd7-f8 looks a better try) 12 b3 ♘a6 13 ♖e1 ♗f7 14 ♗h3 g6 15 ♘f4 ♕d7 16 d5 ♘c7 17 ♗b2 and White's position is a picture of positional superiority thanks to his spatial advantage, and pressure on the a1–h8 diagonal and down the e-file, particularly of course e6; Udovcic–Antoshin, Yugoslavia v USSR 1964.

8   ...   h6

This preludes an aggressive solution to Black's problems. It may be that a purely defensive approach will suffice to hold the balance: 8 ... ♗e7 9 f3 ef 10 ef (Botvinnik has suggested 10 ♘xf3; it is interesting to mull this over with the note on 8 ♘e1 in mind) 10 ... 0-0 11 ♖e1 ♘a6 12 a3 ♖e8 13 b4 h6 14 ♘h3 ♗d7 15 ♕d3 ♗f8 with equality according to Botvinnik, although Black would be wise to maintain his vigilance;

Danov–Knezevic, Skopje 1967.

9 ♘h3 ♛f7

This collected an exclamation mark from Gulko and although it could well be Black's best the alternative may also be playable: 9 ... ♗e6 10 d5 ♗f7 11 f3 cd (White obtained a clear advantage in Yusupov–Yermolinsky, Tallinn 1977, after the unsuccessful pawn offer 11 ... ♘bd7 12 fe fe 13 ♘xe4 cd 14 cd ♘xe4 15 ♗xe4 ♛c5+ 16 ♔h1) 12 cd ♛c5+ 13 ♔h1 ef 14 ef ♘xd5 15 ♖e1+ ♗e7 16 ♘a4!? ♛c7 17 ♘f4 ♘xf4 18 ♗xf4 0-0 19 ♖xe7 ♛xe7 20 ♗xd6 ♛d8 21 ♗xf8 ♛xf8 and Black holds the balance; Razuvayev–Mamatov, Frunze 1979.

10 d5 *(41)* g5!?

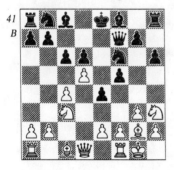

In the game where 9 ... ♛f7 was introduced Black continued with a less radical strategy: 10 ... cd 11 cd ♘a6 (also ! from Gulko) 12 f3 ef 13 ♗xf3 (± Gulko) g5! 14 ♗g2 ♛h5 15 ♘f2 ♗e7 16 ♗e3 0-0 17 ♗d4 (Gulko eschews the win of

a pawn by 17 ♘b5 ♗d7 18 ♘xa7 ♖ae8 19 ♗d4 even though he evaluates it as ±) 17 ... ♗d7 18 e4 ♛xd1 19 ♖axd1 ♘b4! 20 ♖d2 fe 21 ♘fxe4 ♘xe4 22 ♗xe4 ♖xf1+ 23 ♔xf1 ♖f8+ 24 ♔g2 b6 and the ending should be tenable; Gulko–Antoshin, Moscow Ch. 1981.

One important aspect of the text move is that it prevents White capturing on f3 with a piece because of the ... g4 fork.

11 f3 ef
12 ef c5

Black's play is consistently bold; Black locks the centre in preparation for the king taking up residence there. On reflection, this is not so surprising since a return to 'normal' chess by 12 ... ♗e7 13 ♖e1 0-0 14 b3 would leave White all the trump cards of space, development and coordination as well as making Black's advanced kingside pawns look as much a self-inflicted weakness as a vanguard of aggression.

13 ♖e1+ ♔d8
14 b4!?

Correctly seeking to open up the position since then the lack of communication between the black rooks could prove serious.

14 ... ♘a6!

The right response; on 14 ... cb there might follow 15 ♘b5 ♘a6 (not 15 ... ♘bd7? 16 ♗xg5!) 16

♗b2 ♘c5 17 ♕d4 ♗e7 18 ♖xe7! and it all falls apart.

15	bc	♘xc5
16	♘f2	♗d7
17	♖b1	♗g7

Black has marshalled his defences carefully and is optimally poised to counter any offensive and further reduce White's advantage. In the game White failed to find a really testing plan and a draw was shortly agreed: 18 ♘d3 b6 19 ♘b5 (19 ♘xc5 dc! 20 a4 ♘e8 21 ♘b5 ♗xb5 22 ab ♘d6 is unclear, White's domination of the e-file being offset by Black's magnificent knight) 19 ... ♗xb5 20 ♖xb5 ♘fd7 21 f4 g4 22 ♗e3 ♘xd3 23 ♕xd3 ♖e8 24 ♖bb1 ♖c8 ½–½. Probably, White was nagged by a feeling that he could have done better and was happy to call a halt. After, say, 25 a4 ♘c5 26 ♕a3 ♕c7 White would still have no clear method of breaking through.

Gheorghiu–Tal
Moscow 1971

1 d4 f5 2 g3 ♘f6 3 ♗g2 d6 4 ♘f3 c6 5 0-0 ♕c7 *(42)*

6   ♘bd2

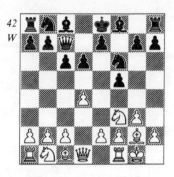

42
W

White aims to threaten to advance his e-pawn as quickly as possible and thus for the time being at least postpones c4. Other systems dispensing with c4 have also been played:

(a) 6 b3 e5 7 de de 8 ♗b2 e4! (8 ... ♘bd7 invites the dangerous pawn offer 9 e4!? ♘xe4 10 ♘bd2 ♘xd2 11 ♕xd2 e4 12 ♘h4 ♘f6 13 ♖ad1 threatening 14 ♕g5 with powerful pressure — Fuchs) 9 ♘d4 ♗e7 10 ♘d2 a6! (threatening ... c5) 11 e3 0-0 12 f3 c5 13 ♘e2 ef 14 ♗xf3 ♘c6 and Black has equalized at least; Gligoric–Kavalek, The Hague 1966. If White is attracted by the idea of the queen's fianchetto then it is probably best effected on move five in order to hinder ... e5. The attempt by Black to throw a spanner in the works by 5 b3 ♕a5+ does not quite come off, e.g. 6 ♘bd2 e5 7 de de 8 0-0 e4 9 ♘c4 ♕d5 10 ♘d4 g6 11 ♗b2 ♗e7 12 f4 0-0 13 ♘e3 ♕f7 14 c4± Vukic–Knezevic, Yugoslav Ch. 1967.

(b) 6 ♘c3!? is another promising method of initiating direct action in the centre. A major inconvenience for Black is that transpositions to a Stonewall leave the queen poorly placed and vulnerable to attack. Normal reactions can backfire badly: 6 ... e5 7 de de 8 e4 ♗b4 (by analogy to note c to White's seventh but here White's development is better and he can strike faster in the centre; 8 ... fe 9 ♘g5 ♗g4 is relatively best) 9 ef 0-0 (or 9 ... ♗xf5 10 ♘xe5! ♗xc3 11 bc ♕xe5 12 ♖e1 ♘e4 13 ♗xe4 ♗xe4 14 ♕d4!±) 10 ♘h4 ♘a6 11 g4 ♕e7 12 g5 ♗xc3 13 bc ♘e8 (thus far Krogius–Otstavokov, USSR 1965) 14 ♕g4! and Black has problems, e.g. 14 ... g6 15 f6! ♗xg4 16 fe ♖f7 17 ♗a3 or 14 ... ♘d6 15 ♗a3 c5 16 ♗d5+ ♔h8 17 ♘g6+! etc. Thus it seems that Black does best to opt for 6 ... g6 with Leningrad-type lines in mind.

6   ...   g6

The hidden sting concealed in the apparently innocuous development of the QN becomes clear if Black innocently proceeds with his plan: 6 ... e5? 7 de de 8 ♘c4! and there is no satisfactory reply, e.g. 8 ... e4 9 ♗f4 or 8 ... ♘bd7 9 ♘fxe5! ♘xe5 10 ♗f4±.

7   ♖e1   d5

As usual, the Stonewall formation proves the best way of keeping the lid on things.

8   c4

8 ♘e5 immediately should be answered as in the game and not by 8 ... ♘bd7?! 9 ♘df3 ♗g7 10

c4± since 10 ... ♘xe5? 11 de ♘g4 12 cd cd 13 ♕xd5 loses a pawn for nothing, Bilek–A. Zaitsev, Debrecen 1970, and Taimanov's recommendation of 10 ... dc is also unappetizing.

8	...	♗g7
9	♘e5	0-0
10	♘df3	♘e4
11	♗f4	*(43)*

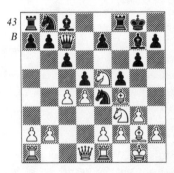

43
B

Clearly, this is a Stonewall which has gone very wrong for Black. White has an iron grip on e5 and has almost completed his development whereas Black's queenside has yet to wake from its slumbers. On top of that, the unhappily placed black queen must move again in view of the threatened discovered attack. That Black manages not to lose this position is a tribute to the resilience of the Stonewall formation — but it helps also to be a former world champion.

The game concluded as follows:

11 ... ♛b6 12 ♛c2 a5 (necessary restraint of the avalanche which would occur after, say, 12 ... ♝e6 13 c5 ♛d8 14 b4) 13 c5 ♛d8 14 h4 ♘d7 15 b3 ♘df6 16 a3 ♝d7 17 ♛c1 (lucky for Black that White did not think of this earlier) 17 ... ♘g4 (Black's first active move of the game ...) 18 ♖f1 (... and it is enough to cow White into curbing his ambitions; 18 ♘xg4 fg 19 ♘e5 would still leave White all the chances) 18 ... ♘ef6! ½–½. For the first time Black has the semblance of an acceptable position and one can well understand both parties being pleased to terminate the proceedings.

6 Staunton Gambit: 2 e4

The Staunton Gambit clearly constitutes one of the most radical and critical challenges to the fundamental soundness of the Dutch Defence. White posits that the gambitting of his important central pawn will best enable him to highlight the negative aspects of Black's first move—that it does not contribute to development, and exposes the king—by getting an advantage in development and mounting a kingside attack. Happily, the Dutch passes this crucial test with flying colours, and the Staunton Gambit is consequently rarely encountered in contemporary praxis.

| 1 | d4 | f5 |
| 2 | e4 | fe *(44)* |

As Steinitz wisely observed, the only way to refute a gambit is to accept it, and that is especially true where an important central pawn is on offer.

3 ♘c3

Obviously White's most natural

44
W

continuation. The artificial alternatives can easily bring White into difficulties:

(a) 3 ♘d2 ♘f6 4 g4 d5! 5 g5 ♘fd7 6 f3 e5! 7 fe ♗e7! (stronger than 7 ... ♕xg5 8 ♘gf3 ♕h5 as played in Bisguier–Bronstein, Goteborg 1955, when 9 ♗g2! would have brought White some play) and White is paying the penalty for flouting the elementary principles of opening play, e.g. 8 h4 0-0 9 ♘gf3 ed 10 ed ♘b6∓.

(b) 3 f3 e5! 4 de ♘c6 (4 ... d5!? certainly deserves attention) 5 ♕d5 ♕e7 (Black could also consider turning the tables with the gambit 5 ... ♗b4+ 6 c3 ♘ge7 7 ♕xe4 d5) 6 f4 d6 7 ed cd 8 ♗b5 ♗d7 9 ♘c3 ♘f6 and Black's active position and strong e-pawn guarantee a promising middle game.

3   ...   ♘f6

Now White must choose between the two major continuations 4 f3 and 4 ♗g5, which we shall examine in detail in the following illustrative games. In addition, there is the unjustifiably wild 4 g4?! which is rarely risked nowadays: 4 ... h6! and by maintaining his knight on f6 Black assures himself of an advantage no matter how White continues:

(a) 5 h4 d5 6 ♗h3 ♘c6 7 ♗f4 g5! 8 ♗e5 (8 hg hg 9 ♗xg5 courts disaster, *viz.* 9 ... ♗xg4 10 f3 ♖xh3! 11 ♖xh3 ♗xh3 12 ♘xh3 ♕d7 13 ♘f2 0-0-0; Yermolinsky–Safarov, Leningrad 1977) 8 ... ♗e6 9 f3 ♕d7 10 ♕d2 0-0-0∓ Byrne and Mednis.

(b) 5 f3 d5 6 g5 (or 6 ♗g2 e5! 7 de ♘xg4!∓ Kuzminikh, while 6 ♗f4 e6 7 ♕d2 ♗d6 8 0-0-0 ef 9 ♗xd6 cd 10 ♘xf3 0-0 leaves Black with an extra pawn and good prospects; Menchik–Sultan Khan, Cambridge 1932) 6 ... hg 7 ♗xg5 ♗f5 8 ♗g2 (after 8 ♕e2 ♘c6 9 0-0-0 ♕d7 10 ♗xf6?! ef 11 fe de 12 ♘xe4 0-0-0∓ White has restored material parity at the cost of positional inferiority; Gasztonyi–Szilagyi, Hungarian Ch.

1953) 8 ... e3! 9 ♘ge2 ♘c6 10 a3 e6 11 ♗xe3 ♗d6 and once again we observe White regaining his pawn but remaining with a considerable positional disadvantage; Tyroler–Araiza, 1928.

(c) 5 g5 hg 6 ♗xg5 d5 7 ♕d2 (7 f3 transposes to note (b)) 7 ... ♗f5 8 0-0-0 c6 9 f3 ♘bd7 10 ♗g2 ♕a5 and White has nothing to show for his pawn deficit; Radugin–Kubbel, Leningrad 1934.

(d) 5 f4?! d5 6 ♗e2 (6 g5 hg 7 fg ♘h5 8 ♗e2 g6∓) 6 ... g6! 7 ♗e3 h5! 8 g5 ♘g8 9 ♕d2 e6 10 f5 (allowing Black to blockade with his knight would be hopeless) 10 ... ef 11 ♘h3 c6 12 ♘f4 ♕d6 and despite White's nice blockade, two healthy extra pawns should be good enough to win; Szabo–Alexander, Amsterdam Ol. 1954.

(e) 5 d5?! e6 6 g5 (6 de d5∓) 6 ... hg 7 ♗xg5 ♗e7 8 ♗xf6 ♗xf6 9 ♘ge2 d6 10 ♗g2 c6! 11 dc d5 12 cb ♗xb7 White's attempt to gain space in the centre has completely backfired leaving Black with a huge strategical advantage in the form of the bishop pair and central pawn mass; Benediktsson–Kristjansson, Reykjavik 1968.

Gulko–M. Gurevich
USSR Ch. 1985

1 d4 f5 2 e4 fe 3 ♘c3 ♘f6

4   f3 *(45)*

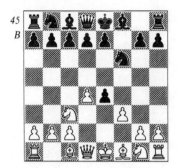

Wxb2 12 ♘xc7+ ♔f7 13 ♗c4+ ♔g6 and White is on the brink of defeat; Krause–Tartakower, Luxembourg 1936.

5 ... de
6 ♗g5

Serves to discourage various ... e5 thrusts. After 6 ♗c4, for example, Black has the pleasant choice between 6 ... e5!? 7 de (7 ♘ge2? ed 8 ♘xd4 ♗g4! is just bad for White, but 7 ♗g5 ed 8 ♘xe4 We7 would produce obscure complications) 7 ... Wxd1+ 8 ♘xd1 ♘g4 with easy equality, and 6 ... ♘c6 7 ♘ge2 e5!? (or Black could equalize by 7 ... ♗f5 8 0-0 Wd7) 8 ♗g5 (8 d5 ♘a5=) 8 ... ed! 9 ♘xe4 ♗b4+ 10 c3 dc 11 ♘4xc3 Wxd1+ 12 ♖xd1 ♘e4 and Black remains a pawn to the good with the endgame fast approaching (analysis by Kovacevic).

6 ... ♗f5 *(46)*

7 ♘ge2

In order to solve the problem of the development of the king's

---

The purest form of the gambit. Experience has shown that capturing this pawn gives White at least sufficient compensation in development and attacking chances, and therefore we shall concentrate on the most critical method of declining.

4 ... d5

By securing the advanced e-pawn Black hopes to obtain a free and easy development while placing some constraints on White's.

5 fe

White gains nothing from delaying this capture, and indeed attempting to get by without it can easily lead him astray, e.g. 5 ♗g5 ♗f5 6 Wd2?! (6 fe de transposing to the game is correct) 6 ... ♘c6 7 ♗b5 e6 8 fe de 9 d5? (a mistaken conception; 9 ♘ge2 was better although it is true that Black would be very comfortably placed after simply 9 ... ♗e7) 9 ... ed 10 ♗xf6 Wxf6 11 ♘xd5 knight and pressurize the advanced e-pawn as quickly as possible. Whether it it is White's best continuation, however, remains to be established. The alternatives are as follows:

(a) 7 ♕e2?! ♘c6 (7 ... ♕xd4? 8 ♕b5+) 8 ♗xf6 (8 0-0-0?? ♗g4) 8 ... ef 9 0-0-0 ♗d6 10 ♘xe4 0-0 11 ♘xd6?! (meets with a surprising rejoinder, but in any case Black has a very comfortable game) 11 ... cd! 12 ♕f2 ♕a5 13 ♗c4+ ♔h8 14 ♘e2 ♘b4 15 ♗b3 ♖ac8∓ Black's queenside attack is becoming very dangerous; Ed. Lasker–Alekhine, match, Paris 1913.

(b) 7 ♕d2 ?! e6 8 h3 ♗d6 9 0-0-0 h6 10 ♗xf6 ♕xf6 11 ♗c4 ♘c6 12 ♘ge2 0-0-0 13 ♖hf1 ♘a5 14 ♗b5 ♕g5 15 ♘f4 a6∓ a useful example of how Black can proceed when White does nothing in particular; Arbakov–Gleizerov, Saratov 1984.

(c) 7 ♗c4!? ♘bd7!? (7 ... ♘c6 is generally featured as Black's best continuation with the main line running 8 ♘ge2 ♕d7 9 0-0 e6 10 ♕e1 0-0-0 11 ♖d1 ♘a5 12 ♗b5 c6 13 ♗a4 ♘c4 — Taimanov suggests 13 ... ♗d6 14 d5 ♕e7 — with an unclear, roughly balanced position: a game Schultz–Wille, E. Germany 1957, went 14 d5?! ♗c5+ 15 ♔h1 ♗e3 16 dc ♕c7 with wild complications, while

Minev has recommended 14 ♗b3 with ♘g3 to follow, again with approximate equality in a mutually difficult position) 8 ♘ge2 ♘b6 9 ♗b3 ♕d7 10 0-0 e6 11 ♕e1 0-0-0 12 ♖d1 c6 13 ♘g3 ♗b4 14 ♗xf6 gf 15 ♘gxe4 with chances for both sides in a sharp position; Danner–Strobel, Austria 1969.

7	...	e6
8	♘g3	♗e7

Black also obtained an advantage in the game Martinez–Byrne, Nice Ol. 1974, after 8 ... ♗b4 9 ♗c4?! ♘c6 10 0-0 ♕xd4+ 11 ♕xd4 ♘xd4 12 ♗xf6 gf 13 ♘cxe4 ♗xe4 14 ♘xe4 f5 15 ♘g5 ♘xc2!, but White could improve at move nine with, say, 9 ♕d2.

9	♕d2	h6!
10	♗e3	

There is no joy for White in 10 ♗xf6 ♗xf6 11 ♘cxe4 ♕xd4 12 ♘xf6+ ♕xf6 13 0-0-0 0-0∓.

10	...	♘bd7
11	♗e2	

Chernin and M. Gurevich analyse 11 ♘xf5 ef 12 ♗c4 ♗d6! 13 ♗e6 g6 as clearly in Black's favour, 14 ♗xh6 being well met by 14 ... ♕e7 with ... 0-0-0 to follow.

11	...	♘b6
12	0-0	♕d7

Simply 12 ... ♗g6 would have avoided the sequence which follows and left Black clearly in control.

13 ♘h5   ♖g8

Understandably fearing the sacrifices which could follow 13 ... 0-0 but unnecessarily so according to Chernin and M. Gurevich who analyse 14 ♘xg7?! ♔xg7 15 ♗xh6+ ♔h7 16 ♕g5 (16 ♗xf8 ♖xf8∓) 16 ... ♖g8 17 ♕h4 ♖g6 and there is no good continuation of the attack.

14 ♘xf6+   ♗xf6
15 ♗h5+!   g6
16 ♗e2

By forcing Black to weaken his kingside pawns White has set up the double threat of g2–g4 and ♘xe4.

16 ...   ♕g7!

A clever tactical counter, utilizing the latent heavy piece power on the g-file.

17 ♗xh6?!

Gives Black an easy time of it. For better or worse, it was practically mandatory to brave the perils of 17 g4 0-0-0! 18 ♖ad1 (not 18 gf? gf+ 19 ♔f2 ♗h4 mate) 18 ... h5!

17 ...   ♗xd4+
18 ♔h1   ♕h8!
19 ♗f4

On 19 g4, Black could reply 19 ... 0-0-0 20 gf ef and White would be hard pressed to cope with the threat of ... ♗e5 and ... g5.

19 ...   0-0-0
20 ♘b5   e5 *(47)*

With this, White's temporary

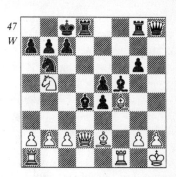

47
W

initiative grinds to a halt and Black slowly takes control of the whole board.

21 ♗e3   a6
22 ♘c3   ♖g7
23 ♖f2   ♖h7
24 g3   ♕e8
25 ♗f1   ♕c6

With his queen optimally regrouped Black is poised for the decisive assault.

26 ♕e2   ♘d7!

Naturally, Black denies his adversary the glimmer of hope which would follow from the double capture on c3. Instead, the knight is sent over to claim control of g4.

27 ♘d1   ♘f6
28 c3   ♗g4!
29 ♖xf6?

Abject capitulation; 29 ♕e1 ♗f3+ 30 ♔g1 ♗b6 31 ♗xb6 ♕xb6 32 ♘e3 g5 with ... g4 to follow would doubtless end in the same result, but at least it would require more effort from Black to secure it.

29	...	♗xe2
30	♖xc6	♗f3+

White's fate is sealed; the end came quickly: 31 ♔g1 ♗xe3+ 32 ♘xe3 bc 33 ♗xa6+ ♔b8 34 ♖f1 ♖d2 35 ♖f2 ♖xf2 36 ♔xf2 ♖xh2+ 0–1.

Shchumitshev–Shaposnikov
7th USSR corr. Ch. 1967–9
1 d4 f5 2 e4 fe 3 ♘c3 ♘f6

4   ♗g5 *(48)*

This is the classical continuation used by Staunton himself. In essence, White hopes to recover the pawn whilst maintaining a central superiority rather than make a real gambit of it.

4   ...   ♘c6

Inaugurating lively piece play in the centre of the board, making use of the fact that should the knight be chased to f7 (via e5) it will attack the bishop.

An alternative defence which is becoming increasingly popular is

4 ... e6 which we have covered in Chapter 8, page 78. Note, however, that Black is unable to hang on to the pawn as in the 4 f3 variation because of the following refutation: 4 ... d5? 5 ♗xf6 ef 6 ♕h5+ g6 7 ♕xd5 pocketing one pawn immediately with a second soon to follow.

5   d5

All the alternatives are very pleasant for Black:

(a) 5 ♗xf6?! ef 6 d5 (6 ♗c4?! f5 7 ♘ge2 ♘a5 8 ♗b3 ♘xb3 9 ab ♗e7 is hopeless for White) 6 ... ♘e5 7 ♘xe4 f5 with a fine game for Black.

(b) 5 ♘h3?! g6 6 ♗c4 ♗g7 7 0-0 d5 8 ♗xf6 ef 9 ♗xd5 ♗xh3 10 gh f5∓ Taimanov.

(c) 5 ♗b5 a6 (5 ... g6 comes into consideration) 6 ♗xc6 bc 7 ♕e2 e6 8 ♘xe4 ♗e7 9 ♗xf6 ♗xf6 10 ♘f3 0-0 and now whether White opts for the aggressive 11 0-0-0 or the prudent 11 0-0, Black's bishops and central pawn mass provide satisfactory middlegame prospects.

(d) 5 f3 e5! (given that it is too risky to accept the pawn, the text move is the most logical way of declining: Black stakes a claim in the centre and entrenches on the dark squares) 6 d5 (White achieves nothing by 6 de ♘xe5, e.g. 7 ♕d4 d6 8 ♘xe4 ♗e7 or 7 fe d6 8 ♘f3 ♗g4) 6 ... ♘d4 7 ♘xe4 (the dark square weakness would be more evident after 7 fe ♗e7 8 ♗c4 d6 9 ♘ge2 ♘g4!; Barda–Rossolimo, Hastings 1949/50) 7 ... ♗e7 8 ♗xf6 ♗xf6 9 ♕d2 (or 9 c3 ♘f5 10 ♕d2 d6 11 ♗b5+ ♗d7 12 ♗xd7+ ♕xd7 13 ♘h3 0-0-0= Wexler–Adler, Mar del Plata 1952) 9 ... 0-0 10 0-0-0 d6 11 c3 ♘f5 with balanced chances; Horberg–Larsen, Stockholm 1966/67.

5   ...   ♘e5

6   ♕d4

Alternatives are not as good:

(a) 6 f4?! ♘f7 7 ♕d4 g6 8 ♘xe4 ♗g7 is fine for Black.

(b) 6 f3 ♘f7 7 ♗xf6 (relatively best; 7 ♗e3 ef 8 ♘xf3 g6 9 ♗e2 ♗g7 10 0-0 0-0 11 ♘d4 c6! as in van Seters–Rossolimo, Beverwijk 1950, and 7 ♗f4 ef 8 ♘xf3 c6 9 ♗c4 cd 10 ♗xd5 e6 11 ♗b3 ♗b4 as in van Seters–Donner, Beverwijk 1951, both leave White with nothing to show for the pawn) 7 ... ef 8 ♘xe4 f5 9 ♘g3 g6 gives Black an active and promising position.

(c) 6 ♗xf6 ef 7 ♘xe4 f5 8 ♘g3 g6 9 ♕e2 ♕e7 10 0-0-0 ♘g4! hands Black the initiative in short order; Alzate–Nilsson, Havana Ol. 1966.

6   ...   ♘f7 *(49)*

7   ♗xf6

Experience with the alternatives strongly suggests that White is well advised to cede the bishop

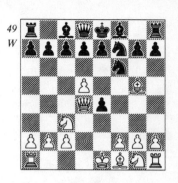

pair rather than lose time:

(a) 7 h4 c6 8 0-0-0 (8 ♗xf6 gf 9 ♕xe4 cd 10 ♘xd5 e6 11 0-0-0 ♗g7∓) 8 ... ♕b6! 9 ♗xf6 gf 10 ♕xe4 ♕xf2 11 ♘f3 ♗h6+ 12 ♔b1 ♕e3 13 ♕a4 ♕f4 14 ♕b3 a5 and in an interestingly unbalanced position Black's bishop pair, potentially powerful central pawns, and dark square play give him the better of it; Yudintsev–Martinov, ½-final USSR corr. Ch. 1964/65.

(b) 7 ♗h4 g5! (stemming from Simagin, the time and activity gained from this bold thrust far outweigh the weakening of the kingside) 8 ♗g3 ♗g7 9 0-0-0 c6! (again we see this important little move which not only challenges White's last central pawn but also lets the queen into play) 10 ♘xe4 (White is left with a similarly bleak ending after 10 d6 ♕b6! 11 ♘xe4 ♕xd4 12 ♖xd4 ♘h5 13 ♖d1 ♘xg3 14 hg ed 15 c4!? b5! 16 cb d5; Matsukevich–Cherepkov, Leningrad 1963) 10 ... ♛b6! (exchanging queens is the correct strategy; Black thereby diminishes White's attacking prospects while enhancing his own positional advantages) 11 ♘xf6+ ♝xf6 12 ♛xb6 ab 13 ♔b1 d6 14 a3 ♖a5 and Black has taken charge; Potter–Jezek, corr. Ol. Final 1959/60.

| | 7 | ... | ef |
| | 8 | ♘xe4 | |

If White does not capture the pawn immediately then Black holds it temporarily in order to return it for positional gains: 8 0-0-0?! f5! 9 f3 ♝d6! 10 fe (10 ♛xg7?? ♝e5) 10 ... ♝e5 11 ♛d3 f4 12 ♘f3 0-0 with a firm blockade on e5, ∓; Kenez–Borisenko, corr. 1958.

| | 8 | ... | f5! |

The most forceful continuation and probably best.

| | 9 | ♘g3 | |

Black would meet 9 ♘c3 in the same way.

| | 9 | ... | g6 |

Making maximum use of the marvellously placed knight on f7.

| | 10 | 0-0-0 | |

The ultra-sharp 10 h4 ♝h6 11 h5 looks more threatening than it actually is on account of 11 ... ♛e7+! breaking the flow of White's attack (but not 11 ... 0-0? 12 hg hg 13 d6!). A game Gudmunsson–Donner, Amsterdam 1950, saw White try 11 d6 (after 10 h4 ♝h6)

but Black emerged on top after 11 ... 0-0 12 ♝c4 ♝g7 13 ♛d3 ♝xb2 14 ♖b1 ♛f6 15 ♘1e2 ♝e5 16 dc ♝xc7.

| | 10 | ... | ♝h6+ |
| | 11 | f4 | |

Attempting to gain some dark square control; 11 ♔b1 0-0 leaves Black with at least equal prospects.

	11	...	0-0
	12	♘f3	♝g7
	13	♛d2	b5!
	14	♘d4	♘d6 *(50)*

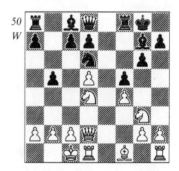

Variously evaluated as 'equal' or 'unclear', it nevertheless seems fairly evident that Black's prospects are the more promising in this unusual and difficult position. The major handicap of White's setup is that he has no equivalent, either literally or figuratively, to the powerful black-squared bishop on g7 which gives energy and purpose to the black position.

| | 15 | c3 | |

Obviously White dare not capture the pawn immediately (15 ♘xb5? ♘xb5 16 ♗xb5 ♖b8 with ... a6 and breakthrough on b2 to follow) so he primes the threat by blunting the bishop's action along the a1–h8 diagonal.

15	...	♖b8
16	♘b3?!	a5!

In trying to slow Black's attack White has inadvertently accelerated it! The rook pawn thrust inaugurates a forceful and instructive sequence which wrests a lasting initiative and positional dominance.

17	♘xa5	♖a8
18	b4	♖xa5!
19	ba	♗b7 *(51)*

51
W

With the white monarch's pawn cover shattered beyond repair and the black KB rampaging unopposed down the long diagonal, White's queenside is ripe for the plucking and his fate practically sealed. Despite desperate defensive efforts, in the end White could find no answer to the concerted action of the black forces: 20 ♕b2 ♕a8 21 ♕b4 ♗xd5 22 ♗xb5 ♘xb5! (22 ... ♖b8 23 a4!) 23 ♕xb5 c6 24 ♕c5 ♖b8 25 ♖xd5 (25 c4 ♕b7 is crushing) 25 ... cd! (not falling for 25 ... ♖b5? 26 ♕xb5 cb 27 ♖hd1 with good chances of holding on) 26 ♖d1 d4! 27 ♘e2 ♕e4 28 ♕c4+ ♔h8 29 ♕d3 ♕b7! 30 ♖d2 dc 31 ♘xc3 ♕c7 32 ♖c2 ♕xf4+ 33 ♔d1 ♕xh2 34 ♕e3 d5 35 ♕f2 d4 36 ♘b5 d3 37 ♖c7 ♕xc7! 38 ♘xc7 ♖b1+ 39 ♔d2 ♖b2+ 40 ♔e3 ♗d4+ 41 ♔xd4 ♖xf2 42 ♔xd3 ♖xa2 43 a6 f4 44 ♔e4 g5 45 ♔f3 ♔g7 46 ♔e4 ♔g6 0–1.

7 The Queen Bishop Attack: 2 ♗g5

The bishop sortie aims to disrupt the normal development of Black's kingside: 2 ... e6 is prevented, and 2 ... ♘f6 permits 3 ♗xf6, downgrading the black pawn structure in a relatively closed position where the two bishops at best offer problematic compensation. Consequently, the two recommended variations we shall examine avoid the structure-damaging exchange by postponing the development of the knight: the restrained 2 ... g6 and the ambitious whiplash 2 ... h6 3 ♗h4 g5.

Kouatly–VI. Kovacevic
Thessaloniki Ol. 1984
1 d4 f5 2 ♗g5

2   ...   g6 *(52)*

Fianchettoing the bishop enables Black to capture on f6 with a piece in the event of a future

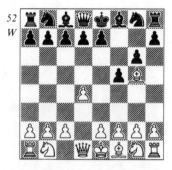

52
W

... ♘f6, ♗xf6 exchange, whilst also observing the eternally important e5 square directly as well as x-raying the long diagonal in general and the weakened b2 spot in particular.

Note that there is no inconsistency here in recommending 2 ... g6 while counselling its avoidance in favour of 2 ... ♘f6 in the Leningrad (see p. 46) since the bishop's presence on g5 gives Black the important additional resource of being able to answer an h-pawn thrust of h4–h5 with ... h6, ♗

retreats g5, thus keeping the king-side sealed.

3 h4

Increasing dark square control and introducing a possible rook pawn rupture form an important part of White's strategic pro-gramme despite the extra defens-ive counters deriving from the exposed bishop.

There are valid alternative treatments:

(a) 3 ♘c3 ♗g7 (3 ... d5 trans-poses to Chapter 8) 4 e4 (delaying this advance brings nothing, e.g. 4 ♘f3 ♘f6 5 ♗xf6 ♗xf6 6 e4 fe 7 ♘xe4 d5!=) 4 ... fe 5 ♘xe4 d5! 6 ♘c5 (nor does retreating promise White any advantage, e.g. 6 ♘g3 ♘c6 7 c3 ♘h6!? 8 ♕d2 ♘f7 with balanced chances in a complex position, or 6 ♘c3 ♘c6 7 ♗b5 ♘h6!? 8 ♗xh6 ♗xh6 9 ♕f3 ♗e6 again with mutual chances and problems; M. Simic–Knezevic, Smederevska Palanka 1977) 6 ... b6 7 ♘b3 ♘f6 8 ♘f3 0-0 9 ♗e2 ♕d6 10 0-0 ♘bd7 with active possibilities for Black; Mik. Zeit-lin–Ivanenko, Central Chess Club Ch. 1984.

(b) 3 ♘d2 ♗g7 4 c3 (a game Bergrasser–Larsen, Monte Carlo 1967, went 4 e3 ♘f6 5 ♘gf3 d6 6 ♗c4 ♘c6 7 c3 a6 8 h4 ♘e4=) 4 ... h6 5 ♗f4 d6 6 e3 e5 7 de de 8 ♗g3 ♕e7 9 f3 ♗e6 and Black has a space advantage and the

more positive position; Kuttner–Mohring, E. German Ch. 1969.

(c) 3 e4 fe 4 ♘c3 ♘f6 5 f3 ef 6 ♘xf3 ♗g7 brings about a vari-ation of the Staunton Gambit con-sidered to offer balanced pro-spects.

3 ... ♗g7 *(53)*

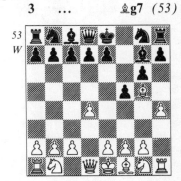

4 e3

Other paths:

(a) 4 ♘c3 c6 (again the trans-position to Chapter 8 by 4 ... d5 is available; ECO suggests an immediate 4 ... h6) 5 ♕d3 d5 6 0-0-0 ♘f6 (6 ... ♕a5 is an active alternative worth attention) 7 ♗xf6!? ♗xf6 8 f4 b5 9 ♘f3 with an interesting middlegame in prospect: White holds the knights in a blocked position but Black has attacking chances on the queenside; Rajkovic–Kovacevic, Yugoslavia 1975.

(b) 4 h5 h6 5 ♗c1 (anywhere else the bishop would just be a nuisance) 5 ... g5 (this instructive sequence sees Black thwart

White's ambitions on the h-file and turn the tables in the battle for the initiative on the kingside) 6 ♛d3 e6 7 e4 d6 8 ♘f3 f4!? 9 e5 ♘e7 10 ed cd 11 ♘bd2 0-0 12 c3 ♘f5 and Black can look to the middle game with confidence; Gipslis–Reize, Leningrad 1960.

4   ...   h6

With the bishop's line of retreat blocked, Black seeks to use it as a target to aid expansion in the centre.

5   ♗f4   d6
6   ♗c4   ♘c6

Naturally Black avoids 6 ... e5? which would leave him with a displaced king and problems with developing after 7 de de 8 ♗f7+ ♚e7 9 ♛xd8+ ♚xd8 10 ♗g3 ♘e7 11 ♘c3.

7   c3   e5

With other factors being equal, this advance always solves Black's opening problems and often gives him the more promising position.

8   ♗g3   ♛e7

The vis-à-vis with White's king means that ... f4 is threatened.

9   ♘e2   ♘f6
10   f3   ...

In order to be able to preserve both QB and h-pawn in the event of ... ♘h5.

10   ...   ♗d7   *(54)*

Black has the more harmonious development and the strategic initiative thanks to his mobile

kingside pawns.

11   a4

Hoping for a compensatory initiative on the other flank.

11   ...   0-0-0

Possibly premature as it permits White to force Black's QN away from the centre and provoke a slight weakening of the queenside pawns. Of course, such a rich position contains several feasible plans, for example immediate kingside expansion with 11 ... g5, or possibly opening the e-file by 11 ... ed and only then castling (so that e5 would be available to the knight in case of d5) followed by vigorous action on the king's flank.

12   d5   ♘b8
13   ♘a3   a6
14   ♗f2   ♛e8!

Subtle prophylaxis designed to hamper a charge by the b-pawn.

15   ♗b3   g5
16   ♗c2   e4
17   ♘g3   ♛e7

Correctly avoiding the tempting 17 ... ♕e5? which would hand the initiative to White after 18 ♘c4 ♕xd5 19 ♕xd5 ♘xd5 20 fe fe 21 ♘h5!

18 ♕d2   ♖df8

This somewhat mysterious rook move brings the piece into play while reserving e8 for the queen.

19 0-0-0

That it is high time to remove the king from its increasingly perilous position in the centre is well illustrated by the combinative refutation of 19 b4?: 19 ... ♘xd5! 20 ♕xd5 ♗xc3+ 21 ♔e2 gh 22 ♘h5 ♗xa1 23 ♖xa1 ♗c6 24 ♕c4 ♕g5 25 ♘f4 ef 26 gf ♗xf3+! with a decisive advantage (V. Kovacevic).

19 ...   gh

At first sight this self-splitting of his pawns seems strange, but further inspection reveals that without this capture it is difficult for Black to open lines and make progress on the kingside.

20 ♘e2

Taking with the rook would allow Black to move his knight with a discovered attack.

20 ...   ♕e8
21 ♘f4   ef
22 gf   ♘h7 *(55)*

Having created a weakness on f3 Black manoeuvres his knight to bring it under pressure.

23 ♗xh4   ♘g5

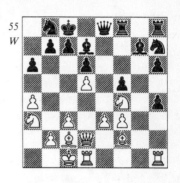

24 ♕f2

Given White's next, the immediate 24 ♕e2 may have been preferable.

24 ...   a5!

In order to bring the inactive knight back into play.

25 ♕e2   ♘a6
26 ♘b5   ♘c5

Consequent, but 26 ... ♖hg8 first was probably more accurate.

27 b4?!

Typical time-trouble lashing out; 27 ♗f2 was more circumspect with a lot of hard fighting still to come.

27 ...   ab
28 cb   ♗xb5

Simultaneously trading White's most threatening piece and shattering his queenside pawns.

29 ab   ♕e5!?
30 ♖d4

Not 30 bc? which would allow Black to run amok on the black squares: 30 ... ♕b2+ 31 ♔d2 ♕b4+ 32 ♔c1 ♗b2+ 33 ♔b1

♗c3+.

30	...	♘d7
31	♘h5	

White is understandably concerned to remove Black's pressure on the long diagonal, but he was probably wrong to forego the obvious 31 ♘g6, e.g. 31 ... ♛e8 32 ♘xf8 when Black would do best simply to recapture by 32 ... ♖xf8 with plenty of tactical chances, rather than allow 32 ... ♗xd4 33 ♘xd7 etc. when the fact that f5 is unprotected makes things awkward.

31	...	f4!

Undermining the d4 blockade which is preventing infiltration down the diagonal.

32	♘xg7	

Even in time-trouble White does not fall for 32 ♘xf4? ♖xf4! 33 ♖xf4 ♛b2+ 34 ♔d1 ♛a1+ 35 ♔d2 ♗c3+ 36 ♔d3 ♘e5 mate! Now at least White is unlikely to fall prey to a mating attack ... immediately, anyway!

32	...	♛xg7
33	♖hd1	

Again, 33 ♖xf4 ♛a1+ 34 ♗b1 ♛a3+ 35 ♔d1 ♖xf4 36 ef ♘xf3 would be asking for trouble.

33	...	♖e8!?

Black is relentless in his determination to get amongst White's dark square weaknesses.

34	♖xf4	♛c3!
35	♖d3	

Not 35 e4? ♘e5 when the rook is out of play and the black cavalry become dangerous.

35	...	♛a1+
36	♗b1	

36 ♔d2 would allow a deadly switch to the opposite flank by 36 ... ♛h1! with 37 ... ♘e5 to follow.

36	...	♘e5
37	♖b3	♖hg8
38	♗f2?!	

Sorely pressed by the clock, White fails to spot 38 ♗e1 intending to transfer the bishop to c3 and drive out the menacing queen. In this case, 38 ... ♛a4 keeps up a multitude of tactical tricks.

38	...	♘h3
39	♖h4	♘g1
40	♛d1	

It would be fatal to invite the enemy's heavy guns to occupy the home base back rank by capturing the frisky horse: 40 ♗xg1? ♖xg1+ 41 ♔c2 ♖eg8 42 ♖h2 ♛a4 and White is hopelessly tied up.

40	...	♘gxf3
41	♖xh6	♖g2
42	♛c2	♖eg8 *(56)*

With this, Black's domination is complete and the outcome no longer in any doubt despite tough resistance: 43 ♖h1 (of course not 43 ♖h7?? ♖g1+) 43 ... ♔b8 44 ♛b2 ♛a4 45 ♖a3 ♛xb5 46 ♛a1 ♛c4+ 47 ♗c2 ♘d3+! (gaining a vital tempo to break White's

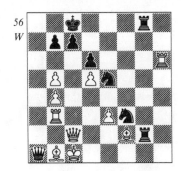

56
W

counterattack) 48 ♖xd3 ♖xf2 49 ♕c3 b5! 50 ♗b3 (it would be worse to give Black a passed pawn and leave the b-pawn exposed to a frontal assault by the black king after 50 ♕xc4 bc 51 ♖c3 ♘e5 with the king march to follow) 50 ... ♕xc3+ 51 ♖xc3 ♘e5 52 ♗c2 ♖g3 53 ♖e1 ♔b7 54 ♗d3 ♔b6 55 ♗e2 ♖h2 56 ♔d1 ♖h4 57 ♖b3 ♖g8 58 ♔d2 ♖h2 59 ♔c1 ♖gg2 60 ♔d1 ♖h4 61 ♔c1 ♖gh2 62 ♔d1 ♖h8 63 ♖a3 ♖2h4 64 ♔c2 (saving the pawn would leave White open to attack from both flanks: 64 ♖b3 ♖a8 65 ♔c2 ♖a2+ 66 ♔c3 ♖h2 with fierce pressure) 64 ... ♖xb4 65 ♔c3 ♖hh4! (dashing White's last hope: 65 ... ♖e4?! 66 ♗xb5! ♔xb5?? 67 ♖b1+ ♔c5 68 ♖a5 mate) 66 ♖a8 ♖he4! (Black sets his own trap: if now 67 ♖ea1 there comes 67 ... ♖xe3+ 68 ♔xb4 c5+ 69 dc ♘xc6 mate) 67 ♖b8+ ♔c5 68 ♖c1 ♘c4 69 ♗d3 ♖xe3 70 ♖b7 ♘e5 71 ♔d2+ (White would lose

both rooks after 71 ♖xc7+ ♔b6 72 ♔xb4 ♘xd3+ followed by 73 ... ♘xc1+ etc.) 71 ... ♔d4 White resigns, as he must acquiesce in simplification to a technically lost ending after 72 ♗f1 ♖b2+ 73 ♖c2 (73 ♔d1 ♖e1+! and mate in two) 73 ... ♘c4+ 74 ♗xc4 ♖xc2+ 75 ♔xc2 bc. This substantial game, packed with incident, is a good example of the rich middlegames which typically arise in this variation.

Magerramov–Avshalumov
USSR 1987
1 d4 f5 2 ♗g5

2	...	h6
3	♗h4	g5 (57)

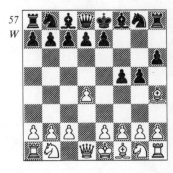

57
W

Played not in the naive expectation of trapping the bishop but in order to develop the KN without it being captured, thereby saddling Black with doubled f-pawns. The danger for Black is that the rapid advance of his kingside pawns may leave him weak on the black squares after a typical h4 thrust and ... g4 response. It then becomes of paramount importance whether Black can achieve the advance of his e-pawn to e5 so as to prevent White obtaining control over the key f4 square.

4 ♗g3

Not forced; the simple transposition 4 e3 ♘f6 5 ♗g3 is equally playable. Violent attempts at refutation come unstuck: 4 e4? ♗g7 5 ♕h5+ ♔f8 6 ♗c4 d5 7 ed ♘f6 8 ♕f3 gh with a winning material advantage; Barnes–Krause, Omaha 1959. It is quite shocking that as recently as 1983 Taimanov could be giving 3 ... g5 a question mark and saying that 4 e4 is good for White through being ignorant of the existence of 4 ... ♗g7 (he considers only 4 ... ♘f6? and 4 ... d5?).

4 ... ♘f6

This is certainly the most natural move here although it has yet to be definitively established whether it is also the most accurate. Examples of the alternatives:

(a) 4 ... ♗g7 5 e3 d6 (5 ... ♘f6 would return to the column) 6 h4 (checking on h5 would involve White in an unwarranted loss of time) 6 ... g4 (the variation 6 ... ♘f6?! 7 hg hg 8 ♖xh8+ ♗xh8 9 ♘h3! g4 10 ♘f4± is a good illustration of what Black should

avoid) 7 ♘c3 e5?! 8 de de 9 ♕xd8+ ♔xd8 10 0-0-0+ ♗d7 11 ♗c4 and White's easy, active development contrasts starkly with Black's sluggish mobilisation and difficulties along the d-file; Lputian–Mik. Zeitlin, Sochi 1985.

(b) 4 ... d6 5 e3 ♘f6 6 h4 ♖g8!? (this bold attempt to avoid ... g4 deserves further investigation) 7 hg hg 8 ♗c4 (this rather simplistic approach tends to leave White with insufficient pawn presence in the centre to be able to affect matters there; Bareev has noted 8 c4 intending to attack f5 by ♗d3, ♕c2, and d5, as a more challenging plan) 8 ... e6 9 ♘c3 a6 (prepares his next by preventing ♘b5) 10 a4?! (mis-reads Black's intentions) 10 ... d5 11 ♗e2 ♗d6 12 ♗e5 ♘c6 13 f4 g4 14 ♗d3 ♔f7 with a very comfortable position for Black; D. Ilic–Bareev, Vrnjacka Banja 1987.

5 e3

Persisting with the original intention of exchanging QB for KN by playing 5 ♗e5 looks rather artificial and should not cause Black any trouble, e.g. 5 ... ♗g7 (5 ... e6!? with the idea of answering ♘c3 by ... ♗b4 is an interesting alternative) 6 h4 g4 7 e3 d6 8 ♗xf6 ♗xf6 9 ♗c4 and now Black should open the queen's path to the flank by 9 ... c6, with a complex and quite promising middle game in view, rather than permit White to diminish the position's dynamism by exchanging queens after 9 ... e5 10 ♘c3 c6 11 de de 12 ♕xd8+ ♚xd8 13 0-0-0+ ♚e7 14 f3 when Black's lagging development is again cause for concern (cf. note (a) to Black's fourth above); Sideif-Zade–Avshalumov, USSR 1987.

5 ... ♗g7 *(58)*

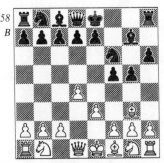

6 ♘d2

Nor have the alternative treatments so far explored given Black any difficulties:

(a) 6 ♘c3 d6 7 ♗d3 ♘c6 8 ♘f3 e6 9 ♕e2 (9 ♗b5 enabled Black to build up a crushing queenside attack quickly in Arkhipov–Mik. Zeitlin, Protvino 1985, after 9 ... ♗d7 10 ♕e2 a6 11 ♗a4 ♕e7 12 0-0-0 b5 13 ♗b3 b4 14 ♘b1 ♘a5 15 h4 g4 16 ♘fd2 ♗b5 17 ♕e1 c5) 9 ... ♕e7 10 ♗b5 (in view of the threatened ... e5 White has little choice; Black's position is already better) 10 ... ♗d7 11 h3

a6 12 ♗a4 b5 13 ♗b3 ♘a5 14 a3 ♘xb3 15 cb ♗c6 (this transference to the long diagonal highlights Black's white square domination of the whole board; in the further course of the game White is unable to find any counterplay while the enemy forces mass for the final assault) 16 ♖c1 0-0 17 0-0 ♗b7 18 b4 ♕f7 19 ♘d2 ♕g6 20 ♕d3 ♖f7 21 f3 h5 22 ♘e2 ♗h6 23 ♖f2 h4 24 ♗h2 ♖af8 25 ♘c3 ♕g7 26 ♖cf1 g4 27 fg fg 28 hg ♘xg4 29 ♖xf7 ♖xf7 30 e4 ♗e3+ 0-1. Smooth, very smooth! Tisdall–Kristiansen, Denmark 1983.

(b) 6 ♗d3 e6 (a game Wheatley-Bellin, England 1981, went 6 ... d6 7 ♘d2 ♘c6 8 c3 e5 9 h4 f4!? 10 hg hg 11 ♖xh8+ ♗xh8 12 ef ef 13 ♗h2 ♕e7+ 14 ♔e2 ♘g4 with a small but distinct advantage for Black; 9 ... g4 would avoid simplification and leave Black with fine prospects) 7 ♘e2 d6 8 f3 ♕e7 9 c4 e5 10 ♘bc3 0-0 11 de (11 ♕c2 ed 12 ed ♘c6 would be in Black's favour) 11 ... de 12 e4 (after the more fluid 12 ♕c2 play might go 12 ... f4 13 ♗f2 ♘c6 14 a3 fe 15 ♗xe3 ♘d4!? with chances for both sides) 12 ... f4 13 ♗f2 c6 14 c5 ♗e6 15 ♕a4 ♕f7 with entirely satisfactory play for Black; Damljanovic–M. Gurevich, Baku 1986.

6 ... d6

Preparing the e-pawn's advance.

7   h4

White must challenge the black pawns in this manner as otherwise he simply concedes that Black has gained space at no cost.

7   ...   g4

A necessary reaction as White is threatening to exchange pawns and rooks and then play ♘h3 advantageously weakening the black pawn structure in the same way as already noted in the 4 ... ♗g7 line.

8   h5

Otherwise the black knight could occupy this square to useful effect.

8   ...   ♘c6

Development aimed at enforcing ... e5.

9   ♗b5

Development aimed at retarding ... e5.

9   ...   ♗d7

10   ♘e2   a6

This is dubious as it gives White the chance to get his knight to f4 from where it can exert a powerful influence on Black's position. The immediate 10 ... e5 would lead to a complex game with balanced chances after for example 11 de de 12 ♘c4 (12 ♗xc6 ♗xc6 13 ♗xe5 could be answered simply by 13 ... ♗xg2 14 ♖h2 ♗c6 or more ambitiously by 13 ... ♕e7, but in both cases White's light square debility presents obvious play for

Black) 12 ... 0-0!

11   ♗a4

White goes along with his opponent's assessment instead of challenging it by 11 ♗xc6 ♗xc6 12 ♘f4 ♕d7 13 c4 e6 14 ♘b3 after which Avshalumov evaluates the position as slightly in White's favour.

11   ...   e5

12   c3

Capturing on e5 would lead to lines similar to those in the note to Black's tenth.

12   ...   ♕e7 *(59)*

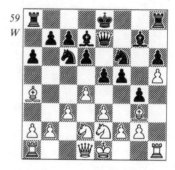

Black's forces are generally more harmoniously coordinated for effective central action, and the black queen is functionally posted in a way difficult for her white counterpart to emulate, while the advanced g-, f- and e-pawns infuse the black position with dynamic potential.

13   ♕b1?!   0-0!

Correctly perceiving that the threat to double the c-pawns is illusory since after 14 ♗xc6 bc 15 de de Black's prospects on the light squares more than outweigh the damaged pawns.

14 ♗b3+?!

Even so, this inconsistent play is misguided, as Black now gets to utilize all the positive aspects of his position without any drawbacks at all.

14 ... ♔h8
15 ♗h4 ♕e8

Underlining the fact that the aggressive h-pawn can also become vulnerable.

16 de de
17 ♘g3 e4!

Now that White's KN has been removed from its observation of f4 to fulfil defensive duties, the time is ripe to cramp White's position further and prepare to swing the QN to e5 when the weakness of d3 will cause the white monarch considerable embarrassment. Black is now clearly in control.

18 ♔f1

18 ♗xf6 would save the h-pawn but leave White's position lifeless and inevitably doomed.

18 ... ♘xh5
19 ♔g1

Thus White has managed to remove his king to relative safety and activate his KR at no greater expense than a pawn.

19 ... ♘xg3

20 ♗xg3 ♗e6?

A miscalculation. Simply 20 ... ♘e5 was indicated, leaving White in dire straits.

21 ♗xc7 ♗xb3

After 21 ... ♕d7 22 ♗f4! (preventing any breakthroughs on the black squares) Black cannot capture on d2 without leaving the QB *en prise* while on 22 ... ♗xb3 White recaptures with the knight.

22 ♘xb3 ♗e5!

Black adjusts well to the changed circumstances and tries to use his better coordination to whip up attacking chances.

23 ♗xe5 ♘xe5
24 ♘d4

Taking the h-pawn would be a fatal error opening the way to the white king.

24 ... ♔g7
25 g3 ♔g6
26 ♕c2 ♕f7
27 ♔g2 h5

With this the writing is on the wall and even with time-trouble looming Black is unlikely to go wrong. The end came as follows: 28 ♖ad1 (28 ♕b3 was the masochistic way to prolong the inevitable) 28 ... ♖ad8 29 a4 ♖h8 30 b3 ♔g5 31 c4 ♘f3 32 ♔f1 ♖d7 33 ♕c3 ♖hd8 34 ♔g2 ♕f6 35 ♕b4 h4 36 gh ♘xh4+ 37 ♖xh4 ♔xh4 38 ♖h1+ ♔g5 39 ♘e2 ♖h8 40 ♖xh8 ♕xh8 41 ♘f4 g3!

Freeing g4 for the king enables Black to proceed with ... ♖d1 without being harassed by the knight check on e6; with his swindle chance gone White resigned.

8 The Queen Knight Attack: 2 ♘c3

This is the sister variation of the Queen Bishop Attack and indeed could reasonably be called the Queen Bishop Attack Deferred as the knight development is almost invariably followed by 3 ♗g5. Black has only two replies which counter the threatened 3 e4: 2 ... ♘f6 and 2 ... d5. We shall examine a promising recent offshoot of the first of these, and the latter in its entirety.

1	d4	f5
2	♘c3 *(60)*	

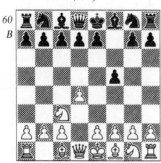

60
B

This logical move renounces

queenside play evolving from advancing the c-pawn in favour of central and kingside activity coupled with rapid piece deployment. As in the Queen Bishop Attack, White hopes to damage Black's pawn structure by capturing the KN on f6 with his bishop when it cannot be recaptured by a piece. Experience has shown that the doubled f-pawns thus inflicted on the black position are a considerable liability obliging Black to play extremely precisely in order to obtain a satisfactory position. Clearly, therefore, it makes sense to prevent White carrying out this strategy if at all possible and that, indeed, is the common factor in our two recommended defences.

Kouatly–Tseshkovsky
Wijk aan Zee II 1988
1 d4 f5 2 ♘c3

2   ...   ♘f6

3   ♗g5   e6

Known for more than a century, until recent years this move had always been considered weak since it allows White to play e4. Many of these earlier games saw Black quickly castling kingside and being crushed by direct attack as a result, whereas the modern strategy looks to effect the much safer long castling.

The reader may care to note that the response previously considered standard here, 3 ... d5, allows White to implement his primary aims mentioned in our introductory comments by 4 ♗xf6.

4   e4

The g-pawn thrust makes more sense here than in other positions; indeed the only example commonly cited from practice, Hort–Holacek, Havirov 1971, produced a preferable position for White after 4 g4 ♗e7 5 gf ef 6 ♗g2 ♘e4 7 ♗xe7 ♕xe7 8 ♕d3 ♘xc3 9 ♕xc3 d6 10 ♘h3. Naturally, this is far from being the last word on the variation, and the search for alternative defensive methods might well profitably begin by examining 4 ... ♗b4.

4   ...   fe

5   ♘xe4

The most natural continuation, but two other moves come into

consideration:

(a) 5 f3 offers a gambit in the Staunton mould which certainly brings White compensatory attacking chances after 5 ... ef 6 ♘xf3 ♗e7 7 ♗d3 0-0 8 h4!? setting up threats of taking on f6 and then h7, but 5 ... e3!? 6 ♗xe3 ♗b4! looks a good way of declining.

(b) 5 ♗xf6 ♕xf6 6 ♘xe4 ♕h6! (Black is in charge of the dark squares) 7 ♗d3 (7 g3 is a sensible attempt to obtain some grip on the black squares which Black could answer either by the straightforward 7 ... ♗e7 or the interesting 7 ... ♗b4+!? 8 c3 ♗e7 when White would be unable to retreat his knight to c3 in the event of a subsequent ... d5; 7 ♘f3 was played in a drastic miniature Laird–Finlayson, 1982, which went 7 ... d5 8 ♘eg5?! ♘c6 9 ♕d2 ♗d6 10 ♗d3?! ♘b4! 11 ♗b5+ c6 12 ♗e2 ♕g6! 13 0-0-0?? ♗f4 0-1) 7 ... d5 8 ♘g3 ♗d6 9 ♘f3 0-0 10 0-0 ♘c6 11 ♖e1 a6 12 c3 ♗d7 13 b4 ♖ae8 and Black's possession of a black-squared bishop more than offsets his inferior pawn structure; Mileika–Liebert, Riga 1961.

5   ...   ♗e7

6   ♗xf6

Capturing this way is the most forceful as it permits White to keep up the momentum. Time, Black's best response to the alternative has yet to be established. After 6 ♘xf6+ ♗xf6 7 h4! capturing on g5 would bring Black an inferior ending following 7 ... ♗xg5 8 ♕h5+ g6 9 ♕xg5 ♕xg5 10 hg, thus Black must seek other ways. A game Veresov–Pohla, Vilnius 1972, went 7 ... 0-0 8 ♗d3 ♕e7 9 ♕e2 ♘c6 10 c3 d5 11 f4 ♗d7 12 0-0-0 with clearly better chances for White. There is clearly no need for Black to declare his hand in castling so quickly, however, and amongst various possible improvements 7 ... ♕e7! springs immediately to mind.

6 ... ♗xf6 *(61)*

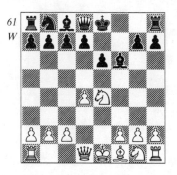

61
W

7 ♕h5+

Introduced by Knaak, this aggressive continuation has superseded the older, straightforward development of 7 ♘f3. That this quieter variation is not without venom is powerfully and instructively illustrated by the famous brilliancy Ed. Lasker–Thomas,

London 1912: 7 ... b6 8 ♗d3 ♗b7 9 ♘e5 0-0 10 ♕h5 ♕e7? 11 ♕xh7+!! ♚xh7 12 ♘xf6++ ♚h6 13 ♘eg4+ ♚g5 14 h4+ (14 f4+!) 14 ... ♚f4 15 g3+ ♚f3 16 ♗e2+ (16 ♚f1!) 16 ... ♚g2 17 ♖h2+ ♚g1 18 ♚d2 mate! Persuasive evidence that Black's safest way of meeting 7 ♘f3 is to remove the king to the queenside: 7 ... ♕e7 8 ♗d3 ♘c6 9 c3 b6 10 ♕e2 ♗b7 11 0-0-0 (if White castles kingside then Black should follow suit since the white forces are better placed to launch flank attacks, whereas homogeneous castling enhances the importance of Black's centralization) 11 ... 0-0-0 12 ♖he1 ♚b8 and Black's harmonious and weakness-free position is entirely satisfactory; Menchik–Flohr, Hastings 1933/34.

7 ... g6
8 ♕h6 ♕e7!?

Whether this latest try is the most accurate remains to be established, but it does appear to be more logical to threaten to preserve the KB before being committed to a particular queenside development (see Fedorowicz–Leow below). Other experience so far:

(a) 8 ... ♘c6 (acceptance of the pawn gives White too strong an initiative after 8 ... ♗xd4? 9 0-0-0 ♗f6 10 h4 etc.) 9 0-0-0!? (the seminal game Knaak–Ftacnik,

Trnava 1980, went 9 ♘f3 ♘xd4?
10 ♘xd4 ♗xd4 11 0-0-0 ♗f6 12
h4 ♛e7 13 ♘xf6+ ♛xf6 14 h5
♖g8 15 ♗d3 and Black was in
bad shape; Knaak gives 9 ... ♛e7
10 ♘xf6+ ♛xf6 11 0-0-0 b6 as
slightly in White's favour, while it
should be noted that 11 ... d6 in
this line would transpose to the
column game) 9 ... b6?! (while
Black can hardly afford to fall
further behind in development by
grabbing the d-pawn, the immediate 9 ... ♛e7 would probably
transpose to the column) 10 ♘e2
♛e7 11 ♛e3 (threatening 12 d5)
11 ... ♗g7 12 ♘2c3 ♗b7 (the
positionally appalling 12 ... d5
was mandatory) 13 d5 and Black
is in trouble; Fedorowicz–Leow,
Philadelphia 1986.

(b) 8 ... b6 9 ♘f3 ♗b7 10 ♗d3
♛e7 11 0-0-0 ♘a6 (11 ... ♘c6?
12 ♛f4) 12 c3 ♗g7 13 ♛e3 0-0-0
14 ♔b1 ♘b8 15 ♖he1 ♘c6 with
approximately equal chances (cf.
Menchik–Flohr above); Ash–
Yusupov, Winnipeg 1986.

Thus we can conclude that if
Black succeeds in setting up the
Ash – Yusupov / Menchik – Flohr
type position then his chances are
satisfactory, but he must be alert
against White's tactical trumps
particularly the d5 breakthrough.

9	♘xf6+	♛xf6
10	0-0-0	♘c6
11	♘f3	d6 *(62)*

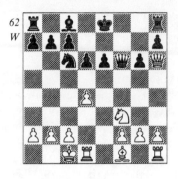

62
W

Thus Black keeps the white
pieces at bay with his small pawn
centre while preparing to complete
his development by 12 ... ♗d7
and 13 ... 0-0-0. After, say, 12
♗c4 ♗d7 13 ♖he1 0-0-0, Black
has no real problems as the e-
pawn is easily defended by ...
♖de8, and he can then think in
terms of ejecting the white queen
either by ♘c6–e7–f5 or ♘c6–d8–
f7 followed by mobilizing his kingside minority and increasing the
pressure along the half open f-file.
Most of the positions arising from
this variation are in fact a kind
of mirror image Sicilian where
White's attacking chances have
been diminished by the loss of
an important bishop. Food for
thought!

Doubtless with some such considerations in mind, White decided
to give up a pawn in order to keep
the black monarch in the centre,
but his initiative comes to nothing
and in regaining the pawn White

permits a decisive counterattack.

12	**d5?!**	**ed**
13	**♗b5**	**♗d7**
14	**♖he1+**	

14 ♗xc6 bc! 15 ♖he1+ ♔d8 would leave Black's king quite safe behind the solid mass of pawns.

14	**...**	**♘e7**
15	**♗xd7+**	**♔xd7**
16	**♘d4**	**♖ae8**
17	**♕h3+**	

The apparently powerful rook incursion 17 ♖e6 would only help Black after the simple retreat 17 ... ♕f7 threatening 17 ... c5 and 17 ... ♘f5.

17	**...**	**♘f5**
18	**♖xe8**	**♖xe8**
19	**♕xh7+**	**♖e7**
20	**♕h3**	

White has counted on this pin to hold the balance but failed to spot Black's knockout counterpunch coming.

20	**...**	**♕g5+**
21	**♔b1**	**♕d2!**
22	**♕f3**	

There is nothing better; 22 ♕d3 would lose a piece after 22 ... ♕xd3.

22	**...**	**♖e1**

Speedily concluding the assault on the opponent's back rank; White resigns.

Halifman–Legky
USSR 1987

1	**d4**	**f5**

2	**♘c3**	**d5**

Putting the Stonewall stopper on White's e2–e4 is especially valid when the c-pawn is blocked from joining in the central struggle. Note that 2 ... g6? would expose Black to the most virulent form of the h-pawn blitzkrieg after 3 h4! (cf. Chapter 4, p. 47).

3	**♗g5** *(63)*

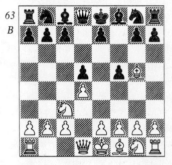

Much the most popular choice in contemporary practice, but Black must also know how to handle the tricky alternatives:

(a) 3 g4 ♘f6! 4 g5?! (4 h3 looks relatively best) 4 ... ♘e4 5 ♘xe4 fe 6 f3 ♗f5 and White's unorthodox aggression has clearly backfired; Spielmann–Mieses, Berlin 1920.

(b) 3 e4 de 4 f3 (4 ♗g5 g6 5 ♗c4 ♗g7 6 ♘ge2 ♘c6∓ Visier–Castro, Costa Brava 1977) 4 ... e5!? is a typical central counter which suffices to bring Black at least equal chances, e.g. 5 de ♕xd1+ 6 ♔xd1 ♘d7 7 ♘d5 ♔d8 8 fe fe 9 ♗f4 ♘c5! 10 ♘e2 ♘e7

11 ♘dc3 ♘g6 with the initiative; Beyen–Zwaig, Nice Ol. 1974.

(c) 3 ♗f4 is a routine developing move which poses no threat, e.g. 3 ... ♘f6 4 e3 e6 5 ♘b5?! (mistakenly attempting to utilize the one special point of his third move) 5 ... ♘a6 6 a4 (artificial, but 6 c4 ♗b4+ 7 ♘c3 ♘e4 is also fine for Black) 6 ... ♗e7 7 c3 0-0 8 ♗d3 c6 9 ♘a3 ♘b8! 10 ♘f3 ♘e4 11 0-0 ♘d7 and Black can enter the middlegame with confidence; V. Raicevic–Psakhis, Troon 1984.

(d) 3 f3 attempts straightforward occupation of the centre but Black can counter with a lightning infantry charge which effectively turns the tables: 3 ... c5! 4 e4 e5! 5 de (alternatives are even less palatable, e.g. 5 ♘xd5 cd and White has problems with e4; 5 ♗b5+ ♗d7 6 ♗xd7+ ♘xd7 7 ♘xd5 cd 8 ♘e2 fe 9 fe ♘fg6∓ again due to the weak e-pawn, Pomar–Larsen, Spain 1975) 5 ... d4 6 ♗c4!? (other moves leave Black in control without a fight) 6 ... ♘c6!? (according to Taimanov, 6 ... ♕a5 7 ♘e2 dc 8 ♘xc3 gives White a strong attack, but this certainly needs confirmation in practice) 7 ♘d5 ♘xe5 8 ♕e2 ♘xc4 9 ♕xc4 ♗d6 10 ♗f4 ♘e7 with a fully satisfactory position for Black; Rossolimo–Pelikan, Argentina 1959.

3   ...   g6

The usual response, but there are alternatives, hitherto barely explored, which are of potentially crucial significance:

(a) 3 ... c6 4 e3 g6 will in all likelihood transpose to lines similar to the column, while other tries have been shown to lose too much time with the queen in one case: 4 ... ♕d6?! 5 ♗d3 e5?! 6 de ♕xe5 7 ♘f3 ♕c7 8 ♘d4 ♕f7 9 ♕f3± Ghinda–Stanciu, Romanian Ch. 1978, and too much time with the knight in another: 4 ... ♘d7 5 ♗d3 ♘df6 6 ♘ge2 e6 7 f3 h6 8 ♗f4 g5 9 ♗e5 ♗g7 10 e4 ♘e7 11 ♕d2 ♗d7 12 0-0-0± Polugayevsky–Liebert, Rostov 1961. The logical follow-up to 3 ... c6 is 4 ... ♕b6!? with the point that gambitting the b-pawn would be dubious in a closed position, while direct methods of dealing with the threat would make queenside castling either less attractive or impossible. That would leave 5 a3, after which at the very least Black would have acquired the additional option of answering 5 ... ♘d7 6 ♗d3 with 6 ... e6. There is clearly much here that remains to be investigated.

(b) 3 ... h6!? is an obvious and critical move which has been almost totally ignored. Since 4 ♗h4 would appear to involve White in unacceptable material loss after 4 ... g5 5 e4 ♗g7 (cf.

Chapter 7, p. 72), the whole *raison d'être* of White's system seems to be called into question. In the only top class example of it so far, White replied 4 ♗f4 and after 4 ... ♘f6 5 e4!? (acknowledging that normal methods give White nothing) 5 ... fe 6 f3 ♗f5 7 fe de 8 ♗c4 e6 Black had obtained a slightly improved version of a Staunton Gambit variation already considered completely satisfactory for Black; Ligterink–Belyavsky, Wijk aan Zee 1984.

4 h4

This advance of the h-pawn is the keystone of White's strategy: strategically, it reinforces the play on the dark squares, while tactically it readies the h4–h5 rupture.

4 ... ♗g7
5 e3 *(64)*

The usual move, opening the queen's path along the d1–h5 diagonal. Alternatively, White may opt for immediately intensifying his dark square play and pre-

paring long castling by 5 ♕d2. This continuation contains hidden venom and Black must tread warily to avoid the many pitfalls as the following variations demonstrate: 5 ... c6 6 ♘f3 ♘d7?! (natural but inaccurate; 6 ... h6 is necessary, with fair chances of maintaining the balance, although it is clear that Black's task is the more onerous, e.g. 7 ♗f4 ♘d7 8 0-0-0 ♘gf6 9 ♘e5 ♘e4! 10 ♘xe4 ♘xe5! and by precise play White is prevented from building any advantage) 7 h5 h6 (were White now to retreat the bishop then all would be fine in the black camp after 8 ... g5, but instead White sacrifices a piece for a dangerous attack) 8 hg! hg 9 ♖h7! ♖xh7 (forced, after 9 ... ♗f6 or 9 ... ♔f8, simply 10 ♘xg5 is crushing) 10 gh ♘gf6 11 ♕xg5 ♔f7 (11 ... ♔f8 puts up stiffer resistance although Black clearly remains under immense pressure after, for example, 12 ♕h4! ♔f7 13 e3) 12 ♕xf5 ♘b6 13 ♘e5+ ♔f8 14 ♕f4 and Black's defensive task is hopeless; Vaganian–Knezevic, Dubna 1973.

White has also occasionally experimented with 5 ♘h3 but this should not cause Black undue problems after simply 5 ... ♘f6 threatening an early ... ♘e4.

5 ... ♗e6

This initially strange-looking

move is aimed at shoring up the kingside defences, a useful task for the otherwise torpid QB. A good example of the type of attack White can whip up if this prophylactic manoeuvre is omitted is provided by the game Bareev–Dreev, Soviet U20 Ch. 1983: 5 ... c6 6 ♗d3 (6 h5 would be premature because after 6 ... h6 the sacrificial continuation 7 hg hg 8 ♖xh8 ♗xh8 9 ♕h5 ♗g7 would be insufficient) 6 ... ♘f6 (the equally unwary 6 ... ♘d7 would run up against 7 ♘f3 ♘gf6 8 h5 ♘xh5 9 ♗xf5 with powerful kingside pressure, but it is still not too late for 6 ... ♗e6, e.g. 7 ♘f3 ♘d7 8 h5!? ♘gf6 — to provoke the sacrifice here would bring disaster after 8 ... h6? 9 hg! hg 10 ♖xh8 ♗xh8 11 ♘xg5 ♘f8 12 g7! ♗xg7 13 ♕h5+ ♔d7 14 ♘xe6 — 9 h6 — Black need not fear the simplifying 9 hg hg 10 ♖xh8+ ♗xh8 11 ♘e2 ♗f7 12 ♘f4 ♘e4 — 9 ... ♗f8 10 ♘e2 ♗f7 with an interesting position where White has cashed in his initiative for a spatial advantage on the king's wing, the advanced outpost of which (the h-pawn) could one day turn into a liability; chances are approximately equal; Palatnik–Legky, Tallinn 1985) 7 h5!? ♘xh5 8 ♖xh5 gh 9 ♕xh5+ ♔f8 10 ♘f3 ♕e8 11 ♕h2 e6 12 0-0-0 (for the exchange, White has lasting pressure due to

the superior coordination of his forces and the vulnerability of the black king) 12 ... ♘d7 13 g4! fg 14 ♘h4 ♘f6 15 f3 ♕h5?! 16 ♕f4 ♕f7 17 ♕d6+ ♕e7 18 ♕g3 ♔e8 19 fg ♖g8?? (cracking under the pressure, but in any case it is difficult to imagine Black surviving in the long run) 20 ♗xh7 ♖h8 21 ♘g6 ♕d7 22 ♘e5! ♕c7 23 ♗g6+ ♔e7 24 ♖f1 ♖f8 25 ♕h4 b5 26 ♗d3 1–0.

This exchange sacrifice attack plays such an important role in this variation that it is worth quoting one further example, this time arising from 5 ... ♘f6: 6 h5!? ♘xh5 7 ♖xh5 gh 8 ♕xh5+ ♔f8 9 ♘f3 ♗e6 10 ♗h6 ♘d7 11 ♗xg7+ ♔xg7 12 ♕g5+ ♔f7 13 ♕h5+ ♔g7 14 ♕g5+ ♔f7 15 ♕h6! (having demonstrated who is in charge White turns the screw) 15 ... ♖g8 (there is no other way of meeting the threatened 16 ♘g5+) thus far we have followed Vaiser–M. Knezevic, Havana 1985, where White decided to restore material parity by 16 ♘g5+ ♖xg5 17 ♕xg5 thus giving Black much needed time to develop and coordinate his pieces, something which would not have been at all easy to achieve after the more ambitious 16 ♕xh7+! ♔e8 17 ♕h5+ ♗f7 18 ♕xf5±.

6   ♘f3

The most natural continuation,

although alternatives such as 6
♘h3 and 6 ♕f3 will doubtless be
explored in the future.

6 ... c6

It is difficult for Black to get by
without this reinforcement of the
d-pawn, e.g. 6 ... ♘d7 7 h5 h6 8
hg! hg 9 ♖xh8 ♗xh8 10 ♘xg5
♘f8 11 ♕h5 ♗g7 12 ♘xe6 ♘xe6
13 ♕xf5 ♕d6 14 ♘xd5 and the
horde of white infantry has every
chance of marching to victory;
Palatnik–Fadeyev, Ukraine Ch.
1984.

7 ♗f4 *(65)*

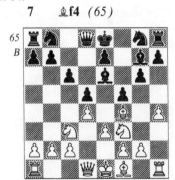

By vacating g5 for the knight,
White indirectly prepares the h-
pawn thrust. The straightforward
7 ♗d3 occurred in Vl. Kovacevic–
Kristiansen, Plovdiv 1983, which
provides us with a good example
of how Black should respond in
the event of an exchange of rooks
along the h-file: 7 ... ♘d7 8 h5
♘gf6 (as is so often the case, Black
dare not allow the passive bishop
sacrifice 8 ... h6? 9 hg! hg 10 ♖xh8

♗xh8 11 ♘xg5 ♘f8 12 g7! ♗xg7
13 ♕h5+ ♔d7 14 ♘xe6 with a
crushing advantage) 9 hg hg 10
♖xh8 ♗xh8 11 ♘e2 (not 11 ♕e2
♘e4!∓ or 11 ♔e2 ♕b6 with ...
c5 in the air) 11 ... ♗f7 12 ♘f4
♘e4 13 ♔e2 and now instead of
13 ... ♘f8?! 14 ♕h1 ♗f6 15 ♗h6
♘e6 16 g4!± as happened in the
game, Vl. Kovacevic gives 13 ...
♗f6 14 ♗xf6 ef 15 ♕h1 ♕e7
16 ♕h6 ♘f8 17 c3 producing an
unclear position with chances for
both sides.

7 ... ♘f6
8 h5! ♘bd7!

Acceptance of the offer would
lead Black into the usual defensive
morass: 8 ... ♘xh5 9 ♖xh5! gh 10
♘g5 ♗g8 11 ♕xh5+ ♔f8 12
♗d3 e6 13 g4 h6 14 ♘f3 ♗f7 15
♕h3 with lasting pressure; Halifman–Lerner, Kubishev 1986.

9 h6

The sacrifice being declined,
there is really very little else for
White to do apart from pushing
back the bishop and gaining space.
We have already seen from the
note to White's seventh that
exchanging along the h-file brings
nothing.

9 ... ♗f8
10 ♕d2 ♗f7
11 ♘e5 e6 *(66)*

This is an appropriate moment
to take stock of the situation. White's advanced h-pawn means that

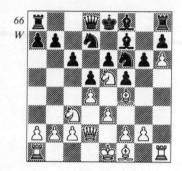

66
W

Black is somewhat cramped on the kingside, but equally the blocked position ensures a fair degree of safety for his king. Black's central grip is satisfactory and there are prospects for creating counterplay on the queen's wing. All in all, chances are nicely balanced.

12   f3

Naturally, White seeks to open up new fronts either by g4 or e4.

| 12 | ... | ♗e7 |
| 13 | g4?! | |

This impetuosity should have backfired; completing development by 13 0-0-0 was correct.

13	...	♘xe5
14	♗xe5	fg
15	fg	0-0
16	♗e2	♗d6?!

Black misses his opportunity. Halifman points out that 16 ... ♘d7! 17 ♗g3 ♗g5 would have given Black a slight advantage, while 17 ♗g7 ♖e8 18 0-0-0 ♗g5 would also leave White poorly placed to create active play.

17	♗xd6	♕xd6
18	0-0-0	e5
19	g5	♘d7?! (67)

67
W

The knight is exposed to attack here and would better have been tucked away by 19 ... ♘e8 with good defensive chances.

20   e4!

Energetically opening up the centre the better to expose the inadequacies of Black's setup.

20   ...   b5

To chase the knight away from c3.

21	ed	b4
22	♘e4	♕xd5
23	♗g4!	

Astutely breaking Black's counterplay by fingering the weak spot in his position.

23   ...   ♕xe4

There is no real choice; 23 ... ♗e6 24 ♗xe6 ♕xe6 25 d5 is crushing, while 23 ... ♕xa2 24 ♕xb4 ♖ab8 25 ♕a3 ♕xa3 26 ba ♗d5 27 ♖he1 also leaves Black in a bad way.

24	♗xd7	♖ad8

Black's prospects in the ending arising after 24 ... ♕xd4 25 ♕xd4 ed 26 ♖xd4 would be grim.

25	de	♕xe5
26	♖he1	♕a5
27	b3!	c5

Of course, 27 ... ♕xa2?? would lose instantly to 28 ♕d4, and 27 ... ♗d5 28 ♖e7 would also be dreadful.

28	♔b1

Avoiding the trap 28 ♕d6 ♖xd7! 29 ♕e5 (29 ♕xd7 c4 would give Black dangerous chances) 29 ... ♕a3+ 30 ♔b1 ♗xb3! 31 ab ♖df7 when Black is still fighting.

28	...	♕c7
29	c4!	

With this the white queen finally gains access to the long diagonal thus compelling Black to shed a pawn and enter into a hopeless end game. The technical part concluded as follows: 29 ... ♕g3 30 ♕b2 ♕c3 31 ♕xc3 bc 32 ♔c2 ♔h8 (pathetically underlining Black's plight) 33 ♖f1 ♗g8 34 ♖xf8 ♖xf8 35 ♔xc3 ♖d8 36 ♗g4 ♖e8 37 ♖d7 a5 38 ♖a7 ♖e5 39 ♖xa5 ♖xg5 40 ♗d7 ♖g3+ 41 ♔d2 ♖g2+ 42 ♔e3 ♖g5 43 ♖a8 ♖e5+ 44 ♔d2 g5 45 ♗c6 1–0.

9   2 ♘f3 and Others

This chapter provides selected recommendations against the less important second moves at White's disposal after the introductory 1 d4 f5. Only 2 ♘f3 has any real importance, although some of the others can be dangerous if not met precisely.

A   2 ♘f3

2   ♘f3   e6 (68)

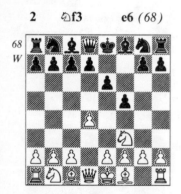

68
W

If Black intends playing a Classical System, then there is much to be said for preferring 2 ... e6 over 2 ... ♘f6. By this means White's most promising lines, based on

pinning the knight by ♗g5, are ruled out.

However, if Black wishes to play a Leningrad Variation then 2 ... ♘f6 is necessary since 2 ... g6 3 h4 is too risky (see p. 47). After 2 ... ♘f6 3 ♗g5 (other moves permit Black to carry on in normal Leningrad fashion) Black has the interesting possibility 3 ... ♘e4, after which White has tried the following:

(a) 4 ♗f4 c5 (naturally, 4 ... e6 is also satisfactory) 5 c3 ♕b6 6 ♕b3 ♕xb3 7 ab d6 8 e3 ♗e6 9 ♗c4 ♗xc4 10 bc ♘c6 and Black has no difficulty holding the balance; Radev–Knezevic, Leningrad 1960.

(b) 4 h4 c6 5 c3 ♕b6 6 ♕c2 d5 7 ♗f4 e6 8 ♘bd2 ♗e7 9 ♘xe4 fe 10 ♘e5 0-0 11 e3 c5 with an equal position where White's advanced h-pawn looks out of place; Pietzsch–Larsen, Dortmund 1961.

(c) 4 ♗h4 g6 5 ♘bd2 ♘xd2 (5 ... ♗g7 comes into consideration)

88

6 ♕xd2 ♗g7 7 c3 d6 8 e3 ♘d7 and Black's game is entirely satisfactory; Eising–Besser, Aibling 1965.

3   ♗f4

Nor do other moves bring White any advantage:

(a) 3 ♗g5 ♗e7 4 ♗xe7 ♕xe7 5 ♘bd2 (or 5 e3 ♘f6=, but not 5 … ♕b4+ 6 ♘c3 ♕xb2 7 ♘b5 ♕b4+ 8 c3 ♕a5 9 ♘e5 with strong threats as shown in Vellner–Duckstein, Vienna 1959; 5 ♘c3 ♘f6 6 e3 d6 7 ♗c4 c6 8 a4 a5 9 0-0 0-0 and Black has nothing to fear, Haygarth–Bellin, British Ch. 1978) 5 … ♘f6 6 e3 b6 7 ♗d3 (or 7 ♗e2 ♗b7 8 0-0 0-0 9 c4 d6 10 b4 ♘bd7= Lasker–Barry, Cambridge Springs 1904) 7 … ♗b7 8 c3 c5 9 0-0 0-0 10 ♖e1 d5 11 ♘e5 ♘bd7 12 ♘xd7 ♘xd7 13 f4 g5 and Black's kingside initiative fully compensates for his slightly inferior bishop; Robatsch–Duckstein, Graz 1961.

(b) 3 c3 ♗e7!? (playing a waiting game in order to prevent White's QB attaining its most active development on g5) 4 ♕c2 d5 5 ♗f4 ♘f6 6 e3 0-0 7 ♘e5 ♘bd7 8 ♘d2 ♘xe5 9 ♗xe5 ♗d6 10 ♘f3 ♗d7 11 ♗d3 ♕e8 with totally satisfactory prospects; Chen De–Bellin, Shanghai 1981.

(c) 3 d5 ♗d6!? (Black secured roughly equal chances by 3 … ed 4 ♕xd5 d6 5 c4 ♘f6 6 ♕d1 ♗e7

7 ♘c3 c6 8 g3 0-0 9 ♗g2 ♘e4 in Silva Rocha–Bolbochan, Rio de Janeiro 1938) 4 de de 5 ♘bd2 ♗c5 6 b3 ♘f6 7 e3 0-0 8 ♗c4 ♘c6 9 0-0 ♔h8 10 ♗b2 ♕e7 (10 … a6!?) 11 ♕e2 e5 12 ♗b5 e4 13 ♗xc6 bc 14 ♘e5 ♗d6 and Black's kingside threats put White on the defensive; Karoly–Karlsson, Gausdal 1987.

(d) 3 g4? fg 4 ♘e5 ♕h4 5 e4 g3∓ White's gambit has backfired; Bogoljubow–Hasenfuss, Kemeri 1939.

3   …   ♘f6
4   e3   b6

Of course, either 4 … ♗e7 or 4 … d5 may also be played.

5   ♘bd2   ♗b7
6   ♗d3

6 h3 was answered challengingly by 6 … ♗d6!? in Baumbach–Mohring, E. German Ch. 1969, giving Black a fine game after 7 ♗xd6 cd 8 ♗d3 0-0 9 ♕e2 ♘e4.

6   …   ♗e7
7   h3

Black's last move contained the positional threat of … ♘h5 gaining the bishop pair.

7   …   0-0
8   c3

The double-step brings nothing, e.g. 8 c4 ♘e4 9 0-0 d6 10 ♕c2 ♘xd2 11 ♘xd2 ♕e8 with excellent kingside play in the offing.

8   …   c5 *(69)*

White's bulwark centre is contested by a pincer formed by

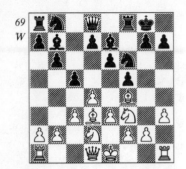

69
W

Black's bishop pawns. Both armies are harmoniously stationed and the stage is set for a complex strategical battle. Given the dearth of practical experience with this position, one can merely observe that after the natural 9 0-0 Black probably does best to immediately occupy his advanced outpost by 9 ... ♘e4, after which 10 ♕c2 ♘xd2 11 ♘xd2 ♕e8 would be a simplification enhancing the positive aspects of Black's position, namely, the raking QB and king-side attacking prospects. The attempt to bring e4 under control by 9 ♕c2 runs into trouble through a *vis-à-vis* with Black's QR on the c-file: 9 ... ♘c6 10 ♗h2 ♖c8 11 a3 (parrying the threat of ... cd and ... ♘b4) 11 ... ♘a5! (threatening to establish a massive white-square bind by 12 ... c4) 12 dc (White must close the c-file) 12 ... bc 13 c4 ♘c6 14 0-0 ♕e8 with a clear positional superiority for Black; Alterman–Bellin, Biel 1987.

B   2 d5

| 2 | d5 | e5!? |
| 3 | de | d5 |

This direct attempt to exploit the d-pawn's advance should suffice to equalize. 2 ... ♘f6 is also good, of course.

C   Dr Krejcik's Gambit: 2 g4

| 2 | g4 | fg |
| 3 | ♗f4 | |

Probably White's best try. The alternatives:

(a) 3 h3 g3! and by returning the pawn Black deprives White of the open h-file and leaves him with a statically weak kingside. This is why White first develops his bishop.

(b) 3 e4 invites sharp counters such as 3 ... e5!? and 3 ... d5!? both of which could well be good for Black. An example of the latter went 4 e5 ♗f5 5 ♘c3 c5 6 ♗b5+ ♘c6 7 ♗xc6+ bc 8 ♘ge2 e6∓ (Callinan–Saidy, USA 1968). In addition, 3 ... d6, as in the column, is also eminently playable.

(c) 3 ♗g5 has little point and could be met by 3 ... ♘f6 4 ♘c3 d5 5 ♕d3 c6! 6 0-0-0 g6 7 e4 ♘xe4! 8 ♘xe4 de 9 ♕xe4 ♕d5∓.

3	...	d6
4	e4	c6
5	♕d2	

On 5 ♘c3, Black can support

the advance of his e-pawn by 5 ... ♕a5.

	5	...	♘d7
	6	♘c3	e5 (70)

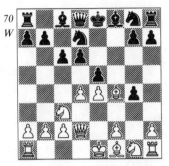

An obscure position, sorely in need of practical trials. It is obvious that much remains to be explored in this crazy gambit.

D   2 h3

	2	h3

This apparently timid move conceals aggressive intentions. As in the preceding variation, White plans to gambit the g-pawn but here the opening of the h-file will be automatic since Black has no opportunity to decline as in note (a) above.

Given its successful introduction by no less a figure than Korchnoi, it is surprising that this quirky continuation has so far singularly failed to attract any followers. Moreover, it is clear that Black's best response has yet to

be worked out.

	2	...	♘f6

As well as this natural move Black could also consider 2 ... d6 and 2 ... d5.

	3	g4

3 ♘f3 would bring about Haik–M. Zeitlin, Sochi 1985, (which actually arose via the move order 2 ♘f3 ♘f6 3 h3) where Black failed to find a good defence: 3 ... d6 (3 ... d5 4 c4 e6 5 ♘c3 c6 comes into consideration) 4 g4 g6 (after 4 ... fg 5 hg ♗xg4 White could play 6 ♘g5 or 6 ♕d3 with compensation for the pawn in an unclear position) 5 ♘c3 ♗g7 6 ♕d3 ♘c6? (6 ... c6 is much better) 7 d5 ♘e5 8 ♘xe5 de 9 gf and Black is in dire straits due to 9 ... gf failing to 10 ♕g3.

	3	...	fg

Although acceptance of the gambit is clearly the acid test, there is much to be said for declining, e.g. 3 ... d6 4 g5 ♘e4 5 ♗f4 c6! 6 f3 ♕a5+ 7 c3 e5 with a wild game which could easily go in Black's favour.

	4	hg	♘xg4
	5	e4	d6 (71)

White has obvious compensation for the pawn in his control of the centre, free development and open h-file. The demands on the defender are considerable and allow no margin of error. The inaugural game for this variation,

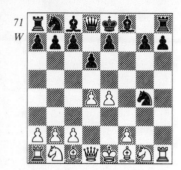

71
W

Korchnoi–Kaenel, Biel 1979, carried on: 6 ♗g5! g6 (6 ... c6) 7 f3 ♘f6 8 ♘c3 c6 9 ♕d2 ♗e6 10 0-0-0 ♘bd7 11 ♔b1 ♗g7 12 ♘h3 ♘h5 13 ♘f4 ♘xf4 14 ♕xf4 ♕b6 15 ♕d2 ♕c7 (15 ... ♗f6 looks more sensible) 16 ♕e3 ♘b6 17 d5 ♗f7 18 a4 a6 19 e5! ♗xe5 20 f4 ♗g7 21 dc bc 22 ♗g2 ♘c8 23 ♘e4 ♔f8 24 ♗h6 and Black's defences are at breaking point. One would imagine this to be sufficient to persuade most players that accepting the gambit is too risky.

E 2 ♕d3

2 ♕d3

An *outré* move which flouts the principles of good opening play but is redeemed by its strategic grounding. White simultaneously threatens the f-pawn and prepares e2–e4 thus compelling Black to adopt a Stonewall formation. Happily for the Dutch Defence

this is no bad thing, and the clumsy placing of White's queen assures Black of a very playable game.

2 ... d5

A classic illustration of what Black must not allow is provided by Fairhurst–Dreyer, Dublin 1957, which went 2 ... g6 3 e4 fe 4 ♕xe4 ♘f6 5 ♕h4 (the queen is powerfully posted here) 5 ... ♗g7 6 ♘f3 b6 7 ♘c3 c5 8 ♗h6 0-0 9 ♗xg7 ♔xg7 10 0-0-0 and Black will experience great difficulty in subduing the active white pieces.

3 g3

Best. More rustic schemes of development leave White passively placed, e.g. 3 ♗f4 e6? (3 ... ♘f6 is correct) 4 ♘f3 (Black's unsuspecting third move could have been exploited by the consistent 4 ♕g3! ♘a6 5 e3 c6 6 ♗xa6!? ♕a5+ 7 ♘c3 ♕xa6 8 ♗d6 — or 8 ♗e5 — with total positional control) 4 ... ♘f6 5 e3 ♗d6 6 ♗e2 (pusillanimous in the extreme; 6 c4 was necessary) 6 ... 0-0 7 ♘e5 c5! 8 c3 ♘c6 9 ♘d2 ♕c7 10 ♘df3 ♘fd7! 11 ♘xd7 ♗xd7 12 ♗xd6 ♕xd6 13 0-0 c4! 14 ♕d2 b5 15 ♘e1 g5! 16 f4 g4 and the black infantry have enveloped the board; Kmoch–Alekhine, Semmering 1926.

3 ... ♘f6
4 ♗g2 e6
5 c4 ♗d6
Simply 5 ... ♗e7 with a later

... ♘c6 would also have its points.

6	♘f3	0-0
7	0-0	c6
8	b3	♗d7!
9	♗a3	♗e8
10	♗xd6	♕xd6
11	e3	♘bd7
12	♘c3	♗h5	(72)

Black has a very comfortable position; his putatively bad bishop is more effective than its theoretically good counterpart, and since the centre is solid and White has yet to generate play on the queen's wing, he can think in terms of developing his initiative on the kingside. The game Gavrikov–Psakhis, Tallinn 1983, continued 13 ♘d2 ♘e4 14 f4 ♖ac8 15 c5 ♕e7 16 b4 g5 17 a4 gf 18 ef ♘df6 (Black's minor pieces are much the more active) 19 ♖ac1 b6 (prophylaxis to nip White's play in the bud) 20 ♘b3 ♖b8 21 ♘a2 ♗e8 22 ♖c2 h5 23 h4 (creates lasting weaknesses, but otherwise Black will constantly have ... h5–h4

available) 23 ... ♔h8 24 ♖f3 ♖g8 25 ♔h2 ♗d7 (the versatile bishop reverts to a more familiar role as mainstay of the queenside) 26 ♗h3 ♖g6 27 ♔h1 (unhappy with the constant possibility of ... ♘g4+ hanging over him, the white king withdraws only to run foul of the advanced cavalry) 27 ... ♖bg8 28 ♖g2 ♖xg3! 29 ♖gxg3 ♖xg3 30 ♖xg3 ♘f2+ 31 ♔g2 ♘xd3 (a degrading demise for her majesty who moved not once since her optimistic emergence at the beginning of the game) 32 ♖xd3 ♘e4 0–1.

F   2 e3

2	e3

Such self-limitation instantly forfeits any prospects of obtaining an opening advantage. Black may respond more or less according to taste; the line given is analogous to that against 2 ♘f3.

2	...	♘f6
3	♗d3	e6

Tolush–Alexander, Hastings 1953/4, went 3 ... d6 4 ♘e2?! (a spiritless deployment which bears no comparison with the natural 4 ♘f3) 4 ... e5 5 de (Black also had an easy time of it in Colle–Nimzowitsch, Baden-Baden 1925, after 5 c4 c5 6 0-0 ♘c6 7 ♘bc3 g5 8 dc dc 9 ♘g3 e4 10 ♗e2 ♗d6 11 ♘b5 ♗e5 12 ♕xd8+ ♔xd8

13 ♖d1+ ♔e7) 5 ... de 6 0-0
♗c5 7 ♘g3 g6 8 ♗c4 ♕e7 and
Black's chances are already superior thanks to his space advantage
on the kingside and concomitant
attacking prospects.

    4   ♘d2

Of course, White would be
better advised to play a quick ♘f3
coupled with c2–c4.

    4   ...   c5

4 ... d5 is also possible but the
text move is more elastic.

    5   ♘gf3   ♘c6
    6   0-0   b6
    7   c3   ♗e7 *(73)*

Black may look to the future
with confidence. In Stahlberg–
Keres, Munich Ol. 1936, White
inconsistently continued with the
sharp 8 e4?! and paid the penalty
after 8 ... cd 9 cd ♘b4 10 ♗b1
♗a6 11 ♖e1 ♘d3 12 ♗xd3
♗xd3 13 ef ♗xf5 14 ♘c4 ♖c8 15
♘ce5 0-0 when he has merely
managed to lose the bishop pair
and obtain an isolated d-pawn.

G The remainder

Of the 28 moves available to White
on his second move only one
(2 ♗h6??) is absolutely unplayable, although it would not be easy
to survive after 2 ♔d2? either.
Those moves apart (and perhaps
also 2 ♕d2 which merely gets in
the way and presents a target), the
advantage of playing first allows
White the luxury of being able to
make a dubious move and get
away with it. When faced with
unorthodox opening play, Black
generally does best to stick as
much as possible to his preferred
development scheme in the knowledge that natural moves are usually the best.

10 The Classical Variation

This chapter covers those variations which arise when White (temporarily at least) avoids the kingside fianchetto and instead follows up his opening move with the direct, classical development of 2 c4 and 3 ♘c3. That this approach is rarely seen in contemporary master praxis is testimony enough to the adequacy of Black's defences.

    1   d4   f5
    2   c4   e6

Of course, Black may equally well play 2 ... ♘f6. The text move-order has been chosen in order to take into account the possibility that Black might transpose into the Dutch via the sequence 1 d4 e6 2 c4 f5.

    3   ♘c3

The usual assortment of offbeat alternatives do not cause Black any trouble:

(a) 3 g4? fg 4 e4 (4 h3 g3! 5 fg c5! 6 d5 ♗d6∓) 4 ... e5! 5 d5 (5 de ♘c6∓) 5 ... ♗b4+ (simply 5

... ♘f6 is also good) 6 ♘c3 ♗xc3+ 7 bc d6∓ *ECO*.

(b) 3 e4? fe 4 ♘c3 ♘f6 5 f3 ♗b4! (rapid development is even better than allowing White the slight compensation he would obtain in return for the pawn) 6 ♗g5 c5 7 dc (7 d5 ed 8 cd 0-0 is also good for Black) 7 ... 0-0 8 ♖c1 ♕c7 9 ♗xf6 ♖xf6 10 fe ♕f4 11 ♘f3 ♕xe4+ and White is in dire straits; Freiman–Model, USSR Ch. 1927.

(c) 3 e3 ♘f6 4 ♗d3 (after 4 f4 b6! 5 ♘f3 ♗b7 6 ♗d3 g6! 7 0-0 ♗g7 8 ♘c3 0-0 9 ♕e2 c5 Black has fully equal prospects; analysis by Pachman) 4 ... d6 5 ♕c2 (it is inadvisable to ignore the threatened advance: 5 ♘e2?! e5 6 ♘bc3 ♘c6 7 d5 ♘e7 8 e4 f4∓ Dubinin–Riumin, USSR Ch. 1934/35) 5 ... g6 6 ♘f3 ♘c6 7 0-0 e5 8 de de 9 ♗e2 e4 10 ♖d1 ♕e7 11 ♘d4 ♘e5 with excellent prospects for Black; Pachman.

(d) 3 ♘f3 is evidently replete

with transpositional possibilities; here we shall merely note some of the more individualistic pathways: 3 ... ♘f6 4 e3 (4 d5 ♗b4+ 5 ♗d2 ♕e7 6 ♘c3 c6! 7 de de 8 a3 ♗d6 9 e4 e5 is good for Black, Vasyukhin–Kolobov, Moscow Ch. 1965) 4 ... b6 5 ♗d3 ♗b7 6 0-0 ♗e7 7 ♘bd2 (or 7 ♕e2 0-0 8 b3 ♕e8 9 ♗b2 d6 10 ♘c3 ♕g6 11 ♘e1 ♘bd7 with complete equality; Pfeiffer–Matulovic, Oberhausen 1961) 7 ... 0-0 8 ♕c2 d5 (a noteworthy method of parrying the e4 threat) 9 cd (on 9 ♘e5 Black will continue with 9 ... c5 and ... ♘c6) 9 ... ♘xd5 10 a3 c5 11 dc ♗xc5 and Black's active centralized pieces balance the chances; H. Frydmann–Tartakower, Lodz 1927.

3   ...   ♘f6 *(74)*

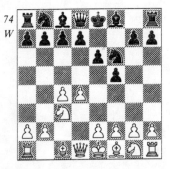

This is the main *tabiya* of the Classical Variation and just about every possible fourth move has been tried at one time or another. Before proceeding with our two

model games we shall summarize these alternatives as follows:

(a) 4 e4? fe transposes to note 'b' to White's third move.

(b) 4 ♕c2 ♗e7 (a game from the world championship match, Bronstein–Botvinnik, 1951, demonstrated that 4 ... ♗b4 is not entirely satisfactory for Black after 5 e3 0-0 6 ♗d3 d6 7 ♘e2 c5 8 a3 ♗xc3+ 9 ♘xc3 ♘c6 10 dc dc 11 b3 ♗d7 12 ♗b2 ♘e5 and now instead of preserving the bishop with 13 ♗e2?! as was played in the game, Botvinnik has pointed out that 13 0-0-0! ♘xd3+ 14 ♖xd3 leaves White the better chances) 5 ♘f3 0-0 6 e4 (White should be content with either 6 e3 or 6 g3) 6 ... fe 7 ♘xe4 ♘c6 8 ♘xf6+ (not 8 ♗d3 ♘b4 9 ♘xf6+ ♔h8!) 8 ... ♗xf6 9 ♗e3 e5= 10 de ♘xe5 11 ♘xe5 ♗xe5 12 ♗d3 ♕h4 13 g3?! ♕h5 14 0-0 d6 15 f4 ♗f6 16 ♖fe1 ♗h3 with some advantage for Black; Pachman–Larsen, Havana Ol. 1966.

(c) 4 ♗g5 ♗e7 (4 ... ♗b4 also comes into consideration) 5 e3 (White achieves nothing by 5 ♗xf6 ♗xf6 6 e4, e.g. 6 ... fe 7 ♘xe4 0-0 8 ♘f3 d6 9 ♗d3 ♘c6=) 5 ... 0-0 6 ♗d3 (long castling produces double-edged positions, e.g. 6 ♕c2 ♕e8 7 ♘f3 d6 8 0-0-0 ♘c6 9 d5 ♘b4 10 ♕b3 ♘a6 11 de ♘c5 12 ♕c2 ♘xe6 13 ♗h4 ♘c5 14 ♘d4 ♕h5 15 ♗g3 a5; Polugayevsky–Guimard, Buenos Aires 1962) 6 ... b6 7 ♘f3 (Harrwitz–Morphy, Paris 1858, went 7 ♘ge2 ♗b7 8 0-0 ♘h5! 9 ♗xe7 ♛xe7 10 ♘g3 ♘xg3 11 hg d6=) 7 ... ♗b7 8 0-0 ♛e8! 9 ♛e2 ♘e4 (Botvinnik has suggested 9 ... ♛h5 10 e4 ♘c6! producing a rich and unclear position) 10 ♗xe7 ♘xc3 (this important zwischenzug was made possible by Black's eighth) 11 bc ♛xe7 12 a4 ♗xf3!? (this bold and interesting capture has been universally criticized in favour of 12 ... ♘c6 13 ♖fb1 ♖ab8 with a consensus evaluation of =) 13 ♛xf3 ♘c6 14 ♖fb1 ♖ae8?! (but this is where I would point the finger; by playing 14 ... g6! instead Black could not be prevented from achieving the vital ... e5 advance) 15 ♛h3 ♖f6 (and here Alekhine's recommendation of 15 ... g5 is more to the point) 16 f4± Black's e-pawn has been prevented from advancing while the white counterpart will shortly do so to considerable effect; Capablanca–Tartakower, New York, 1924.

(d) 4 e3 b6! 5 ♗d3 (Najdorf's 5 ♗e2 ♗b7 6 ♗f3 is most simply answered by 6 ... ♗xf3 7 ♛xf3 ♘c6 with approximately even chances, while Fraser–Steinitz, Dundee 1867, demonstrated that unambitious opening play by White enables Black to adopt a typically flexible setup guaranteeing pleasant middlegame prospects: 5 ♘f3 ♗b7 6 ♗e2 ♛e7 7 ♗d2 ♘c6 8 ♖c1 g6 9 ♛c2 ♗g7=) 5 ... ♗b7 6 ♘f3 (6 f3 is an important alternative, best met by 6 ... g6, when Dus-Hotimirsky–Maroczy, Carlsbad 1907, saw Black equalize after 7 ♘ge2 ♗g7 8 ♛c2?! ♘c6 9 a3 e5; ECO gives 7 ♘h3 ♗g7 8 0-0 0-0 9 e4±, but 8 ... c5!, exploiting the decentralized white knight, is more logical) 6 ... ♗b4! (Black increases his control of e4) 7 ♗d2 (nor has Black any problems after 7 0-0 ♗xc3 8 bc 0-0 9 a4 ♘c6 10 ♘d2 d6; Rubinstein–Maroczy, Teplitz-Schonau 1922) 7 ... 0-0 8 ♛c2 (Black has an extremely comfortable game after 8 0-0 d6 9 a3 ♗xc3 10 ♗xc3 ♘e4) 8 ... a5 9 a3 ♗xc3 10 ♗xc3 ♘e4 11 0-0-0 d5 (utilizing the fact that White dare not countenance a further weakening of the king's pawn cover by b2–b3 to obtain a second central light square base for his pieces) 12 ♘e5 ♘d7 13 ♘xd7 ♛xd7 14 ♗e1 dc 15 ♗xc4 ♗d5 with fine chances for Black; Flohr–Bondarevsky, USSR Ch. 1951.

(e) 4 ♘f3 b6 5 e3 ♗b7 6 ♗d3 ♗b4 transposes to note (d).

(f) 4 f3 ♗b4 5 ♗d2 0-0 (not 5 ... c5 6 a3) 6 a3 ♗e7 7 e3 c5 8 ♗d3 ♘c6 9 ♘ge2 d6 10 ♛c2 ♗d7 11 0-0-0 a6 12 g4 b5, with a typical opposite wing castling maelstrom of a middlegame to come, was the course of Volovich–A. Zaitsev, match, Moscow 1962. Clearly there remains much to be discovered here.

It should be noted that Black may, of course, transpose to a Stonewall in many of these variations should he so prefer.

Maroczy–Tartakower
Teplitz-Schonau 1922
1 d4 f5 2 c4 e6 3 ♘c3 ♘f6

    4   a3 *(75)*

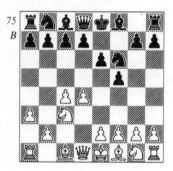

This modest looking move is logical enough given that the major theme of the Dutch is control of e4 and that the move ... ♗b4 often plays a vital role in Black's efforts toward this end. By switching to the Stonewall, however, Black can simultaneously maintain control of e4 and highlight the lack of bite behind the a-pawn advance.

4	...	♗e7
5	e3	0-0
6	♗d3	d5
7	♘f3	c6

Sidestepping an instructive error easily made by inexperienced Stonewallers: 7 ... ♘e4? 8 cd ed 9 ♕b3 and the double attack on d5 and e4 makes the proud black knight untenable.

| 8 | 0-0 | ♘e4 |
| 9 | ♕c2 | |

White unsuspectingly continues with natural-looking routine moves which surprisingly rapidly lead him into a passive and vulnerable position. 9 ♘e5 followed by 10 f4 would stabilize White's kingside and produce an equal position.

9	...	♗d6
10	b3	♘d7
11	♗b2	♖f6 *(76)*

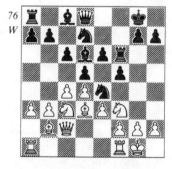

Tally-ho! Black has sighted his quarry and is after it without further ado. It was this game which established the rook manoeuvre as the most effective method of pursuing the attack in such optimum conditions. An alternative idea, noted by Tartakower, would be ... ♛f6 followed by ... g7–g5–g4.

12 ♖fe1

Preparing to shore up the defences.

12 ... ♖h6

Threatening the bishop sacrifice on h2 followed by ... ♛h4.

13 g3 ♛f6
14 ♗f1

White would dearly like to reposition his knight at f1 by 14 ♘d2, but this would allow the devastating sacrifice 14 ... ♘xf2! 15 ♔xf2 ♖xh2+ 16 ♔g1 (or 16 ♔f3 e5) 16 ... ♗xg3 and 17 ... ♛h4.

14 ... g5
15 ♖ad1

At first sight it seems incredible that there can be anything seriously wrong with White's position given that all of his pieces are developed and occupy sensible looking squares while most of Black's queenside is still asleep. Two key factors supply the answer: king safety and purpose. That the white monarch is in grave danger is clear enough, but even that might not be decisive if only his forces were actually *doing* something — which they manifestly are not. And therein lies the

overriding problem: whilst White's army is optically plausible, functionally it is impotent.

15 ... g4
16 ♘xe4

Forced, since once again 16 ♘d2 would allow the decisive knight offer 16 ... ♘xf2 17 ♔xf2 ♖xh2+ 18 ♗g2 ♗xg3+!

16 ... fe
17 ♘d2 (77)

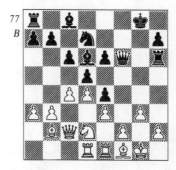

77
B

17 ... ♖xh2!!

A glorious conception, which Réti, writing in 1933, described as '... a type of combination without precedent in the literature of chess'. The astonishing and distinguishing feature is that Black does not follow up his heavy sacrifice with a forcing sequence, but calmly completes his development, thus leaving his opponent all the time and choice in the world with which to organize his defences!

18 ♔xh2 ♛xf2+
19 ♔h1!

The best defence. After the

obvious 19 ♗g2, Black plays neither 19 ... ♕xg3+ nor 19 ... ♗xg3+ 20 ♔h1 ♕f6! 21 ♖e2 ♗f2! 22 ♖xf2 ♕xf2 etc., but rather brings up extra firepower by 19 ... ♘f6! after which White is helpless, e.g. 20 ♕c3 ♕xg3+ 21 ♔g1 ♕h2+ 22 ♔f1 ♘h5 23 ♘xe4 (otherwise there follows 23 ... ♗d7 and ... ♖f8+) 23 ... de 24 d5 e5 25 dc ♘g3+ 26 ♔f2 ♗e6 and wins (analysis by Tartakower).

19   ...   ♘f6!

Naturally, Black does not relinquish the pin on the knight which is a key factor in the successful prosecution of his attack; after 19 ... ♕xg3 20 ♘b1 the white queen would be able to transfer to the kingside immediately.

20   ♖e2   ♕xg3
21   ♘b1   ♘h5
22   ♕d2   ♗d7!

With remarkable *sang-froid* Black goes about completing his development.

23   ♖f2

Against the natural 23 ♕e1 Tartakower gives 23 ... ♕f3+ 24 ♖g2 ♕h3+ 25 ♔g1 ♖f8 26 ♘d2 ♗g3 27 ♖xg3 ♕xg3+ 28 ♕xg3 ♘xg3 29 ♗c3 ♘f5 30 ♖e1 h5, and the pawn mass advances threateningly.

23   ...   ♕h4+
24   ♔g1   ♗g3

The Soviet Grandmaster Ragozin suggested 24 ... g3 as possibly

an even stronger continuation of the attack, e.g. 25 ♖g2 ♖f8 and Black threatens either 26 ... ♖f6 and ... ♖h6 or 26 ... ♖f3 followed by ... ♘f6 and ... ♘g4.

25   ♗c3

White is obliged to give back some material in an effort to break the attack, for, as Tartakower pointed out, after 25 ♖g2 ♖f8 26 ♕e2 ♖f3 27 ♗c3 ♗d6 28 ♗e1 g3 29 ♘d2 ♕g4, an incredible position arises where White, despite his great material superiority, is powerless to prevent Black carrying out the decisive knight regrouping ... ♘h5–g7–f5.

It would, however, have been better to give back the exchange by 25 ♖h2 ♗xh2+ 26 ♕xh2 ♕g5 27 ♗c1 g3 28 ♕h1! when the final outcome would remain a moot point.

25   ...   ♗xf2+
26   ♕xf2   g3
27   ♕g2   ♖f8

Black finally completes his development and at the same time threatens 28 ... ♖f2 29 ♕h1 ♖h2 trapping the queen.

28   ♗e1 *(78)*
28   ...   ♖xf1+!

Tartakower crowns his attack with another beautiful sacrifice!

29   ♔xf1   e5
30   ♔g1   ♗g4
31   ♗xg3

On 31 ♖d2, Black liquidates

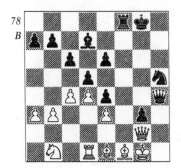

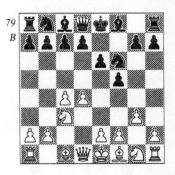

into an easily won ending: 31 ...
ed 32 ed ♗f3 33 ♗xg3 ♘xg3 34
♕h2 ♕xh2+ 35 ♖xh2 ♘e2+ and
36 ... ♘xd4.

31	...	♘xg3
32	♖e1	♘f5
33	♕f2	♕g5
34	de	

After taking such a buffeting it is
hardly surprising that Maroczy's
resistance finally snaps. Not that
the better 34 ♔f1 would have
altered the result; Tartakower
gives 34 ... ♕h5 35 ♕g1! ♕h4 36
♘c3 ♘g3+ 37 ♔g2! ♘h1! 38
♔f1 ♕f6+ with mate in two.

34	...	♗f3+
35	♔f1	♘g3+

0-1

One of the greatest attacking
games of all time!

K. Grigorian–Balashov
USSR Ch. 1974
1 d4 f5 2 c4 e6 3 ♘c3 ♘f6

4	g3 *(79)*

The fianchetto updates the
Classical Variation into the
modern approach, inviting various transpositions. Although playable, it is hard to commend this
move order by White as it permits
Black to enter one of the most
reliable versions of the Dutch
Indian.

4	...	♗b4

Of course, Black may also
choose 4 ... ♗e7, or 4 ... d5.

5	♗d2

It is natural to prevent the
doubled pawns but not obligatory;
for 5 ♗g2 see Chapter 11, p. 106.

5	...	0-0

The normal continuation and
probably best, although it is worth
noting the course of the game
Vark–Keres, Parnu 1971, where
Black successfully provoked novel
strategical complications: 5 ...
♘c6 6 a3 ♗e7 (6 ... ♗xc3 7
♗xc3 ♘e4 leads to equality) 7
d5!? ♘e5 8 ♕b3 ♗c5 9 ♗g2 ♕e7
10 ♘h3 ♗b6 11 ♘a4 ♘e4 12
♗b4 d6 13 ♘xb6 ab 14 ♘f4 0-0

and Black had no reason to be dissatisfied with his prospects.

6	♗g2	d6
7	♘f3	♗xc3
8	♗xc3	♘e4

Black has implemented the standard procedure in such positions: remove White's protection of e4 by the exchange ... ♗xc3 and then occupy the outpost with the knight.

9   ♕c2

This time White must attend to the threatened capture since hand in hand with the appearance of doubled pawns would go the disappearance of the compensatory bishop pair.

9   ...   ♘d7

The correct way to develop the queen's knight; from d7 the knight can either support the advance ... e6–e5 or reinforce the outpost by ... ♘d7–f6. Note that here 9 ... ♘c6 would be mistaken as it would allow White to open up the centre, downgrade Black's pawn structure and disrupt the flow of his development after 10 d5! The consequences of this response must always be weighed very carefully whenever Black is contemplating playing ... ♘c6.

10   0-0   ♘df6 *(80)*

10 ... ♕e7 is also eminently playable after which a game Flohr–Botvinnik, match 1933, meandered to a correct draw via

11 ♖fd1 ♘xc3 (now that White's KR has been developed the retreat ♗e1 preserving the two bishops is a real threat) 12 ♕xc3 ♘f6 13 ♘e1 e5 14 de de 15 ♖d2 e4! 16 ♘c2 ♗e6 17 ♖ad1 ♖ad8 18 ♘e3 ♖xd2 19 ♖xd2 g6 20 ♗f1 ♖d8 21 ♖xd8 ♕xd8 22 ♘c2 ½–½.

11   ♗e1

An ambitious and controversial idea: can the bishops really be worth the disruption visited on the white position by this retrograde manoeuvre? The answer to that is evidently closely bound up with matters of taste and personal preference, but I for one would be very happy as Black to see such a move appear on the board.

11   ...   ♗d7

In contrast to White's sophistication Black continues his development with rustic simplicity.

12   ♖d1

It is interesting to note that after this *ECO* evaluates the position as ±, an assessment with which it is not at all easy to agree. The rook move is explained through dissatisfaction with the immediate 12 ♘d2 ♗c6 and therefore White prepares to advance his d-pawn.

12 ... ♕e8

The queen is much more effective here than on e7; now she is poised for activity on the king's flank whilst also glancing prophylactically to the queenside (13 b4?? ♗a4).

13 d5 e5

Invariably the right response in such situations: the position is kept closed thus minimizing White's bishop pair, the knight on f3 is denied access to d4, and Black creates a healthy, mobile pawn duo on f5 and e5.

14 ♘d2 ♘c5

It stands to reason that Black will not readily acquiesce in exchanges which would only serve to relieve the congestion in White's camp.

15 f3?!

While this gives *luft* to the confined cleric and prepares the additional central pawn advance e2–e4, it also weakens the king's defences. The most logical continuation is 15 b4 ♗a4 16 ♘b3, although after 16 ... ♘xb3 17 ab ♗d7 White's impaired pawn structure is a considerable hindrance to his normal queenside play.

15 ... a5

16 ♗f2 b6
17 b3 *(81)*

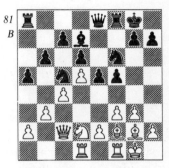

17 ... f4!

Having secured his position on the queenside Black now signals the attack on the opposite flank.

18 e4

This advance is dictated by the necessity of preventing Black from decisively deflecting the f-pawn from guarding g4, e.g. 18 e3 fg 19 hg e4 20 ♘xe4 ♘cxe4 21 fe ♕h5 and 22 ... ♘g4.

18 ... ♕g6

Immediately utilising the cover inadvertently provided by the e-pawn.

19 ♖fe1

In order to provide further protection for g3.

19 ... fg
20 hg h5!

A multi-purpose move which fixes White's pawns, prepares a breakthrough by ... h4, and frees h7 so that the KN can be optimally re-positioned. In the meantime

White's passive forces can do no more than await the storm.

21	♘f1	♘h7
22	♗e3	♘g5
23	♗xg5	

An inglorious end for the prelate of once grand pretensions.

23	...	♕xg5
24	♕d2	♕f6
25	♘e3	

Since Black can always prepare ... h4 at his leisure White does not bother to postpone matters by 25 ♕f2.

| 25 | ... | h4 |
| 26 | g4 | |

The position must be kept closed at all costs.

| 26 | ... | g6 |
| 27 | ♖b1 | |

A forlorn gesture at queenside expansion.

| 27 | ... | ♖f7 |
| 28 | ♖e2 | |

28 a3 a4 29 b4 ♘b3 and 30 ... ♘d4 would only add to White's troubles.

| 28 | ... | ♖af8 |
| 29 | ♗h1 | ♕g5 *(82)* |

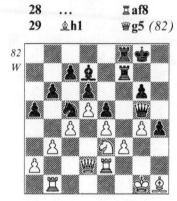

82
W

A more perfect outcome for Black's strategy is hard to imagine! The outcome is no longer in doubt, and it is something of a blessing in disguise that White makes a blunder in time-trouble which puts a mercifully swift end to the proceedings.

30	♘d1??	♘xe4!
31	fe	♕xg4+
32	♖g2	♖f1+
33	♔h2	♕h3 mate

11 The Dutch Indian

After the introductory

1	**d4**	**f5**
2	**c4**	**e6**

... White may choose to revert to the fianchetto variations by playing

3	**g3**	♘**f6**
4	♗**g2**	

... in which case Black may either lead into the major variations with 4 ... d5 or 4 ... ♗e7 (for which see Chapters 12–16), or take advantage of the weakness created on the a5–e1 diagonal by White's second move and deliver check with the bishop:

4	...	♗**b4**+*(83)*

This continuation often produces positions which have much in common with the Nimzo-Indian and Queen's Indian — hence the designation Dutch Indian. After the check Black must choose between two radically different courses: either to seek enhanced prospects of equalization through simplification (the early exchange of a pair of minor pieces), or to interpret the check as essentially a spoiler operation designed to prevent the best deployment of White's pieces, albeit at the cost of a tempo. Both approaches appear to be viable, but the latter has come increasingly into favour in recent years.

Before going on to consider White's two main replies, 5 ♘d2 and 5 ♗d2, we note how Black should meet 5 ♘c3. This move allows Black to bring about a kind of Sämisch Variation of the Nimzo-Indian defence where White has tamely tucked away his

KB on g2 instead of developing it aggressively on d3 as is normally the case. Thus the logical response is 5 ... ♝xc3+ 6 bc 0-0 7 ♘f3 d6 8 0-0 ♘c6 (probably the surest route to equality; Meulders–Short, Brussels 1987, went 8 ... ♛e7 9 ♝a3 ♘bd7 10 ♘d2! c5 11 e4 fe 12 ♘xe4 ♘xe4 13 ♝xe4 and now the precise 13 ... ♘f6 would leave White with only slightly the better of it) 9 ♛c2 (or 9 ♝a3 ♜e8 10 ♛c2 e5 11 de de 12 ♜fd1 ♝d7 13 ♘h4 ♛c8 with level chances; de Winter–Spassky, Lugano Ol. 1968) 9 ... e5 10 de ♘xe5 11 ♘xe5 de 12 ♝a3 ♜f7 13 ♜ad1 ♛e8= White's active pieces and bishop pair offset the weak pawns; Colon–Spassky, San Juan 1969.

Botvinnik–Larsen
Leiden 1970
1 d4 f5 2 c4 e6 3 g3 ♘f6 4 ♝g2 ♝b4+

5   ♘d2 *(84)*

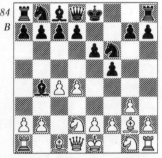

By parrying the check in this fashion White hopes either to obtain the bishop pair 'for free' (i.e. without suffering doubled pawns as in 5 ♘c3), or to oblige Black to lose time withdrawing the bishop to the safety of its own lines. However, Black can utilize the indirect disadvantage of the knight's placement at d2 — the diminished control of d5 as a result of the queen being blocked — to develop the QB actively in fianchetto without having to face a timely d4–d5. These factors tend to balance out, producing rich middlegames of considerable strategic complexity.

5   ...   0-0
This natural move has been accepted as the norm for many years, but nevertheless may well not be the most precise. The reason for this assertion is to be found in the note to White's ninth move where a recent game has cast serious doubt on the validity of Black's setup. It may well be that by playing 5 ... a5!? (always a useful move), with the intention of fianchettoing before castling, Black can circumvent the problems posed by this latest White improvement. For example, after 6 ♘f3 b6 7 ♘e5 ♜a7 8 0-0, in addition to 8 ... ♝b7 Black may also play 8 ... ♝xd2!? 9 ♛xd2 (a standard recapture, hoping to develop the bishop at b2 on

the long diagonal; 9 ♗xd2 is no better) 9 ... d6!? with many promising possibilities. This certainly deserves testing in practice.

6 ♘f3

Expending a tempo on 6 a3 allows Black instant equality after 6 ... ♗xd2+ 7 ♗xd2 d6 8 ♘f3 ♕e7 9 ♗c3 ♘e4. Nor does 6 ♘h3 seem appropriate, e.g. 6 ... d6 7 0-0 e5 8 ♕b3 ♗xd2 9 ♗xd2 ♘c6 10 de de 11 ♗b4 ♘xb4 12 ♕xb4 ♘e4! 13 ♖ad1 ♕f6 14 f4 ♗e6!∓ thanks to his better coordinated forces; Opocensky–Keres, Prague 1937.

6 ... a5

It is instructive to note the way straightforward play backfires on Black after 6 ... d6 7 0-0 ♗xd2 8 ♕xd2! ♕e7 9 b4 e5 10 de de 11 ♗b2 e4 12 ♘d4 (White's control of the dark squares is evident) 12 ... ♘a6 13 b5 ♘c5 14 ♗a3 and Black is suffering; Furman–Antoshin, Voroshilograd 1955.

By contrast, the immediate 6 ... b6 is a very playable alternative:

(a) 7 0-0 ♗b7 8 a3 (8 ♕c2 a5 9 ♘e1 ♗xg2 10 ♘xg2 ♘c6 11 ♘f3 ♗e7 12 a3 ♕e8 13 d5 ♘d8 14 ♖d1 a4 15 ♗e3 ♘e4 produced an unclear and difficult position for both sides in Bertok–Larsen, Vinkovci 1970) 8 ... ♗xd2 9 ♕xd2 ♘c6 10 b4 ♘e7 11 ♗b2 (in Popov–Makarychev, Amsterdam

II 1974, Black cleverly exploited the light square weaknesses in his opponent's camp which arose via 11 a4 a6 12 ♘e1 ♗xg2 13 ♘xg2 b5! 14 cb ab 15 a5 ♘ed5 16 f3 ♘b6!∓) 11 ... ♕e8 12 a4 ♕h5 13 a5 ♗e4 and with a firm grip on e4 Black has no problems; Sokolov–Cvetkovic, Yugoslav Ch. 1962.

(b) 7 ♘e5!? (clearly more challenging than castling) 7 ... c6 8 0-0 ♗b7 9 ♘b3 ♗e7 10 a4 ♘a6 11 a5 ♕c7 12 ♗g5 d6 13 ♘d3 c5 and Black's elastic disposition of his forces should prevent White's slight spatial superiority and initiative from growing; Stein–Bronstein, USSR Ch. 1971.

The text move not only restrains queenside expansion by White but also provides a flight-square for the rook so that after a subsequent ... b6, ♘e5 sequence Black will not be obliged to play ... c7–c6 as in the example above.

7 0-0 b6
8 ♘e5 ♖a7 *(85)*

The point!

9 ♘d3

Perhaps it is not too surprising that White has recently discovered a big improvement on this voluntary retreat, but it *is* surprising that the improvement is yet another voluntary retreat! The astonishing 9 ♘b1! provides a prime example of *reculer pour*

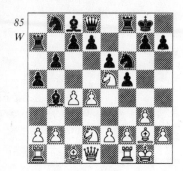

85
W

mieux sauter: redeploying the knight to c3 transforms White's strategy at a stroke as it instantly puts the crucial advance d4–d5 back on the agenda. Not only that, but from c3 the knight also observes b5 thus giving Black some cause for concern over his eccentric rook. The following convincing example strongly suggests that a satisfactory answer to this imaginative innovation by the Soviet player Shabalov is likely only to be found by reconsidering the introductory sequence (see note to Black's fifth). After 9 ♘b1!, Gelfand–Knaak, Halle 1987, went 9 ... ♗e7 (with nothing left to capture, the bishop is menaced by 10 c5 and 11 a3) 10 ♘c3 ♗b7 11 d5 ♕c8 (Black's plight is made manifest by the way the natural 11 ... d6 12 ♘f3 e5 falls foul of 13 ♘g5 ♗c8 14 ♘e6 ♗xe6 15 de c6 16 e4 stirring up play in the centre which he is ill prepared to meet) 12 e4 (those who play against the

Dutch dream of such positions!) 12 ... fe 13 ♘xe4 ♘a6 14 ♗e3! ♕e8 (14 ... ♘c5 15 ♘xc5 ♗xc5 16 ♗xc5 bc 17 ♘d3±) 15 d6! (even better than the 15 ♘c3 ed 16 ♘xd5 ♗xd5 17 ♗xd5+ ♔h8 18 ♖e1 ♗b4 19 ♗d2± of Shabalov–Naumkin, Norilsk 1987) 15 ... ♘xe4 (15 ... cd 16 ♘xd6 ♗xd6 17 ♕xd6 ♗xg2 18 ♔xg2±) 16 de ♕xe7 17 ♕xd7 ♕f6 18 ♘c6 ♘ec5 19 ♕d2 ♗xc6 20 ♗xc6 e5 21 ♗g2 and with two bishops on an open board plus the better pawn structure, not to mention Black's queenside exiles, White's positional superiority is massive.

After that it is a relief to note 9 ♘df3 which brought White no advantage in J. Watson–Ginsburg, US Ch. 1982: 9 ... ♗e7 (again, there is a threat to trap the bishop by 10 c5) 10 ♘d3 (a game Portisch–Kristiansen, Luzern Ol. 1982, went 10 b3 ♘e4 11 a3 ♗b7 12 ♗b2 ♗f6 13 ♘d3 and now with 13 ... c5 Black could have transposed to the column game) 10 ... ♗b7 11 ♘f4 ♘e4 12 h4 ♕e8 13 ♗e3 ♗f6 14 ♖c1 ♘c6 with balanced chances.

9 ... ♗b7

This position is evaluated as equal by Larsen.

10 ♘f3

10 ♘xb4 ♗xg2 11 ♔xg2 ab would give Black excellent

counterplay along the a-file and long diagonal especially after the arrival of the queen on a8.

10	...	♗e7
11	b3	♘e4
12	♗b2	♗f6
13	a3	c5!

There is no point in playing for ... e5 with so many white pieces trained on it, so Black contests the centre with the aid of his c-pawn.

14	e3	♘c6
15	♘fe5	*(86)*

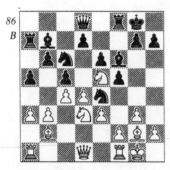

| 15 | ... | cd! |

Black instigates a very important and instructive alteration of pawn structure which brings his pieces to life.

16	ed	♘xe5
17	de	♗e7
18	a4	

White is concerned that his c-pawn might be undermined at some future time by ... a5–a4, but the cure is more debilitating than the disease as it leaves his queenside pawns permanently crippled

and the useful c5 square securely in Black's hands.

18	...	♕c7
19	♕c2	♗c6
20	f3?!	

The beginning of a faulty plan which exacerbates White's problems; simply 20 ♖ad1 was in order.

20	...	♘c5
21	♘f4?!	♗g5
22	♘e2?	♗e3+
23	♔h1	f4! *(87)*

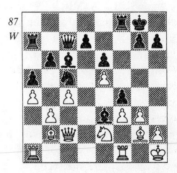

This advance nearly always spells trouble for White. No matter how he reacts his king is bound to become less secure.

| 24 | ♘d4 | |

This is criticized by Larsen, albeit without attempting to suggest an improvement. It takes a skilful trading of advantages to show the deficiency of the text move.

24	...	fg
25	♘xc6	

Not 25 hg? ♕xe5! and the threat of 26 ... ♕h5+ prevents White doing damage with a discovered attack by the knight.

25	...	dc
26	hg	♕f7
27	♗h3	

The queen check must be prevented.

| 27 | ... | ♖d8! |

This clever switch exploits the bishop's desertion of the f-pawn and enables Black to dominate the d-file since the attempt to contest it by 28 ♖ad1 ♖xd1 29 ♕xd1 would be unacceptable after 29 ... ♖d7.

| 28 | ♗c3 | ♖ad7 |

An extremely satisfying conclusion to the manoeuvre begun twenty moves ago with 8 ... ♖a7!

| 29 | ♖a2 | |

There is nothing active for White to undertake.

| 29 | ... | ♖d3 |

Larsen points out that 29 ... ♖d1 30 ♕e2 ♖1d3 31 ♖c2 ♘xb3 also came into consideration.

30	b4	ab
31	♗xb4	♕h5
32	♕h2	♕xe5

With the fall of this pawn and the continuing central dominance of the black pieces White's fate is sealed. The game concluded as follows: 33 f4 ♕e4+ 34 ♕g2 ♕xc4 35 ♗xc5 ♗xc5 36 ♕xc6 (White is fighting hard, his temporary sacrifices having produced opposite coloured bishops) 36 ...

♖e3 37 ♖af2 ♔h8 (37 ... h6!) 38 ♕g2? (the last chance lay in 38 ♖f3! ♖e2 39 ♖3f2 ♖e4 40 ♖d2) 38 ... h6 39 ♗g4 ♕xa4 40 ♖e2 e5 41 ♖a2 ♕c4 42 ♖c2 ♕b4 43 ♗f5 ef 44 gf ♖e1 45 ♖e2 ♖xf1+ 46 ♕xf1 ♖f8 47 ♗e4 ♕d4 48 ♔g2 ♕f6 49 f5 ♕g5+ 50 ♔h1 ♕h4+ 51 ♔g2 ♖d8 52 ♗c2 ♖d4 0–1.

M. Gurevich–Dolmatov
USSR Ch. 1987

1 d4 f5 2 c4 e6 3 g3 ♘f6 4 ♗g2 ♗b4+

| 5 | ♗d2 | *(88)* |

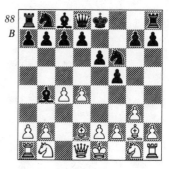

88
B

This natural move has long been White's most popular choice. Theoretically speaking, the exchange of dark squared bishops should work to White's advantage unless Black can rapidly achieve the vital ... e6–e5 advance.

| 5 | ... | ♗e7 |

The idea behind this paradoxical retreat is that the inconvenience caused White by luring the bishop to d2 will adequately off-set the tempo loss incurred. At the same time, Black ensures that a more complicated struggle will ensue than would be the case after the disappearance of the bishops.

If Black prefers the simple life, then 5 ... ♕e7 is a reliable alternative which promises good chances of equality as the following variations show:

(a) 6 ♘h3 0-0 7 0-0 ♗xd2 followed by ... d6 with full equality.

(b) 6 ♗c3 0-0 7 a3 ♗xc3+ 8 ♘xc3 d6 again with an easy game for Black.

(c) 6 ♘c3 0-0 7 ♘f3 d6 8 0-0 ♗xc3 9 ♗xc3 ♘e4 10 ♕c2 ♘d7= brings about Flohr–Botvinnik, match 1933, given in Chapter 10, p. 103, note to Black's tenth.

(d) 6 ♕b3 ♗xd2+ 7 ♘xd2 0-0 8 ♘gf3 d6 9 0-0 e5 10 c5+ ♔h8 11 cd cd 12 de (after 12 e4 fe 13 de de 14 ♘g5 ♘c6 15 ♘gxe4 ♘d4 Black's pieces are very active; Peterson–Uusi, Parnu 1960; Hebert has suggested that 12 ♕a3 gives White the advantage, but this seems unlikely, e.g. 12 ... e4 13 ♘e5 ♕d8!? 14 ♘ec4 ♘c6 and Black should be OK) 12 ... de 13 ♘c4 (Heberg–Spraggett, Toronto Open 1985, went 13 e4?! ♘xe4 14 ♘xe4 fe 15 ♘d2 ♘c6 16 ♗xe4 ♗h3∓) 13 ... ♘c6 14 ♕c3 e4 15 ♘fe5 ♘xe5 16 ♕xe5 ♕xe5 17 ♘xe5

♗e6 with Black for choice; Whiteley–Bellin, England 1976.

(e) 6 ♘f3 ♗xd2+! 7 ♕xd2 d6 8 ♘c3 e5 9 dxe5 (9 0-0 e4=) 9 ... dxe5 10 e4 (Gulko–Speelman, Amsterdam 1989) and now Black's most natural move is 10 ... ♘c6 (10 ... fxe4 11 ♘g5 ♘c6 is also possible) when Black's free development offsets the vulnerability of his e-pawn.

6 ♘c3

White can also fight for an advantage with other moves:

(a) 6 ♗c3?! 0-0 7 ♘d2 d5! (the Stonewall is the best formation for exploiting White's substitution of bishop for knight on c3) 8 ♘h3 c6 9 0-0 b5 10 b3 a5 11 ♕c2 a4 and Black's position is already preferable; Sliwa–Sebestyen, Sopot 1951.

(b) 6 ♘f3 0-0 (6 ... d6 is more precise, avoiding the possibility of 7 d5!) 7 0-0 d6 8 ♘c3 ♕e8 9 ♕c2 (it is interesting to note that with the bishop on d2 White is unable to adopt the normal procedure against the Ilyin-Zhenevsky since now after 9 ♖e1 ♕g6 10 e4 fe 11 ♘xe4 ♘xe4 12 ♖xe4 ♕xe4 13 ♘h4 the d-pawn would be *en prise*) 9 ... ♕h5 10 e4 e5 11 de de 12 ♘d5 (12 ♘xe5? fe is good for Black) 12 ... ♘xd5 13 ed (the inferior 13 cd gives Black active play after 13 ... ♗d6 14 ♖fe1 ♘a6 15 ef ♗xf5 16 ♕c3 ♗h3!; Shelotshilin–Shestoporov, corr. 1955) 13 ... ♗f6 14 ♗c3 ♘d7 and White has a marginal positional edge; Szabo–Bronstein, Budapest 1950.

(c) 6 ♕b3 c6 (6 ... 0-0 comes strongly into consideration as 7 ♘c3 would transpose to the column game, whilst 7 ♗xb7 ♗xb7 8 ♕xb7 ♘c6 9 ♗c3 ♖b8 10 ♕a6 ♘e4 clearly offers compensation for the pawn) 7 d5 cd!? 8 cd e5 (both 8 ... ed? 9 ♘c3 and 8 ... ♘xd5 9 ♗xd5 ed 10 ♘c3 leave White clearly better) 9 ♘c3 d6 10 ♘f3 ♘bd7 (of course not 10 ... 0-0? 11 ♘xe5!) 11 0-0 0-0 12 ♘g5 ♘c5 13 ♕c4 h6 14 b4 (14 ♘e6 ♘xe6 15 de e4 is in Black's favour) 14 ... ♘cd7! 15 ♘e6 ♘b6 16 ♕b3 ♗xe6 17 de d5 with complicated play perhaps somewhat favouring White; Sosonko–Abramovic, New York Open 1986.

| 6 | ... | 0-0 *(89)* |

89
W

| 7 | ♕b3 |

This queen sortie is more forcing than the alternatives:

(a) 7 ♘h3 d6 8 0-0 e5 9 d5 h6 10 f4 e4 produced a difficult game for both sides in Kmoch–Judovic, Leningrad 1934.

(b) 7 e3 d6 8 ♘ge2 c6 9 0-0 ♔h8 10 b4 e5 11 d5 cd 12 cd ♘bd7 13 ♖c1 ♘b6 14 ♕b3 ♗d7 and Black has almost imperceptibly taken control of the game in instructive fashion; White suffers from inactive minor pieces, a sensitive d-pawn and incipient light square weaknesses; Cobo–Larsen, Havana 1967.

(c) 7 ♘f3 ♘e4 (7 ... d6 would transpose to note (b) to White's sixth; adopting a Stonewall formation would allow White to take advantage of the position of the bishop on d2 by 7 ... d5 8 0-0 c6 9 ♕c2 ♕e8 10 a3! ♕h5 11 ♘a2 ♘bd7 12 ♗b4 bringing about the strategically favourable exchange of dark squared bishops; Flohr–Szabo, Moscow–Budapest 1949) 8 0-0 ♗f6 9 ♕c2 (9 ♘xe4 brings no advantage, e.g. 9 ... fe 10 ♘e5 d6 11 ♘g4 ♗xd4 12 ♗xe4 e5 13 ♘e3 ♘d7= Nogueiras–Murey, Luzern Ol. 1982) 9 ... ♘xd2 10 ♕xd2 d6 (10 ... d5 might contain White's advantage more successfully) 11 e4 fe 12 ♘xe4 ♘c6 13 ♖ad1 with a clear positional superiority for White; Grünfeld–Spielmann, Vienna 1935.

| 7 | ... | c6 |

This dynamic continuation concedes White some structural advantage in return for active piece play in the style of the Leningrad Variation.

8 d5! d6

Black must beware of the hidden dangers along the a2–g8 diagonal; thus 8 ... e5?? loses to 9 d6! ♗xd6 10 c5+.

9 de ♞a6

10 ♞h3

This mode of development leaves the KB unhampered and thus permits White's minor pieces to work at maximum efficiency.

10 ... ♞c5

11 ♛c2 ♞g4

The best way of meeting the threat to the f-pawn as 11 ... ♗xe6 12 b4 would be awkward.

12 0-0 a5

Securing the c5 square and generally restraining White's queenside pawns.

13 b3 ♗xe6

14 ♞f4 ♗d7 *(90)*

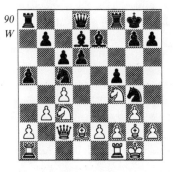

90
W

With the opening almost over,

it is time to take stock. White's pawn structure is somewhat sounder but the black infantry secure a share of the centre and provide the foundation for kingside action whilst restraining enemy ambitions on the opposite wing. Piece coordination in general is roughly balanced. Although the white prelates currently enjoy slightly greater scope than their counterparts, the success of Black's diversionary check in deflecting White's QB from its natural long diagonal is quite notable. Black's major problem is to find a suitable deployment for the queen.

15 ♞d3 ♞e6

16 e3 ♛c7?!

The course of the game shows that Black should have sent his queen to the king's flank by 16 ... ♛e8 intending to cover the weak b6 square with the KB, *viz.* 17 ♞a4 ♗d8.

17 ♖ad1 ♗e8

Heading for the h7–b1 diagonal, this redeployment is consistent with his sixteenth.

18 ♞e2 g5

Depriving the white knights of the use of f4 as well as building long-term attacking chances.

19 ♞d4!

A classical central counter to Black's wing demonstration.

19 ... ♞xd4

20   ed   h6

With the action of White's QB opened up, the g-pawn needs support so that the knight may retreat to f6 if attacked.

21   ♖de1   ♗g6
22   f4

This gives Black tactical chances due to the weakening of the g1–a7 diagonal. Dolmatov indicates 22 ♖e6 as a safer way for White to keep in control.

22   ...   ♗f6
23   d5   ♖ae8
24   ♔h1   ♗d4
25   dc   bc
26   ♕c1! *(91)*

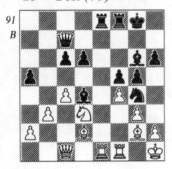

91
B

By keeping e3 under control and thus introducing h3 as a threat White's advantage becomes clear.

Even so, Black's position contains many tactical resources and the game provides a perfect example of how to muddy the waters when things go wrong: 26 ... ♖e4! 27 fg (27 h3 ♘f6 28 fg ♘h5 would be awkward to meet) 27 ... hg 28 ♗xg5! (28 ♗xe4? fe would give Black a dangerous attack) 28 ... ♕h7 29 h4 ♖fe8 30 ♗f3! (gives the king air and thereby prepares the decisive consolidation ♘f4) 30 ... ♘e3 31 ♗xe3? (a mistake in time pressure; this was the correct moment to simplify by 31 ♗xe4! ♘xf1 32 ♗xc6 ♘xg3+ 33 ♔g2 ♘e4 when White would clearly be on top) 31 ... ♗xe3 32 ♕b2 f4!∓ (with the undermining of his h-pawn White's king becomes extremely vulnerable) 33 ♘xf4? (the decisive error; 33 gf ♖4e7 was relatively best) 33 ... ♗xf4! 34 ♖xe4 (34 ♗xe4 ♗xe4+ is crushing) 34 ... ♗xe4 35 gf ♕xh4+ 36 ♔g1 (36 ♔g2 fails to the neat 36 ... ♕g4+ 37 ♔h2 ♗xf3 38 ♖g1 ♖e2+) 36 ... ♗xf3 37 ♖xf3 ♖e1+ 38 ♖f1 ♖xf1+ 39 ♔xf1 ♕h1+ and the queen is lost, so White resigns.

12 Classical System: Auxiliary Variations

This chapter deals with various rare deviations by White from the main introductory sequence to the Classical systems. Accurate defence by Black generally results in interesting middlegames with balanced chances.

1	d4	f5
2	g3	♘f6
3	♗g2	e6

Reshevsky–Botvinnik
The Hague 1948

4 ♘h3 *(92)*

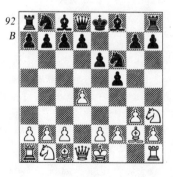

Blackburne's variation, named after the British grandmaster who introduced it over a century ago. Developing the knight this way avoids blocking in the KB and prepares ♘h3–f4 putting pressure on d5 and e6. Furthermore, White is ready almost immediately to carry out the important advance e2–e4, supported by f2–f3 if necessary. On the debit side, the diminished control of e5 makes it easier for Black to advance his own e-pawn, possibly with gain of tempo (should the knight be on f4) or positional advantage (should the knight remain offside on h3).

Other fourth moves are relatively innocuous:

(a) 4 e3 ♗e7 5 ♘e2 0-0 6 0-0 d6 7 b3 e5 8 de de= Euwe–R. Byrne, New York 1951.

(b) 4 ♗g5 ♗e7 (as usual, 4 ... d5 is a safe alternative) 5 ♗xf6 ♗xf6 6 e4 0-0 7 f4 fe 8 ♗xe4 d5 and Black's KB provides the basis

115

for strong counterplay on the dark squares; Cobo–Pritchett, Siegen Ol. 1970.

(c) 4 ♘c3 d5 (invariably the best response when White develops the QN in front of his c-pawn) 5 ♘f3 c5!? (an aggressive approach; the usual Stonewall formation might in fact be more suitable) 6 0-0 ♘c6 7 dc (a game Mestrovic–Sines, Yugoslav Ch. 1968, produced a mutually difficult position after 7 ♗f4 a6 8 ♘a4 c4) 7 ... ♗xc5 8 a3 0-0 9 b4 ♗e7 10 ♗b2 ♕b6 with satisfactory play for Black; Tartakower–Treybal, Hamburg Ol. 1930.

(d) 4 ♘d2 d5 (Black probably does best not to allow White to play e2–e4; 4 ... c5!?, while usually not good, may be feasible here; 4 ... ♘c6 5 c3 d5 6 ♘df3 ♗e7 7 ♘h3 ♘e4 8 ♘f4 0-0 is a strategically rich alternative; Ftacnik–Bellin, Hastings 1980/81) 5 ♘df3 ♗d6 6 ♘h3 0-0 7 ♘f4 ♘e4 8 ♘d3 ♕f6 9 e3 ♘d7 10 0-0 g5 with fine play for Black; Forintos–Szabolsci, Hungarian Ch. 1972.

4	...	♗e7
5	0-0	0-0
6	c4	d6

Much more logical than a 6 ... d5 Stonewall formation which gives White improved chances of obtaining an advantage, e.g. 7 ♘c3 c6 8 ♕b3 ♘a6 (8 ... ♕e8 9 ♘f4 ♔h8 10 ♘d3 ♘e4 11 f3 ♘xc3 12

♕xc3 ♘d7 13 b3 is assessed as only ± by Petrosian, but it seems to me that Black's prospects are extremely bleak) 9 ♘f4 ♔h8 10 ♘d3 ♘c7 11 ♗f4 ♘ce8 12 c5 and White is clearly in charge; Capablanca–Botvinnik, Hastings 1934/35.

7   ♘c3

This natural developing move must be best. Less forceful continuations allow Black an easy time of it:

(a) 7 ♘f4 c6 (blunting the bishop's diagonal and taking control of d5) 8 ♘c3 e5 9 de de 10 ♘d3 ♕c7 and Black has an excellent Hort–Antoshin type of position; Nemet–Djurasevic, Yugoslavia 1950.

(b) 7 ♕b3 c6 8 ♘d2 a5 (8 ... e5!? is an interesting and good alternative, e.g. 9 c5+ d5 10 e3 ♕c7, or 10 de ♘g4) 9 ♘f4 a4 10 ♕c3 ♕c7 11 e4 e5 12 de de 13 ♘d3 fe 14 ♘xe4 ♗f5 with active piece play; Forintos–Farago, Hungarian Ch. 1965.

(c) 7 b3 ♕e8 8 ♗b2 ♗d8 9 ♘f4 e5 10 de de 11 ♘d5 ♘bd7 12 ♘bc3 c6 13 ♘xf6+ ♘xf6 14 ♕d6 ♘d7 15 ♘a4 ♖f6 and Black has a solid position plus kingside attacking chances; Udovcic–Alexander, Belgrade 1952.

These examples clearly demonstrate that a soundly executed ... e6–e5 advance invariably brings

Black full equality.

7 ... ♕e8 *(93)*

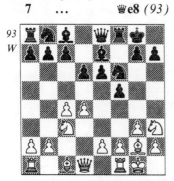

The immediate 7 ... e5?! condemns Black to a cheerless defence in the ending arising after 8 de de 9 ♕xd8 ♗xd8 (9 ... ♖xd8? 10 ♘d5) 10 b3 ♘a6 11 ♗a3 ♖e8 12 ♘b5, as was shown in the game. E. Vladimirov–Psakhis, USSR 1985.

7 ... c6 may be an acceptable alternative, e.g. 8 e4 fe 9 ♘xe4 e5 10 de de 11 ♘hg5 ♘a6 12 ♘xf6+ gf 13 ♘e4 ♕xd1 14 ♖xd1 ♗g4 15 f3 ♗f5 with full equality; Olafsson–Ivkov, Birmingham 1951.

8 e4

Consequent and active, although some of the alternatives can lead to even more complex play:

(a) 8 b3 should simply be met by the usual 8 ... c6 rather than 8 ... ♘c6?! 9 d5 or 8 ... e5?! 9 de de 10 ♘d5 ♗d8 11 ♗a3 when White has the initiative.

(b) 8 ♕b3 c6 9 d5!? cd 10 cd e5 11 ♘g5 ♘a6 12 ♘e6 ♗xe6 13 de

♘c5 14 ♕c2 e4 15 f3 d5 with a complex, double-edged position; Fesche–Schmeisser, Kuortone 1976.

(c) 8 ♘f4 is probably best answered by Keres's recommendation 8 ... g5 9 ♘d3 ♕g6 which has yet to be tested in practice. After the standard 8 ... c6, White can use tactical means to gain a positional advantage: 9 d5! e5 10 dc bc 11 ♘fd5! ♘xd5 12 ♘xd5 ♗d8 13 b3 ♗b7 14 ♘c3 and Black's pawns are decidedly shaky; Taulbut–Rumens, London 1977.

8 ... fe

9 ♘f4

Against the immediate recapture 9 ♘xe4, I recommend 9 ... ♘xe4 10 ♗xe4 e5! 11 ♘g5 ♗xg5! (the consequences of 11 ... h6 12 ♘h7 are not at all clearly in Black's favour) 12 ♗xg5 ♘c6, and the harmony of the black forces offsets White's bishop pair.

9 ... c6

10 ♘xe4 ♘xe4

11 ♗xe4 e5

12 ♘g2

12 de would isolate Black's e-pawn, but after 12 ... de 13 ♘d3 (otherwise Black's KB will occupy the a7–g1 diagonal) 13 ... ♗h3 14 ♖e1 ♘d7, Black's dynamic compensation can easily become more than sufficient.

12 ... ♘d7

13 ♘e3 *(94)*

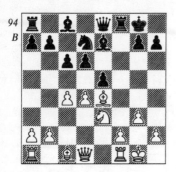

94
B

13   ...   ed
Introducing a simplifying manoeuvre which completely equalizes. Keres notes that 13 ... ♘f6 14 ♗g2 e4 15 d5! c5 16 ♗d2 followed by ♗c3 is in White's favour.

14   ♕xd4   ♘e5
15   f4
Covering the weakness on f3.

15   ...   ♘g4
16   ♘xg4   ♗xg4
Black may look to the future with confidence on account of White's weakened king's position. The game concluded as follows: 17 ♖e1 ♗f6 18 ♕d3 (18 ♕xd6? ♖d8 19 ♕a3 ♗d4+ 20 ♔h1 ♕h5 would give Black a dangerous attack) 18 ... ♕h5 19 ♗d2 ♖fe8 20 ♖ab1? (20 ♖e3!) 20 ... ♖e7? (20 ... ♖e6! was better) 21 ♗b4 ♖ae8 22 ♗xd6 ♖e6 (perhaps Black had intended 22 ... ♖xe4 23 ♖xe4 ♖xe4 24 ♕xe4 ♗f5 25 ♕e1 ♗d4+ winning, and only now noticed that 25 ♕e3! turns

the tables on account of 25 ... ♗xb1 26 ♕e6+, and it is Black who is mated) 23 ♖e3 ♖xd6! (a temporary sacrifice to force the draw) 24 ♕xd6 ♖d8 25 ♕c7 ♕c5 26 ♖e1 ♖c8 27 ♕xb7 ♗d4 28 ♔f2 ♗xe3+ 29 ♖xe3 ♕d4 30 ♕b3 ♕d2+ 31 ♔g1 ♕c1+ 32 ♔f2 ♕d2+ 33 ♔g1 ♕c1+ ½-½.

Botvinnik–Bronstein
World Ch. (1) 1951
1 d4 f5 2 g3 ♘f6 3 ♗g2 e6

4   c4   ♗e7
5   ♘c3

Some interesting nuances can arise when White plays 5 ♘f3 and delays castling after 5 ... 0-0, for example:
(a) 6 ♘c3 d5 (a game Bogoljubow–Alekhine, World Ch. 1934, went 6 ... d6 7 ♗f4 ♕e8 8 ♖c1 ♘c6 9 d5 ♘d8 10 ♘b5 ♕d7 11 ♕b3 a6 12 de ♘xe6 13 ♘c3 ♘xf4 14 gf ♔h8=) 7 ♘e5 c6 8 ♗f4 ♕e8 (Selezniev–Model, USSR Ch. 1927, went 8 ... ♘bd7 9 ♕c2 ♘xe5 10 de ♘e4 11 ♘xe4? fe 12 ♗d2 ♗c5 13 f3 ♕b6 14 0-0-0 e3 and White was in trouble) 9 ♕b3 ♔h8 10 0-0-0?! (10 0-0=) 10 ... ♘bd7 11 h3 ♘xe5 12 ♗xe5 ♘d7 13 ♗c7 b6 and with ... ♗a6 to follow, Black has the better chances; Selezniev–Riumin, USSR 1927.
(b) 6 d5!? ♗b4+ (*ECO* gives 6

... d6 7 de ♘c6 8 ♘d4 ♘xd4 9 ♕xd4 c6 and ... ♗xe6 as equalizing, but I for one do not find this convincing) 7 ♗d2 ♕e7 8 0-0 ♗xd2 9 ♕xd2 e5 10 d6! (a deep positional pawn sacrifice) 10 ... cd? (it would be better to remove the queens by 10 ... ♕xd6 11 ♕xd6 cd 12 ♘c3 ♘c6 13 ♖fd1 ♘e8 14 ♖d2, as indicated by Robatsch, but even so White has good compensation) 11 ♘c3 ♘a6 12 ♕g5! d5 (or 12 ... g6 13 ♘h4 ♗h8 14 ♕xg6!) 13 ♘h4! ♔h8 14 ♘xf5 ♕f7 15 cd with a crushing advantage; Robatsch–Jamieson, Buenos Aires Ol. 1978.

It seems to me that until a reliable antidote is found to Robatsch's 6 d5, Black should refrain from castling on move five and effect a simple transposition according to choice.

5   ...   0-0 *(95)*

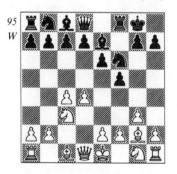

6   e3

It is important to be *au fait* with the alternatives:

(a) 6 e4 fe 7 ♘xe4 d5! (both 7 ... ♘xe4 8 ♗xe4 d5 9 ♗d3 and 7 ... d6 8 ♘e2 ♕e8 9 0-0 are good for White) 8 ♘xf6+ ♗xf6 9 ♘f3 c5 10 0-0 cd 11 ♘xd4 dc 12 ♗e3 ♘c6 13 ♘xc6 bc 14 ♗c5 ♖f7 15 ♕xd8+ ♗xd8 and with pressure to come against White's b-pawn, Black has no problems; Boutteville–Duckstein, Le Havre 1966.

(b) 6 d5 ♗b4 (better than leaving the bishop locked behind the pawn chain after 6 ... e5 7 ♘f3 d6, although that is also playable) 7 ♗d2 (7 ♕b3 awaits testing) 7 ... e5 8 e3 d6 9 ♘ge2 a6!? (intending to weaken the d5 pawn by attacking its support) 10 ♕c2 ♕e8 11 f3 b5! 12 ♕b3 (Botvinnik–Bronstein, World Ch. 1951, ninth game) and now simply 12 ... ♗xc3 13 ♘xc3 bc 14 ♕xc4 ♕f7 would give Black excellent play thanks to the dual threats of 15 ... c6 and 15 ... a5 combined with ... ♗a6.

(c) 6 ♗g5 d6 (6 ... c6!? is possible, with 7 ♗xf6 ♗xf6 8 e4 ♕b6 leading to unclear play and 7 ♘f3 d5 bringing about a Stonewall) 7 ♗xf6 (7 ♘f3 ♘bd7 8 0-0 e5 is fine for Black) 7 ... ♗xf6 8 e4 fe 9 ♘xe4 ♘c6 10 ♘e2 e5 with a position assessed as unclear by Garcia–Palermo. This whole line awaits further practical tests.

(d) 6 ♕b3 (usually known as the Anti-Stonewall Variation, for obvious reasons; cf. Chapter 11, p.

112) 6 ... c6 (Black's best response has yet to be established; 6 ... a5!? 7 ♘f3 — 7 ♗xb7? a4 costs material — 7 ... d6 is natural and sensible, while the gambit continuation 6 ... c5!? 7 d5 e5 8 e4 d6!? 9 ef ♗xf5 10 ♛xb7 ♘bd7 certainly offers some compensation in return for the pawn) 7 d5 d6 (7 ... e5?? 8 d6 will win the bishop) 8 de ♘a6 (cf. Gurevich–Dolmatov, p. 110) 9 ♘f3 ♘c5 10 ♛c2 ♘fe4 11 ♘d4 ♘xc3 12 bc ♗xe6 13 ♘xe6 ♘xe6 14 0-0, and it seems that White's bishop pair and open lines outweigh the weakened pawns; Euwe–Opocensky, Venice 1948. Thus Black's defences currently stand in need of reinforcement in this variation, but, with so much yet to be explored, this is a task which may be approached with optimism.

The text-move, first played in Staunton–Horwitz, London 1851, and re-introduced in the present game, aims for flexible and harmonious development, but has the big strategic drawback of allowing Black to achieve ... e6–e5 without difficulty.

6 ... d6

A much more logical reaction to White's restrained development than adopting a Stonewall formation, although that was Botvinnik's response when Bronstein confronted him with the psychological ploy of using the same variation.

7 ♘ge2 c6
8 0-0 e5

In notes to this game, Botvinnik himself observed, 'Black has achieved a good game ... White has already lost his opening advantage'. The immobility of the knight on e2 is particularly notable.

9 d5

Gaining space at least; other moves bring nothing:

(a) 9 e4 ♘xe4! 10 ♘xe4 fe 11 ♗xe4 ♗h3 ∓

(b) 9 de de 10 ♛xd8 ♖xd8 11 e4 ♘a6 =.

9 ... ♛e8
10 e4

Bolstering the centre rather than ceding it by 10 dc bc 11 ♘b5? which would get nowhere after 11 ... ♛d7 and 12 ... ♗b7.

10 ... ♛h5
11 ef

Hoping to use e4 for his pieces at a future date while also defusing dangerous attacking ideas based on ... f5–f4.

11 ... ♗xf5 *(96)*
12 f3

Bringing e4 under control with tempo gain due to the fork threat g3–g4. The dangerous tactical thrust 12 c5 (based on the fact that 12 ... dc? 13 ♛b3! is very strong for White) can be satisfactorily

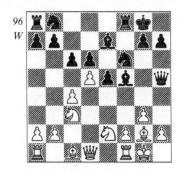

96
W

countered by 12 ... ♗h3 as Botvinnik's following instructive variations demonstrate:

(a) 13 dc ♘xc6 14 ♛b3+ ♚h8 15 ♛xb7 ♖ac8 with a promising attack in the offing.

(b) 13 cd ♗xd6 14 dc ♘xc6 15 ♛xd6 ♖ad8 16 ♛c5 ♘g4 17 f3 ♗xg2 18 fg (or 18 ♛c4+ ♚h8 19 fg ♛h3 20 ♖f2 ♗f3) 18 ... ♖xf1+ 19 ♚xg2 ♛f7, and White is in trouble.

(c) 13 f3 ♗xg2 14 ♚xg2 dc 15 ♛b3 b5 16 dc+ ♛f7 17 c7 ♘a6 18 ♘xb5 ♘d5 and Black maintains the balance.

(d) 13 ♛b3 ♘g4 14 dc+ ♚h8 15 cb ♗xg2 16 h4 ♗f3! 17 ba♛ (after 17 ♘d5 ♗xh4 18 ♛xf3 ♖xf3 19 ba♛ ♗d8 20 ♚g2 ♖xf2+ Black gives perpetual check) 17... ♗xa8 18 ♘d5 ♘h2! and again Black has sufficiently strong counterplay. Wonderful stuff!

| 12 | ... | ♛g6 |
| 13 | ♗e3 | ♘bd7 |

It is interesting to observe that

all the black pieces are more actively placed than their white counterparts.

| 14 | ♛d2 | cd |
| 15 | cd | |

15 ♘xd5 is better, with approximately even chances after 15 ... ♘xd5 16 cd, but not 16 ♛xd5+ ♗e6 17 ♛xb7? ♛d3 winning a piece.

| 15 | ... | ♗d8 |

An excellent regrouping, but it would have been preferable to preface it with 15 ... h5 keeping White contained on the kingside.

| 16 | ♖ac1 | |

Missing the chance to play 16 g4 ♗d3 17 ♖fd1 ♗a6 18 ♘g3 with increased activity. 16 ♘b5 ♘e8 gets nowhere.

| 16 | ... | ♗a5 |
| 17 | g4 | |

Better late than never. Bronstein points out that 17 ♖fd1 runs up against 17 ...♘b6 18 g4 ♘c4! 19 gf ♛xf5 and 20 ... ♘xe3.

17	...	♗d3
18	♖fd1	♗c4
19	♛c2	

White understandably seeks salvation in the ending, but even so Black's pressure persists.

19	...	♛xc2
20	♖xc2	♘b6
21	♖cd2	(97)
21	...	♗a6

Missing the favourable liquidation 21 ... ♗xe2 22 ♖xe2 ♗xc3

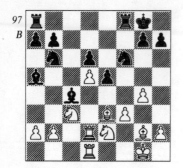

97
B

23 ♗xb6 ab 24 bc g5, with a winning position according to Bronstein.

| 22 | ♗f2 | ♘c4? |

In time-trouble, Black not only forgoes the above line once again but also misses 22 ... e4! threatening 23 ... e3 24 ♗xe3 ♘c4, thus obliging White to play 23 g5 ef 24 ♗xf3 ♘fd7 when Black is still clearly in control.

23	♖c2	♗b6
24	♗xb6	ab
25	♖e1!	

With this, White is out of the woods.

25	...	♘e3
26	♖d2	♘c4
27	♖c2	♘e3
28	♖d2	♘c4

White claimed a draw by threefold repetition.

13 Alekhine's Variation:
6 ... ♞e4

Alekhine's Variation is reached after the moves

1	d4	f5
2	g3	♞f6
3	♝g2	e6
4	♞f3	♝e7
5	0-0	0-0
6	c4	♞e4 (98)

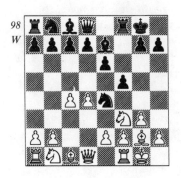

98
W

This provocative move was introduced by the great former World Champion Alexander Alekhine in his game against Sämisch at Dresden 1936, and thoroughly tested by him in other games played that same year. Black's main idea is to preserve his option on d-pawn placement as long as possible: 'It is generally in the interests of the second player to delay as long as logically possible the advance of his d-pawn in this opening, so as to keep the choice between the two points, d6 and d5' — Alekhine. Another important point is that the early advance of the KN vacates f6 for the KB which can thus exert pressure along the h8–a1 diagonal.

The potential dangers of delaying the development of the queenside make considerable demands on the accuracy, sophistication and resourcefulness of the second player, but for those able to rise to the challenge Alekhine's variation provides a viable and intriguing alternative to the established classical lines.

123

Capablanca–Alekhine
Nottingham 1936

7   ♕b3

This move has its logic: White pressurizes b7 and makes d1 free for the rook. Its main drawbacks are that the queen is somewhat exposed to harassment by Black's minor pieces and the QB is deprived of development in fianchetto.

Other uncommon lines also fail to upset Black's equanimity:

(a) 7 ♘e1 d5 8 f3 ♘f6 9 cd ed 10 ♘d3 b6 11 ♗e3 ♗d6 12 ♘c3 c6 13 ♖c1 ♕e7 14 ♕d2 ♗a6 15 ♗f4 ♘bd7 16 ♗xd6 ♕xd6 with a fully satisfactory position for Black; Flohr–Alekhine, Podebrady 1936.

(b) 7 ♘fd2 d5 8 cd (White is concerned to cover the weak d-pawn) 8 ... ed 9 ♘c3 c6 10 ♕c2 ♗f6 and Black has no problems whatever; Incutto–Emma, Buenos Aires Ch. 1972.

(c) 7 ♕c2 ♗f6 (as is frequently the case, Black may perfectly well produce a Stonewall by 7 ... d5) 8 ♘c3 (the seminal encounter Sämisch–Alekhine, Dresden 1936, went 8 ♖d1 d6 9 ♘bd2 ♘xd2 10 ♗xd2 ♘c6 11 ♗c3 ♕e8 12 d5 ♗xc3 13 ♕xc3 ♘d8 14 de ♘xe6 15 ♘d4 ♘c5 with equality; 8 ♘bd2 would transpose to the second featured game) 8 ... ♘xc3 9 bc (9

♕xc3 c5 would leave White's d4 more sensitive) 9 ... d6 10 e4 ♘c6 11 ef ef 12 ♖e1 ♘a5 13 ♕d3 c5 with a difficult and roughly equal game where White's greater activity is tempered by his structural weakness;   Foltys–Alekhine, Prague 1943.

7   ...   ♗f6

Alekhine observes that this bishop placing '... is strong both for attack or defence'.

8   ♖d1   ♕e8

8 ... ♕e7 is an equally good alternative.

9   ♘c3   ♘c6!
10   ♘b5

A contentious sortie, disparaged by Alekhine but lauded by others. Although it may not bring White any advantage, it can equally do no harm to force Black to retreat his bishop. In any case, it is certainly better than the superficially attractive 10 d5 which would invite the troublesome 10 ... ♘a5.

10   ...   ♗d8
11   ♕c2

According to Capablanca, he should have preferred 11 d5 ♘a5 12 ♕c2 c6 13 dc and 14 ♘d6 with the better chances. However, that would only be true if Black recaptured with 13 ... dc, whereas 13 ... bc would produce an unclear position charged with strategic complexity.

11   ...   d6 (99)

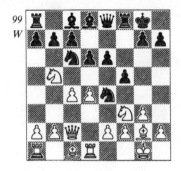

99
W

12   d5

Alekhine's observations on this advance are very instructive: 'In the majority of cases the exchange involved by this move is in White's favour. It gives him control of the square d5 ... but in this particular position White has already lost too much time with his queen and knight, thus permitting Black to complete his development and to take advantage of the open e-file'.

12   ...   ♘b4

This manoeuvre occurs quite often; by attacking the enemy queen Black gains the time for optimum repositioning of the knight.

13   ♕b3   ♘a6
14   de

Naturally, White cannot allow Black to advance ... e6–e5 which would instantly deaden the white position while giving Black a dangerous mobile pawn duo and a strong initiative on the king's wing.

14   ...   ♘ac5
15   ♕c2   ♘xe6
16   ♘fd4

Simple development by 16 ♗e3 a6 17 ♘bd4 was preferable.

16   ...   ♘xd4
17   ♘xd4   ♗f6
18   ♘b5

Causing even less inconvenience than the first time; 18 ♗e3 was still indicated.

18   ...   ♕e7
19   ♗e3   a6
20   ♘d4   ♗d7
21   ♖ac1   ♖ae8
22   b4   b6
23   ♘f3?!

This knight's inability to keep still ought to have cost White dear. After the correct 23 ♕b3 the chances would be approximately even.

23   ...   ♘c3!

The direct 23 ... g5 would also generate strong threats, but the text move throws the enemy camp into even greater disorder.

24   ♖d3 *(100)* f4?

Beginning an hallucinatory miscalculation. The straightforward 24 ... ♗a4 25 ♕d2 ♘e4 26 ♕e1 g5 would have left Black with a big, perhaps decisive, positional advantage according to Alekhine.

25   gf   ♗f5
26   ♕d2   ♗xd3
27   ed   c5?

Black persists in the delusion

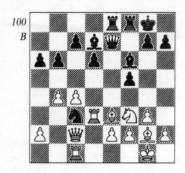

100
B

that he is winning two exchanges when in fact he is losing three minor pieces for two rooks. After 27 ... ♘a4 28 d4 (or 28 ♘g5) White's generally active position and Black's wayward knight would give White more than sufficient compensation for the exchange, but Black would not be entirely without hope. After the move played, the life goes out of Black's position and against Capablanca there is no hope.

| 28 | ♖xc3 | ♗xc3 |
| 29 | ♕xc3 | ♕f6 |

Retaining the queens would also be hopeless.

| 30 | ♕xf6 | gf |
| 31 | ♘d2 | f5 |

31 ... cb 32 ♗d5 + ♔g7 33 ♘e4 is no improvement.

32	b5	a5
33	♘f1	♔f7
34	♘g3	♔g6
35	♗f3	♖e7
36	♔f1	♔f6
37	♗d2	♔g6

38   a4

Black resigned. There is nothing to be done about the winning plan given by Capablanca: White plays ♗c3 followed by h2–h4–h5; Black must respond with h7–h6 and ♔h7; then comes ♗f3–g2–h3 forcing ... ♖e7–f7 after which Black can only oscillate his king between h7 and g8 while White posts his king on f3 and manoeuvres the knight to d5; in this position Black must protect the b-pawn, but whichever way he does it the check on f6 by the knight is decisive.

Ree–Bronstein
Budapest 1977
1 d4 f5 2 g3 ♘f6 3 ♗g2 e6 4 ♘f3 ♗e7 5 0-0 0-0 6 c4 ♘e4

7   ♘bd2 *(101)*

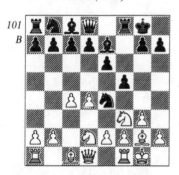

101
B

This immediate challenge to the advanced cavalry is evidently a critical continuation. Its drawback is that the QB is blocked in and the necessity of solving this problem limits White's flexibility. Consequently, the continuation 7 b3 suggests itself, with practical experience so far indicating that Black must react carefully: 7 ... ♗f6 8 ♗b2 (a game Cebalo–Pytel, Liege 1980, saw White obtain an edge after 8 ♕c2 c5 9 ♗b2 cd 10 ♘xd4 ♘c6 11 ♘xc6 bc 12 ♘d2 d5 13 ♗xf6 ♖xf6 14 e3; one wonders if Black was correct to eschew the natural 13 ... ♕xf6) 8 ... b6 (both 8 ... c5 and 8 ... d5 come into consideration, as does 8 ... a5 which produced a position teeming with strategic complexity after 9 a3 ♘c6 10 ♘e5 ♘e7 11 f3 ♘d6 12 ♕d3 b6 13 ♘d2 ♗b7 in Andersen-Bronstein, Munich Ol. 1958) 9 ♘bd2 ♗b7 10 ♘e5 d6 11 ♘d3 ♕e7 (11 ... c5 12 e3 is worth testing) 12 ♕c2 ♘c6 13 e3 ♘xd2 14 ♕xd2 ♘d8 15 d5! ♗xb2 16 ♕xb2 e5 17 f4 e4 (17 ... ♘f7 is rather better) 18 ♘b4 a5 19 ♘c2 ♗a6 20 ♘d4 and Black's position is cramped and passive; Gaprindashvili–Gurieli, match, Tbilisi 1980.

7 ... ♗f6

Once again, Black may adopt a Stonewall formation: 7 ... d5 8 b3 ♘c6 9 ♗b2 ♗d7 10 ♘e5 (10 e3 is less committal, with a mutually difficult game) 10 ... ♘xe5 11 de c6 12 ♘f3 ♕b6 13 ♕d3 ♖ad8 with fine prospects; Rovner–Hasin,

½-final USSR Ch. 1956.

8 ♕c2

Natural and logical, but the forthright capture 8 ♘xe4 poses a much more radical challenge to Black's opening. After 8 ... fe 9 ♘e5 d5, experience has shown that the immediate attempt to open the centre by 10 f3 backfires on account of 10 ... c5 11 ♗e3 (11 ♘g4 ♗e7! 12 fe dc is good for Black) 11 ... ♗xe5 12 de d4 13 ♗c1 ♘c6 (13 ... e3 straightaway has to reckon with the consequences of 14 b4 which may nevertheless go in Black's favour) 14 f4 e3 15 b3 ♕b6 and Black's extraordinary pawn chain severely hampers the communication between White's flanks; Vaganian–Bronstein, USSR Ch. 1971. Subsequently 10 ♘g4 was successfully employed in Didishko–Yuferov, USSR 1976, bringing an edge after 10 ... ♗e7 11 ♗f4 c6 12 ♕c2 ♘d7 13 f3 ef 14 ♗xf3 ♕e8 15 ♖ae1. It remains to be seen whether the possible improvements 11 ... c5 or 13 ... ♘f6 will sustain the viability of Black's set-up.

8 ... d5

It is essential for Black to maintain a grip on e4; meekly exchanging the knight by 8 ... ♘xd2 9 ♗xd2 d6 10 ♗c3 ♕e8 11 e4 gives White an advantageous Ilyin-Zhenevsky-type position (see

Chapter 14).

9   b3

Much the most natural. Black met 9 ♖d1 in traditional Stonewall manner in the game Borisenko–Korchnoi, USSR 1965: 9 ... c6 (9 ... ♘c6 is also playable) 10 ♘f1 ♘d7 11 b3 g5 12 ♗b2 ♕e7 13 ♘e1 ♕g7 14 f3 ♘d6 with a mutually difficult game.

9   ...   c5 (102)

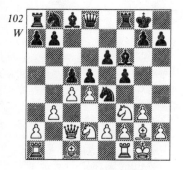

This rapid sharpening of the central conflict is characteristic of Alekhine's Variation. Black trusts that his pieces will become sufficiently active to balance any loosening of his pawn structure.

The relatively restrained 9 ... ♘c6 once again provides a serviceable alternative as demonstrated in Farago–Pytel, Bagneux 1980, which went 10 ♗b2 a5 (typically restraining the white queen's wing and providing a possible later white-square softener in ... a5–a4) 11 e3 ♗d7 12 a3 ♕e7 (12 ... g5!?) 13 ♖ac1 and here Pytel rec-

ommends 13 ... ♖fc8!? preparing to answer 14 ♘e5 with 14 ... ♗e8 and then play on the queenside.

10   ♗b2

Acquiescing in the dissolution of his own pawn centre in the hope of saddling Black with structural weakness. To this end White is successful, but it turns out that the secure foothold in the centre and active piece play provide more than enough compensation. Other tries:

(a) 10 e3 is recommended as best by Bronstein which he feels should conserve White's opening edge; this has yet to be tested in practice.

(b) 10 ♗a3 cd 11 ♗xf8 ♕xf8 12 cd ed is a somewhat exotic variation, again emanating from Bronstein, which he evaluates as slightly in Black's favour; this also remains to be confirmed in practice.

(c) 10 cd ed (not 10 ... cd 11 ♗b2 ♘c3 12 ♘xd4!) 11 ♗b2 cd 12 ♘xd4 ♕b6 13 ♘2f3 ♘c6 14 ♖ad1 ♗d7 15 e3 ♖ac8 and although White has an iron grip on d4 Black's pieces are extremely active; Bukic–Barle, Yugoslav Ch. 1976.

10   ...   cd

11   ♗xd4

White fared no better with the alternative capture in Fine–Alekhine, AVRO 1936: 11 ♘xd4 ♘c6 12 ♘xe4 fe 13 ♖ad1 ♕b6 14 ♘xc6

bc 15 ♗xf6 ♖xf6 and the upshot
of all the exchanges has been to
give Black a powerful centre and
strong pressure on f2.

11	...	♘c6
12	♗xf6	♕xf6
13	cd	ed
14	a3	a5!

Preventing the expansion on the
queen's wing which would enable
the QN to find useful work via b3.

| 15 | ♕d3 | ♗e6 |
| 16 | e3 | ♖ad8(*103*) |

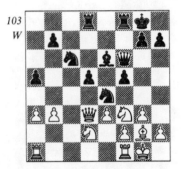

103
W

The right rook. Although at
present the play is all in the centre
or on the queenside, the massive
presence of the knight on e4
ensures that the kingside will one
day come to life.

17   ♖fd1

Bronstein supplies the following
variation to show that White cannot afford to ignore the growing
pressure on the d-file: 17 ♖fc1 d4
18 ed ♘xd4 19 ♘xd4 ♖xd4 20
♘xe4 fe 21 ♕e3 ♖d3 22 ♕xe4
♕xf2+ 23 ♔h1 ♗d5 and Black

wins.

| 17 | ... | ♗f7 |
| 18 | ♘d4 | |

18 ♖ac1 would invite the awkward pin 18 ... ♗h5.

| 18 | ... | ♘e5 |
| 19 | ♘xe4 | |

This is queried by Bronstein but
his proposal of 19 ♕f1 hardly
seems any better after 19 ... ♘g4.

| 19 | ... | fe |
| 20 | ♕b5 | b6! |

A quiet move of high class
avoiding the overimpetuous 20 ...
♘d3? 21 ♖xd3! ed 22 ♕xd3 with
excellent prospects of holding the
draw, or 20 ... ♗e8? 21 ♕xa5
♕xf2+ 22 ♔h1 ♗h5 23 ♖f1
♕xe3 24 ♖xf8+ ♖xf8 25 ♕xd5+
and White turns the tables.

| 21 | ♖ac1 | ♘d3! |
| 22 | ♖c2 | |

Now 22 ♖xd3? would come
unstuck against 22 ... ♗e8! 23
♕a6 ♕xf2+ etc.

22	...	♖c8
23	♖dd2	♖c5
24	♕a6	♗e8
25	h3	♗d7!

Black naturally wants nothing
to do with the premature 25 ...
♖xc2 26 ♖xc2 ♘xf2 27 ♕b7! but
instead strengthens the threat by
planning 26 ... ♗c8 27 ♕a7 ♖xc2
28 ♖xc2 ♘xf2 and the h-pawn is
en prise.

26   ♖xc5

White feels obliged to liquidate

to the ending which, however, rapidly proves untenable. The middlegame following 26 f4 ♗c8 27 ♕a7 ♕d6 28 ♗f1 ♘e1 would scarcely be more palatable.

26	...	bc
27	♕xf6	♖xf6
28	♘c2	♖b6
29	f3	♗c6
30	fe	de
31	♘a1	a4

White's quietus.

32	b4	cb
33	ab	♖xb4
34	♘c2	♖b2

0–1

Huerta–Nogueiras
Santa-Clara 1980
1 d4 f5 2 g3 ♘f6 3 ♗g2 e6 4 ♘f3 ♗e7 5 0-0 0-0 6 c4 ♘e4

7   d5 *(104)*

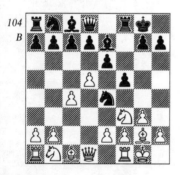

This advance, which simultaneously gains space and prevents Black shoring up the knight with ... d5, was long regarded

as tantamount to a refutation of Black's play. The present game, however, has been instrumental in revising that assessment, and at the time of writing the ball remains quite clearly in White's court.

7   ...   ♗f6

8   ♕c2

Not 8 ♘d4 c5! 9 ♘c2 ♘d6! with the initiative (Simonovic–Kostic, Yugoslav Ch. 1946), or 8 ♘fd2 ♘xd2 9 ♘xd2 e5 tamely handing Black an easy game (Haugli–Gausel, Gausdal 1990).

8   ...   ♘a6!
(105)

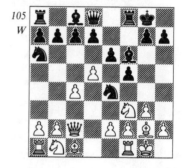

White's queen move prevents 8 ... e5 because of the crafty retreat 9 ♘e1 winning a pawn. In the debut game with 7 d5, Reshevsky–Suesman, US Ch. 1938, Black tried 8 ... a5 but was overwhelmed after 9 ♘bd2 ♘c5 (9 ... ♘xd2 is relatively better but White still keeps the upper hand after 10 ♗xd2 d6 11 e4 fe 12 ♕xe4 ♘a6 13 ♗e3; 10 ♘xd2 also comes into consideration) 10 e4 fe 11 ♘xe4 ♘xe4 12 ♕xe4 ed 13 ♕xd5+ ♔h8 14 ♘g5 ♕e8 15 ♗f4 and White's massive positional superiority is virtually decisive.

The only real alternative to the text move is 8 ... d6 intending to answer 9 ♘e1 ♘c5 10 ♘c3 e5 11 e4 by 11 ... f4 stirring up complications, while 11 b4 ♘cd7 12 ♖b1 would also not be without counterchances.

The knight move has several plus points: it continues Black's development, it prepares tactical harassment of the white queen, and it reinforces Black's growing pressure on the dark and queen-side squares weakened by the advance of White's d-pawn.

9 ♘e1

This is unsuitable here and leads White into difficulties. As a possible improvement, Nogueiras mentions 9 ♘bd2, but Taimanov is of the opinion that Black stands well after 9 ... ed 10 cd ♕e7 and himself suggests that White should investigate either 9 ♗e3 or 9 ♘c3. It is hard to believe that these moves will bring White much joy, particularly the positionally inept knight move.

9 ... ♘b4

Causing mischief in the best tradition of knights developed on a6.

10 ♕d1

If 10 ♕b3 or ♕a4 then 10 ... a5 will prime a further tempo-gaining attack by ... ♘c5.

10	...	a5
11	f3	♘c5
12	♘c3	d6
13	♖b1	c6!

Cleverly using tactical means to pursue his positional ends.

14 e4

14 a3 founders on 14 ... ed! 15 ab ab when Black regains his material with advantage.

14	...	ed
15	ed	cd
16	cd	♖e8

Takes the newly opened file and prevents the QB going to e3.

17 a3 ♕b6! (106)

18 ♔h1

18 ab ab 19 ♘e2 ♘d3+ 20 ♔h1 ♘f2+ 21 ♖xf2 ♕xf2 would be fatal.

18 ... ♕a6!

Black continues to manoeuvre with great verve and exploits his initiative to the utmost.

19 ♖f2

19 ab ab would certainly not ease White's defensive task.

19	...	♘bd3
20	♘xd3	♘xd3
21	♖e2	♗d7
22	♗f1	♖xe2
23	♕xe2	♘xc1
24	♖xc1?	

A grave inaccuracy just when it was beginning to look as if the worst of his troubles were behind him. By interposing 24 ♕xa6 ba 25 ♖xc1 White would have kept his disadvantage to a minimum after 25 ... ♖b8 26 ♖c2 ♖b6.

24 ... ♕xe2

25 ♗xe2 ♖c8

The combined pressure from the c-file pin and the dominating bishop pair leave White scant hope of saving the game. With time-trouble approaching Black concludes the proceedings as elegantly as he began them: 26 ♖c2 b5 27 ♗d3 ♖c5 28 ♔g2 g6 29 f4 ♔f8 30 ♔f2 b4! 31 ab ab 32 ♘a2 ♗a4! 33 ♖e2 ♗d4+ 34 ♔f3? (a time-induced blunder, but there could be no doubt about the final outcome even after the best play 34 ♔g2 ♗d1! 35 ♖d2 b3! 36 ♘b4 ♗h5) 34 ... ♗d1
0–1.

14 Ilyin-Zhenevsky System

The Ilyin-Zhenevsky System is established by Black's sixth move in the sequence

1	d4	f5
2	g3	♘f6
3	♗g2	e6
4	♘f3	♗e7
5	0-0	0-0
6	c4	d6 *(107)*

Named after the Soviet master who developed and refined it during the 1920s and 30s, this is Black's most direct attempt to force through the advance of his e-pawn. Left unhindered, the basic plan of ... ♛e8, ... ♗d8 and ... e5 guarantees Black lively play in the centre and on the kingside. Experience suggests, however, that by judiciously mixing prophylaxis against ... e6–e5 with preparation for e2–e4 himself, White can manipulate the strategical battle in his favour. Even so, Black's resources, tactical in particular, are considerable, and are quite capable of yielding the one or two improvements in key areas which would be sufficient to challenge the current assessment.

We shall examine the material under the broad divisions of 7 b3 (in conjunction with ♘bd2) and 7 ♘c3 when Black has the choice between 7 ... ♛e8 and 7 ... a5.

Goldberg–Ilyin-Zhenevsky
Leningrad 1932

7 b3

Although the fianchetto development is an important weapon in countering Black's plans, it requires vigorous support in order to be effective. This game shows just how easily an optically attractive and apparently harmonious development can turn out to be functionally inadequate.

Of White's other seventh moves, only 7 b4 has any independent significance. This attempt to pep up the fianchetto needs to be countered energetically lest White obtain too much space too quickly: 7 ... e5! 8 de de 9 ♘xe5 (9 ♕b3 e4 would produce a complex balanced middlegame) 9 ... ♕xd1 10 ♖xd1 ♗xb4 11 ♗b2 c6 12 ♘d2 ♘a6 13 ♘b3 ♗e6 with reciprocal chances; Djaja–Duckstein, Gloggnitz 1970.

7 ... ♕e8 *(108)*

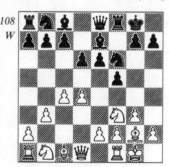

108
W

8 ♘bd2

A refinement designed to reserve the possibility of answering 8 ... ♗d8 with 9 ♗a3 which would paralyse Black's position at a stroke. It suffers though from the drawback of diminishing control of d5, thus permitting Black's

QN to join the central battle immediately without being exposed to the push d4–d5 which would downgrade the black pawn structure.

Thus White's best eighth move is the simple 8 ♗b2 ruling out 8 ... ♘c6 on account of 9 d5. After the correct response 8 ... a5 (a typical all-purpose waiting move) White can transpose to variations considered later by 9 ♘c3, or carry on with 9 ♘bd2 satisfied at having gained a tempo over the column game. The game Averbakh–Boleslavsky, Zurich 1953, provides a good example of likely developments in this latter case: (8 ♗b2 a5 9 ♘bd2) 9 ... ♘c6 10 a3 ♗d8 11 ♘e1 e5 12 e3 ♗d7 13 ♘c2 ed 14 ♘xd4 (14 ed f4!) 14 ... ♘xd4 15 ♗xd4 ♗c6 (Black has a very comfortable position) 16 ♘f3 ♗e4 17 ♘e1 b6 18 a4 ♘d7 19 ♘d3 g5! (denying the knight access to d5 via f4) 20 ♘c1 ♘e5 (20 ... ♗f6 was a better way to strengthen Black's position) 21 ♗xe4 fe 22 ♗xe5 ♕xe5 23 ♕d5+ ♕xd5 24 cd (the exchanges have helped White considerably, but accurate play enables the position to be held without much difficulty) 24 ... ♖b8 25 ♖d1 b5 26 g4 ♗f6 27 ♖a2 ♗e5 28 ♔g2 ♖f7 29 ab ♖xb5 30 ♖a4 ♗b2 31 ♖xe4 ½–½ (in view of 31 ... ♗xc1 32 ♖xc1 ♖xd5).

8   ...   ♘c6
9   ♗b2   ♗d8

This subtle retreat uncovers the support from the queen which is necessary to effect the strategically vital ... e6–e5 advance. Black is able to get away with such 'undeveloping' because of the generally closed nature of the position and the somewhat sluggish disposition of White's forces.

10   ♕c2

Alternatively, 10 ♘e1 e5 12 e3 would parallel Averbakh–Boleslavsky above, while 10 ♖e1 takes away protection from the king and also enables Black to utilize the possibility of threatening a ... ♘d3 fork, e.g. 10 ... e5 11 e4 f4! 12 d5 (12 gf ♘h5 would be extremely risky) 12 ... ♘b4 13 ♕b1 (thus far a game Shatskes–Neishtadt, Moscow 1963) and now by 13 ... fg 14 hg c5 Black could secure the centre in preparation for pursuing his attacking ambitions on the kingside. Note also that 10 ♗a3 ♗e7 instantly renews the threat of ... e5.

10   ...   e5
11   de

White hopes to distract Black from the kingside by opening up the centre. Closing the centre would be a positional error freeing Black to concentrate on building his attack, e.g. 11 d5 ♘e7 12 ♖ae1 ♕h5 13 e4 ♘g6 and already the storm clouds are gathering over White's king; Lisitsin–Ilyin-Zhenevsky, USSR Ch. 1931.

11   ...   de
12   e4 *(109)*

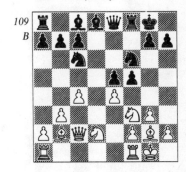

109
B

12   ...   fe

This simple move brings Black open lines galore and obvious attacking chances for no more than acceptance of an isolated pawn. It is a measure of the inadequacy of White's opening that Black also has the option of sacrificing a pawn for a more complex type of attack based on establishing a knight on f4: 12 ... f4!? 13 gf ♘h5 14 f5 (an attempt to limit the activity of the black pieces) 14 ... ♘f4 15 ♔h1 ♗f6 16 a3 g6 17 fg ♕xg6 18 ♖g1 ♔h8 19 ♗h3 ♕h5 20 ♗xc8 ♖axc8 21 ♖g3 ♘e2 22 ♖g2 ♖g8 23 ♖xg8+ ♖xg8 24 ♕d1 ♘f4 25 ♕f1 ♖d8 26 ♖d1 ♘d3 27 ♗c3 ♗h4 28 ♘xh4 ♕xh4 0–1   Budo–Ilyin-Zhenevsky, USSR Ch. 1931. Although White's defence was rather feeble, the impression remains that this type of attack must be very difficult to withstand in practice. Thus despite the fact that Ilyin-Zhenevsky played 12 ... fe after 12 ... f4, it would probably be mistaken to deduce from this that he considered the capture superior. Both approaches are valid and the choice is largely a matter of personal preference.

| 13 | ♘xe4 | ♕h5 |
| 14 | ♘xf6+ | |

White is understandably anxious to remove the potentially very dangerous Knight but in so doing he relieves Black of the problem of his back rank bishops and encourages occupation of the outpost on d4.

14	...	♗xf6
15	♘d2	♗h3
16	♘e4	♖ad8
17	f4?	

A panicky attempt to force matters which backfires in spectacular fashion. The prudent 17 f3 would have been much more appropriate.

| 17 | ... | ♘d4 |
| 18 | ♕f2? *(110)* | |

Compounding the previous error; the uninviting 18 ♗xd4 was essential.

18	...	ef!
19	♘xf6+	♖xf6
20	♗d5+	

On 20 ♗xd4 comes 20 ... fg 21

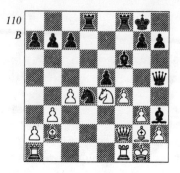

♕xg3 ♖g6 etc.

| 20 | ... | ♖xd5! |

Shattering White's dreams of 20 ... ♔h8? 21 ♗xd4 fg 22 ♕xf6!

21	cd	fg
22	♕xd4	♕e2!
	0–1	

A fittingly elegant *coup de grâce* with which to conclude this wonderfully instructive miniature from the Master's own hand.

Flohr–Sokolsky
Semi-final USSR Ch. 1953
1 d4 f5 2 g3 ♘f6 3 ♗g2 e6 4 ♘f3 ♗e7 5 0-0 0-0 6 c4 d6

| 7 | ♘c3 | |

It is not surprising that this active and natural development poses Black far more serious problems than the previous variation.

| 7 | ... | ♕e8 |

The standard and most explored continuation; other possibilities will be examined further on.

8 ♖e1

White's most direct procedure, aiming to open the centre with e2–e4 as quickly as possible.

8 ...♦ ♘e4!? *(111)*

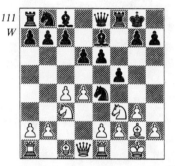

This obstructive occupation of e4 is probably the most promising of Black's less explored paths in the classical Ilyin–Zhenevsky. That such relatively fresh ideas need to be investigated is plain from the well established main lines where Black is reduced to trying to hang on for a draw. For example, 8 ... ♕g6 9 e4 fe 10 ♘xe4 ♘xe4 11 ♖xe4 ♘c6 (11 ... ♕xe4 12 ♘h4 traps the queen) 12 ♕e2 ♗f6 13 ♗d2 e5 14 de ♘xe5 (in the famous game Aronson–Tal, USSR Ch. 1957, the 'magician from Riga' typically sought complications by 14 ... de 15 ♗c3 ♗f5 16 ♘h4 ♗xh4 17 ♖xh4 ♖ae8 18 ♕e3 h6 19 b4 ♕f6 20 b5 ♘d8, and although he was rewarded with the full point some moves after 21 ♗d5+? ♔h8 22 f4? ef!

23 ♕d2 ♕b6+! 24 ♗d4 ♕g6 25 ♕xf4 ♔h7 26 ♕xc7 ♗b1!, simply 21 c5 would have underlined White's positional supremacy on the queen's wing in complete safety) 15 ♘xe5 ♗xe5 16 ♗c3! ♗xc3 17 bc c6 18 ♖e1 (another line is 18 ♖e7 ♗g4 19 f3 ♗f5 20 ♖xb7 ♗d3 21 ♕f2 ♗xc4 22 ♖xa7 ♖xa7 23 ♕xa7 c5 with compensation for the pawn because of White's uncoordinated pieces; Matulovic–Minic, Yugoslav Ch. 1959) 18 ... ♗d7 (18 ... ♗f5 19 ♖e7 ♗d3 20 ♕b2) 19 ♕e3 ♖fe8 20 ♕d4 ♗f5 21 ♖xe8+ ♖xe8 22 ♖xe8+ ♕xe8 23 h4! ♕b8 24 c5 dc 25 ♕xc5 ♗e6 26 a4 ♗f7 27 a5 a6 28 ♕e7 and White went on to squeeze out a win in Bukic–Maric, Kraljevo 1967. Even with improvements, such barren positions would hold little attraction for warriors of the Dutch.

9 ♕c2

The most natural method of disputing control of e4. Alternatively:

(a) 9 ♘d2 ♘xc3 10 bc e5 11 c5 is Konstantinopolsky's artificial-looking suggestion.

(b) 9 ♕d3 can hardly be better than the column move, but in Cvetkov–Hermann, Halle 1954, Black incurred a slight disadvantage after 9 ... ♕g6 10 ♗f4 ♘c6 11 ♖ad1 ♔h8 (certainly not essential) 12 ♘b5 ♗d8 13 ♘d2

♘xd2 14 ♕xd2 a6 15 ♘c3 ♗f6 16 d5 ♘d8 17 de ♘xe6 18 ♘d5.

(c) 9 ♘xe4 de is sharp and critical: 10 ♘d2 (in Martin–Piazzini, Argentina 1954, the tactics following 10 ♘g5 d5 11 cd ed 12 ♕b3 c6 13 ♘xe4?! ♕f7 14 ♗g5 ♗xg5 15 ♘xg5 ♕xf2+ 16 ♔h1 ♕xd4 went in Black's favour; 13 f3 is better) 10 ... d5 11 f3 ♗f6!? (11 ... ef 12 ef ♘c6 also merits attention) 12 fe ♗xd4+ 13 e3 ♗b6 14 cd (Bertok–Milic, Yugoslav Team Ch. 1958, went instead 14 ed ed 15 ♗xd5+ ♔h8 16 ♘b3 c6 17 ♗g2 ♘d7 18 ♘d4 ♘e5 19 b3 ♗g4 20 ♕d2 and now 20 ... ♖d8 would have been the best way to augment Black's dangerous compensation) 14 ... ed 15 ed ♘d7 (Black's active pieces and the many weaknesses in White's camp provide fine play in return for the pawn) 16 ♘c4 ♘e5 17 ♘xb6 ♗g4 18 ♕d4 ab 19 ♗d2 c5 20 dc ♖d8 21 ♗c3 ♖xd4 22 ed ♕f7 23 ♖xe5 ♕f2+ ∓ White's attempt to break Black's initiative by giving up his queen has not been successful; Bilek–Milic, Gotha 1957.

9 ...   ♕g6 *(112)*
10 b3

White must decide how to develop his QB, an important question which will determine the shape of the middlegame. The fianchetto declares an intention to

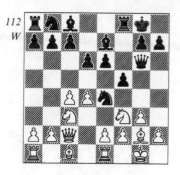

112
W

concentrate on the centre in stark contrast to the important alternative 10 ♗e3 which renounces central play in favour of a space-gaining pawn storm on the queenside. The encounter Olafsson–Korchnoi, Hastings 1955/56, provides an excellent illustration of typical play for both sides: (10 ♗e3) ♘xc3 (White is threatening 11 ♘xe4 and 12 ♘d2 with advantage; note that 10 ♘xe4 fe 11 ♘d2 loses instantly to 11 ... e3) 11 ♕xc3 ♗f6 12 b4 (12 ♖ad1 ♘c6 13 ♕b3 e5! is fully acceptable for Black) 12 ... ♘c6 (this appears somewhat more precise than 12 ... ♖e8 13 c5 e5 14 cd cd 15 de de 16 ♖ac1 ♘c6 17 b5 ♘d8 18 ♖ed1 ♘f7 as in Furman–Boleslavsky, semi-final USSR Ch. 1954) 13 b5 ♘d8 14 c5 ♘f7 (White's spatial advantage is clear, but the knight on f7 helps both to cover potential entry points along the d-file and ensure that the central counterpunch ... e6–e5 cannot be pre-

vented) 15 cd cd 16 ♘d2 e5 17 de
de 18 ♗d5 e4 19 ♗d4 ♗xd4 20
♕xd4 ♗e6! 21 ♗xe6 (it would be
risky to take the pawn, e.g. 21
♗xb7 ♖ad8 22 ♕c3 ♘g5 with …
f5–f4 to follow) 21 … ♕xe6 22
♖ec1 ♖ad8 23 ♕c4 ♖d5 24 ♘f1
♘d6 25 ♕b3 ♖e8 (25 … ♘xb5??
26 ♖c5) 26 a4 f4 27 ♖d1 ♖xd1 28
♕xe6+ ♖xe6 29 ♖xd1 g5 30 ♖d5
h6 ½–½.

10 … ♘xc3

Deflecting the queen away from
its observation of e4 and on to the
sensitive a1–h8 diagonal.

11 ♕xc3 ♗f6
12 ♗a3

Black would be entirely satisfied
with 12 ♗b2 ♘c6 13 ♕d2 e5 14
de de.

12 … ♘c6
13 ♖ad1 ♗d7
14 ♕c1 a5 *(113)*

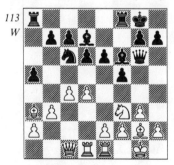

113
W

15 d5

Having completed his development White proceeds with the central breakthrough only to find that
it accomplishes very little.

15 … ♘b4
16 de ♗xe6
17 ♕d2

Against 17 ♘d4 the retreat 17
… ♗c8 would be surprisingly
effective in renewing the threat on
the a-pawn.

17 … f4!
18 ♖c1?

This passive prevention of 18 …
♘c2 merely loses a tempo as he
can find nothing better than to
accept the pawn sacrifice later on
anyway. The f-pawn is immune:
18 ♕xf4? ♗c3 or 18 gf? ♗h3 19
♘g5 ♗xg2 20 ♔xg2 h6. After 18
♗xb4 ab 19 ♕xb4 Black could
choose between 19 … b6 20 a4 fg
21 hg h5 and 19 … fg 20 hg ♖xa2
21 ♕xb7 ♕f7, in both cases with
active pieces, the bishop pair, and
attacking chances in compensation for the pawn.

18 … fg
19 hg h5!

Single-mindedly pursuing the
storming of the white monarch's
citadel.

20 ♗xb4 ab
21 ♕xb4 h4!
22 ♘xh4 ♗xh4
23 gh ♕f6

Not 23 … ♗h3? 24 ♕xb7, but
Sokolsky notes that both 23 …
♖f4 24 ♖c3 and 23 … b6 24 ♕c3
came into consideration.

24 ♖f1 ♖xa2

25   ♕xb7?

Loses quickly, but the line given by Sokolsky as relatively best is also unpleasant: 25 c5 d5 26 ♕xb7 ♖xe2 27 ♗xd5 ♕xh4 28 ♗xe6+ ♖xe6 29 ♕d5 ♖f6.

25   ...   ♖xe2
26   ♕xc7   ♕d4!

Black bludgeons away the last line of defence in a mercifully swift onslaught.

27   ♕e7

27 ♖cd1 would not deter Black: 27 ... ♖fxf2! with mate in three on acceptance of the queen.

27   ...   ♖fxf2
28   ♔h1   ♗h3!

Black throws in the kitchen sink as well, dashing White's last hope of 28 ... ♖xg2?? 29 ♕e8+ ♔h7 30 ♕h5+ with perpetual check. White resigns.

Csom–Szabolcsi
Hungarian Ch. 1972
1 d4 f5 2 g3 ♘f6 3 ♗g2 e6 4 ♘f3 ♗e7 5 0-0 0-0 6 c4 d6 7 ♘c3 ♕e8 8   b3 *(114)*

This elastic continuation makes for a sophisticated positional battle where White hopes to outfox his opponent by virtue of greater flexibility of position.

White's remaining eighth moves are mostly minor and of a more rustic character:

(a) 8 e4?! fe (8 ... ♘xe4 is more ambitious) 9 ♘g5 d5 10 cd ed 11 ♕b3 c6 12 ♘gxe4 ♔h8 13 ♘c5 b6 14 ♘d3 ♗a6 15 ♕d1 ♘bd7 with excellent play for Black; Purdy–Koshnitzky, match 1934.

(b) 8 b4 ♕h5 (Taimanov recommends 8 ... e5 9 de de 10 ♘d5 ♗d8 11 ♗b2 e4=) 9 ♕b3 ♔h8 10 c5 ♘c6 11 b5 ♘d8 12 ♗a3 ♘f7 gives a mutually difficult position; Vaganian–Andersson, Groningen 1968/69.

(c) 8 ♕d3 ♕h5 9 e4 e5 10 de de 11 ♘d5 ♘c6 12 ♘xe7+ ♘xe7 13 ♘xe5 fe 14 ♕c3 ♗h3 with attacking prospects on the light squares; Steiner–Duckstein, Vienna 1969.

(d) 8 ♗f4 c6 9 ♕b3 ♘bd7 10 a4 a5 11 ♘g5 e5 12 ♗e3 ♕h5 with a very tense and complicated position; Szily–Farago, Hungarian Ch. 1967.

(e) 8 ♗g5 ♘e4 9 ♗xe7 ♘xc3 10 bc ♕xe7 and White's pieces show little dynamism to offset the doubled pawns; Rossolimo–Pachman, Beverwijk 1950.

(f) 8 ♕b3 ♚h8 (8 ... c6) 9 ♗f4 ♘c6 10 ♘b5 (10 d5 ♘d8 11 de ♘xe6 would bring the black knights to life) 10 ... ♗d8 11 d5 ♘e7 12 de ♗xe6 13 ♘fd4 ♗d7 14 ♘c3 ♘c6 with very satisfactory play for Black; Palfi–Schneider, Budapest 1952.

(g) 8 e3 has little independent significance and may be met according to taste.

(h) 8 ♘e1 invites 8 ... e5 which Black may either play or prepare as he wishes.

(i) 8 ♕c2 is a much more important continuation than the foregoing; after Black's most active reply, 8 ... ♕h5 (taking advantage of the fact that White can no longer profit from a manoeuvre of the type e2–e3 and ♘f3–e1 proposing the exchange of queens) White has three main possibilities:

(1) 9 ♗g5 h6! 10 ♗xf6 ♗xf6 11 e4 ♘c6 12 ♘b5 ♕f7 13 ♖ad1 (thus far Olafsson–Kan, Nice Ol. 1974) and now by advancing ... e6–e5, either immediately or after 13 ... a6 14 ♘c3, Black would get an equal game.

(2) 9 e4 e5 10 de de 11 ♘d5 (both 11 ♘xe5? fe and 11 ♗g5 ♘c6 12 ♖fe1 f4! are good for Black) 11 ... ♘xd5 12 ed (12 cd ♗d6 13 ef ♗xf5 14 ♕b3 ♘d7 15 ♗e3 h6 leaves Black with a solid

centre and the initiative on the kingside; E. Richter–Skalicka, 1934) 12 ... ♗f6 13 c5 e4 14 ♘e1 ♘d7 15 ♗f4 ♘e5 and Black's play is the more purposeful; Kozlovskaya–Kakabadze, USSR Women's Ch. 1971.

(3) 9 b3 (let us note in passing Geller–Milic, USSR v Yugoslavia 1957, which saw the whole board in turmoil after 9 b4 ♘c6 10 b5 ♘d8 11 a4 ♘f7 12 ♗a3 g5 13 ♖ad1 f4) 9 ... a5 (secures b4 as a blocking outpost in the event of White's QB moving to the a3–f8 diagonal) 10 ♗b2 (10 ♗a3 ♘a6 11 d5 e5 12 ♘xe5? ♘b4∓ demonstrates the usefulness of ... a5, and 10 e4 merely loosens the white position after 10 ... fe 11 ♘xe4 e5 12 de de 13 ♗b2 ♘c6 14 ♖ael ♗g4!) 10 ... ♘a6 11 ♖ae1 c6 12 a3 ♗d8 13 e4 e5 14 de de 15 ♘xe5 ♘c5 with compensation for the pawn; Flohr–Kotov, USSR Ch. 1949, went 16 b4? ♘cxe4 17 ♘xe4 fe 18 c5? ♗e6 19 ♗xe4 ♘xe4 20 ♖xe4 ♗d5 and the white-squared bishop dominated the board. There is a forced repetition by 16 ♗f3 ♕h3 17 ♗g2 etc., and Taimanov has suggested that White may play for the win by 17 ef ♗xf5 18 ♕d1.

8 ... a5

White's basic idea would be seen in its clearest form after 8 ... ♗d8? 9 ♗a3 paralysing Black's position. Similarly, the standard 8 ... ♕h5 runs up against 9 ♗a3! x-raying the now undefended bishop and preparing a favourable alteration of pawn structure: 9 ... a5 (Black's best bet might be the consistent 9 ... g5 10 e3 ♖f7 11 c5 ♗d7 12 ♘d2 ♕xd1 13 ♖axd1 d5 14 ♘f3 ♖g7 15 ♘e5 ♗e8; Kozma–Bhend, Munich Ol. 1958) 10 d5! and the centre is opened up to White's advantage as 10 ... e5? loses to 11 ♘xe5.

9 ♖e1

Once more maximizing flexibility: whilst introducing the possibility of e2–e4 White is also waiting to see how Black plays before committing his QB.

The simpler 9 ♗b2 ♘a6 10 e3 c6 11 ♕e2 ♗d7 12 e4 fe 13 ♘xe4 ♕h5 would bring about a standard type of position where White has greater freedom but Black's set-up is very resilient and not without counterchances on both sides of the board.

9 ... ♕g6

By analogy with other positions it could be that 9 ... ♘e4 deserves further investigation.

10 ♗a3

As in the old 8 ♖e1 main line White could also continue 10 e4 fe 11 ♘xe4 ♘xe4 12 ♖xe4 ♘c6 13 ♕e2 although the extra pawn moves would ease Black's task somewhat.

10 ... ♘a6

This typical edge-development serves several functions: generally restraining White's queenside ambitions, protecting the c7 weak spot, and last but by no means least, avoiding central congestion (... ♘bd7) or offering White a target (... ♘c6, d4–d5!).

11 e3

Flashy manoeuvring by 11 ♘e5 ♕e8 12 ♘d3 would allow 12 ... e5, while 11 d5 would also be ineffective because of 11 ... ♘e4! The move played secures the central dark squares and can hope to lull the opponent into the inattentive 11 ... ♗d7? 12 ♘e5!

11 ... ♘b4
12 ♗b2 *(115)*

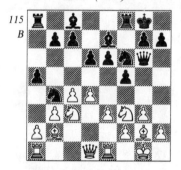

115
B

Having accomplished a good deal behind the scenes on the a3–f8 diagonal, the bishop retires with honour in order to eject the trespasser on b4.

12 ... c6

Construction of an elastic,

defensive pawn wall is an integral part of Black's strategy in such positions, but here White can utilize the opposition of queen rooks to make immediate and important spatial gains and therefore the preliminary 12 ... ♖b8 would be preferable.

13	a3	♘a6
14	b4	ab
15	ab	♗d7
16	♕b3	♕h5
17	♘d2	

White inconsistently opts to prepare the central advance e3–e4 before completing his queenside action; 17 b5 cb 18 cb ♘c7 19 ♘d2 (19 d5 intending 19 ... ♘cxd5 20 ♘xd5 ♘xd5 21 ♘d4 ♕f7 22 ♗xd5 ed 23 ♖fc1 is interesting) 19 ... d5 20 f3 was the correct way to preserve White's strategic initiative.

17 ... d5!

The delayed transition to a Stonewall formation is an important weapon in Black's positional armoury. Here, there is also the concrete point of opening up an attack on b4.

18 b5 ♘b4! *(116)*

Astute tactical exploitation of White's lapse on the seventeenth; it may well be that this possibility had escaped White's attention.

19 ♘a2

Sensibly taking immediate steps to eliminate the frisky intruder.

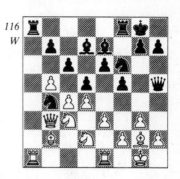

Simply defending d3 by 19 ♗f1 looks suspiciously passive, whilst the blunt 19 ♗a3?! would fall foul of 19 ... ♖xa3! 20 ♕xa3 ♘g4 21 h3 ♘xf2! with a vicious attack.

19	...	♘xa2
20	♖xa2	♖xa2
21	♕xa2	♘e4

21 ... ♗b4 would have obliged White to meekly hold the balance by 22 ♗c1 ♘e4 23 bc bc 24 ♕c2.

22	♘xe4	fe
23	bc	♗xc6
24	c5	g5

Inaugurating an extremely brash plan which was probably unnecessary in view of the attractive alternative 24 ... ♗d8 intending to activate the bishop on the b8–h2 diagonal.

25	♗c3	g4
26	♖b1	♖f6
27	♕a8+	♗f8
28	♕c8	♖h6
29	♖xb7	

Naturally, White is only too

happy to make the trivial material investment required to clear the path for his dangerous c-pawn.

29	...	♗xb7
30	♕xb7	♕xh2+
31	♔f1	♖f6
32	♕b8	h5?

The delicate equilibrium of opposite flank play would have achieved a fitting finale in the variation 32 ... ♕h6! 33 ♔g1 ♖f7 34 c6 ♕f6 35 ♗e1 ♕e7 36 ♗a5 ♕f6 etc., but Black mistakenly plays for a win, not appreciating that the self-incarceration of his queen paves the way for an imaginative and amusing finish: 33 ♕e5!++ ♗g7 34 c6 ♖xf2+ 35 ♔xf2 ♗xe5 36 de h4 37 c7 h3 (37 ... ♕xg3+ 38 ♔f1 h3 is no improvement: 39 c8♕+ ♔h7 40 ♕d7+ ♔h8 41 ♕e8+ ♔g7 42 ♕e7+ ♔h8 43 ♕f8+ ♔h7 44 ♕f7+ ♔h8 45 ♕h5+ ♔g7 46 ♕g5 ♔h7 47 ♗h1) 38 c8♕+ ♔g7 39 ♕d7+ ♔g6 40 ♕xe6+ ♔h5 41 ♕f5+ ♔h6 42 ♕f6+ ♔h5 43 ♕h4+ 1-0.

Suetin–Rashkovsky
Sochi 1973
1 d4 f5 2 g3 ♘f6 3 ♗g2 e6 4 ♘f3 ♗e7 5 0-0 0-0 6 c4 d6 7 ♘c3

7	...	♘e4!?(117)

In view of Black's theoretical difficulties in the accepted main lines of the Ilyin-Zhenevsky,

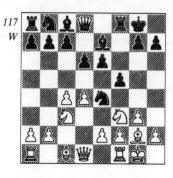

117
W

this neglected byway certainly deserves deeper investigation. The similarities with Flohr–Sokolsky above are evident and there are also instructive and informative parallels to be drawn with Notaros–Maric below.

8	♕c2

Other moves are unlikely to worry Black, e.g. 8 ♗d2 ♗f6 9 ♕c2 ♘xd2! or 8 ♘xe4 fe 9 ♘d2 d5 10 f3 ♗f6 with a superior version of the analogous variation of note 'c' to White's ninth move, p. 138.

8	...	♘xc3
9	♕xc3	

After 9 bc Black could transpose to an acceptable Alekhine variation by 9 ... ♗f6 10 e4 ♘c6 if unable to find anything better.

9	...	♗f6
10	b3	

Two other moves have been played:

(a) 10 b4 ♘d7 (clearly, alternatives await testing, amongst them

10 ... c5) 11 ♗b2 c5 (thus far Savon–Rashkovsky, USSR 1974) and now 12 ♕b3 leaves White somewhat the better of it.

(b) 10 ♗e3 ♘c6 11 ♖ad1 ♕e7 12 b4 ♘d8 13 ♕b3 ♘f7 14 c5 and now it should not prove too difficult to improve on the loosening 14 ... g5?! 15 ♘e1 ± of Hasin–Simagin, USSR Ch. 1956.

    10   **...**   **♘c6**
    11   **♗b2** *(118)*

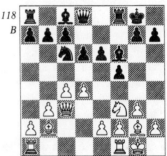

Obviously, Black should now seize the opportunity to play the thematic 11 ... e5 after which his position would appear to be completely satisfactory. Instead, in our game there occurred 11 ... ♗d7 12 ♖ad1 ♕e8 13 ♕d2 ♕h5 14 ♖fe1 (Suetin recommends 14 e3 ± and notes that 14 d5 ed 15 cd ♘e5 16 ♘xe5 de 17 d6 c6 would be unclear) 14 ... ♘e7 15 ♘e5!? ♗c8? (15 ... ♗g5 16 f4 de 17 de ♗c6 18 fg f4! was the way to make a fight of it) 16 ♘d3 ± after which White instructively increased his

positional superiority to decisive proportions: 16 ... ♗g5 17 f4 ♗f6 18 e4 fe 19 ♖xe4 (Black's sickly e-pawn is completely pinned down) 19 ... ♗d7 20 ♘e5! (an amusing echo) 20 ... ♗xe5 (the ignominious 20 ... ♗c8 would leave Black doubly shamed and still struggling after 21 ♗f3 and 22 ♘g4) 21 de d5 22 ♖ee1 ♖fe8 23 ♗a3 ♗c6 24 ♗xe7 ♖xe7 25 cd (the rest is basic technique and best passed over in silence) 25 ... ♖ad8 26 d6 ♗xg2 27 ♔xg2 ♖ed7 28 ♕b4 ♕f5 29 ♖d2 a5 30 ♕xb7 cd 31 ♕c6 d5 32 ♕c2 ♕f7 33 ♖c1 d4 34 ♕e4 d3? 35 ♖c3 h6 36 ♖cxd3 ♖xd3 37 ♖xd3 ♖xd3 38 ♕xd3 ♕b7+ 39 ♔h3 ♕h1 40 ♕c4 ♔f7 41 f5 ♕f3 42 ♕xe6+ ♔f8 43 ♕c8+ ♔e7 44 ♕e6+ ♔f8 45 ♔h4 h5 46 ♕c8+ 1–0.

Notaros–Maric
Novi Sad 1974
1 d4 f5 2 g3 ♘f6 3 ♗g2 e6 4 ♘f3 ♗e7 5 0-0 0-0 6 c4 d6 7 ♘c3

    7   **...**   **a5** *(119)*

By taking b4 under control Black not only impedes queenside expansion by White but also provides protection for knight forays to that square. The critical main line features a pawn sacrifice by Black in return for active piece play, but with the refinement of White's defences has come the

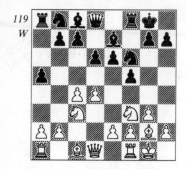

119
W

growing suspicion that the compensation is insufficient. Unless an improvement can be found this attractive variation seems doomed to oblivion.

8   ♖e1

Other continuations make fewer demands on Black's resources, e.g.:

(a) 8 ♕c2 ♘c6 9 e4 (Smyslov–Filipowicz, Bath 1973, went 9 a3 e5 10 d5 ♘b8 11 ♘g5?! c6 12 ♖d1 and now 12 ... ♘g4 would have been more active than the 12 ... ♘e8 played) 9 ... fe 10 ♘xe4 e5 11 de de 12 ♘fg5 (Tomovic–Maric, Yugoslav Ch. 1956, saw 12 ♖d1 ♕e8 13 ♘xf6+ ♗xf6 14 ♗e3 ♕h5 15 ♗c5 ♖e8 with Black's kingside chances at least as important as White's central pressure) 12 ... ♘xe4 13 ♘xe4 ♘d4 14 ♕d1 ♗e6 15 b3 (Pytel–Bednarsky, Poland 1971) and now Pytel gives 15 ... a4 16 ♗b2 ab 17 ab ♖ax1 ∓.

(b) 8 b3 ♘a6 9 ♗b2 c6 10 ♕c2

♗d7 11 ♖ae1 (11 e4 permits the interesting tactical counter 11 ... ♘b4 12 ♕e2 fe 13 ♘xe4 ♘xe4 14 ♕xe4 e5! with the strong threat of 15 ... ♗f5) 11 ... b5 12 ♘d2 bc 13 ♘xc4 ♖c8 14 e3 ♗e8 15 ♕e2 and White's prospects are perhaps slightly the more positive in this mutually difficult middlegame; Vilela–Rantanen, Tallinn 1979. This particularly rich example will repay careful examination. It seems likely that a search for Black alternatives and improvements will be rewarded.

8   ...   ♘e4

Once again we see the knight blockade White's attempted advantageous opening of the centre.

9   ♘xe4

This capture changes the character of the game completely. White's basic aim is to induce ... d6–d5 and then uncover the resulting weakness by means of f2–f3. The drawback is the danger of the white pieces remaining bottled up while Black's gain in mobility.

The best move, 9 ♕c2, is examined in the following game.

9   ...   fe
10   ♘d2   d5
11   f3   ef
12   ♘xf3

The d-pawn is too weak to allow 12 ef ♗f6 etc.

12   ...   c5 *(120)*

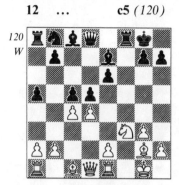

Faced with this challenge to his centre White has no time to settle to quiet exploitation and occupation of e5.

13   cd   ed
14   &e3   c4!

This pawn has a bright future.

15   ♘e5   ♘c6
16   ♘xc6   bc
17   b3?!

Priming the long-awaited advance e2–e4 by 17 &f2 was the correct continuation; neglecting this positional imperative, White falls inexorably into passivity.

17   ...   c3! *(121)*

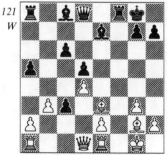

18   ♕c1

Hastening to pluck the irritating thorn from his flesh, but it turns out not to be so easy to accomplish. 18 ♕c2 &f5 would be worse.

18   ...   ♕b6
19   ♖d1   &g4
20   &f1

20 ♕xc3 &b4 21 ♕d3?? &f5 would be tragi-comic curtains, and 21 ♕c2 ♖ae8 likely as not the beginning of the final act with the black pieces in full cry.

20   ...   ♕b4
21   ♖d3   c2!
22   ♕xc2

The white position has turned septic and a radical solution must be attempted.

22   ...   &f5
23   ♕xc6   &xd3
24   ♕xd5+   ♔h8
25   ed   &f6
26   ♖c1   ♖ae8

With this it becomes clear that despite a temporary rallying the case is terminal. The final throes: 27 ♖c4 ♕e1 28 &f2 ♕d2 29 ♕g2 &g5 30 d5 ♖xf2 0–1.

Kavalek–Bednarsky
Skopje Ol. 1972
1 d4 f5 2 g3 ♘f6 4 &g2 e6 4 ♘f3 &e7 5 0-0 0-0 6 c4 d6 7 ♘c3 a5 8 ♖e1 ♘e4

9   ♕c2 *(122)*

Natural and clearly strongest.

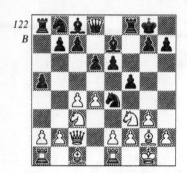

122
B

9 ... ♘c6

There are three other possibilities:

(a) 9 ... d5 produces a rather poor Stonewall.

(b) 9 ... ♘xc3 10 ♕xc3 (10 bc also gives chances of advantage) 10 ... ♘c6 11 e4! d5 (11 ... fe 12 ♖xe4 ♗f6 13 ♗f4 is relatively best but cedes White an undeniable positional superiority) 12 ed! ♗b4 13 ♕d3 ed 14 ♗g5 ♘e7 15 c5! ♗xe1 16 ♖xe1 ♖e8 17 ♕e2 ♔f8 18 ♘e5 with massive compensation for the exchange; Shashin–Korzin, semi-final Moscow Ch. 1966.

(c) 9 ... ♘a6!? will transpose to the column in all likelihood.

10 ♘xe4 ♘b4
11 ♕b1

Consistency is essential; in Raicevic–Maric, Bar 1977, White wavered with 11 ♕c3?! which encouraged the energetic response 11 ... fe 12 ♘d2 d5 13 f3 c5 14 e3 e5!∓.

11 ... fe
12 ♕xe4 e5

With the strong threat of 13 ... ♗f5.

13 g4!

Boldly controlling f5, albeit at the cost of some weakening of the kingside.

13 ... ed *(123)*

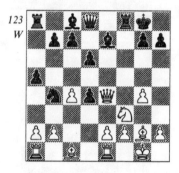

123
W

14 a3

Much stronger than the recapture with the knight which lets Black drum up counterplay, e.g. 14 ♘xd4 ♗h4! 15 ♖f1 (the game Reshevsky–Larsen, Santa Monica 1966, was drawn by repetition after 15 ♗e3 ♖e8 16 ♕f4 ♖f8 17 ♕e4 etc.) 15 ... ♖e8 16 ♕f3 ♖f8 17 ♕h3 h5 18 ♘f5 hg 19 ♕xh4 ♗xf5 20 ♗g5 ♕c8 (or 20 ... ♕e8 21 a3 ♘c6 22 ♗d5+ ♗e6 23 ♕xg4 Havsky–Karasev, Leningrad Ch. 1968) 21 a3 ♘c6 22 ♖fd1 ♘e5 with approximately even chances; Podzielny–Bellin, Winterthur 1974.

14 ... ♘a6

Larsen has mentioned the moves 14 ... ♘c6 15 ♘xd4 ♗h4.

15 ♕xd4

15 ♘xd4 is inferior on account of 15 ... ♘c5 16 ♕d5+ ♔h8 17 h3 c6 18 ♕h5 ♗f6 when 19 ♗e3 fails to 19 ... g6 20 ♕h6 ♗g7.

15 ... ♘c5

16 h3 ♘b3 *(124)*

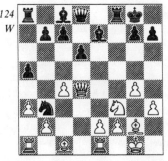

124
W

Other attempts appear equally ineffective:

(a) 16 ... ♗f6 17 ♕d1

(b) 16 ... ♗e6 17 ♕c3 ♗f6 18 ♕c2 a4 19 ♗e3 ♘b3 20 ♖ad1 ♘a5 21 ♘d2 and Black has very little to show for the pawn; Kavalek–Jamieson, Buenos Aires Ol. 1978.

17 ♕d5+ ♔h8

18 ♖b1 a4

19 ♗d2

Stopping ... ♖a5 and ... h5 softening up White's kingside.

19 ... ♗f6

20 ♗b4 ♕e8

21 e4

Black's temporary initiative has ground to a halt and with normal play White will simply consolidate his extra pawn and win. This explains the last desperate fling by Black before bowing to the inevitable: 21 ... ♗e6 22 ♕xb7 c5 23 e5! de 24 ♗c3 ♖b8 25 ♕e4 ♕f7 26 g5 ♗e7 27 ♕xe5 ♖b6 28 ♖bd1 ♗d8 29 ♖d6 ♗xc4 30 g6! hg 31 ♖xd8! ♖xd8 32 ♘g5 ♕f8 33 ♕e4 1–0. It must be admitted that it is very difficult to imagine this variation being rehabilitated.

15   Classical Stonewall

'Stonewall' is the descriptive term for the craggy pawn configuration ... f5, ... e6, ... d5, ... c6. This creation of a rock-solid pawn barrier is essentially aimed at stabilizing the centre in order to free Black's hands for play on the flanks. Early interpretations of the Stonewall often saw this in its crudest form: Black would leave the centre and queenside to take care of themselves and throw everything into a *va banque* offensive on the kingside. This would typically be built up by occupying the e4 outpost with the KN, shifting the heavy pieces to the h-file by means of ... ♛d8–e8–h5 and ... ♜f8–f6–h6 and further mobilizing the infantry by ... g5. Such an attack can be very dangerous, and constantly figures in Black's plans, although nowadays it is likely to be deferred, if not abandoned, in favour of central and queenside action. This modern interpretation posits that Black's central spatial parity, strategic initiative on the kingside, and adequate queenside prospects provide sufficient compensation for ceding White permanent control of e5. This is the nub of the ongoing debate on the viability of the Stonewall formation.

Non-fianchetto Stonewall

Practice has shown that these lines tend to favour White, particularly when his QB is developed outside the pawn chain, thus Black should probably prefer the more flexible type of development seen in Chapter 10. This variation has produced many horror stories for Black, but none more instructive than the following game which is *the* classic warning of the inevitable consequences of chronic dark-square debility.

Schlechter–John
Barmen 1905

| 1 | d4 | f5 |

2	c4	e6
3	♘c3	d5

As indicated above, 3 ... ♘f6 is more promising.

4	♗f4

There are also two rather dubious gambit continuations:

(a) 4 g4?! fg 5 e4 de 6 ♕xg4 (or 6 ♘xe4 ♗b4+ 7 ♘c3 ♘f6) 6 ... ♘f6 7 ♕g3 ♘c6∓ Shainswit–Breitman, Tbilisi 1961.

(b) 4 cd ed 5 e4 de (5 ... fe?? 6 ♕h5+) 6 ♗c4 ♘f6 7 ♘ge2 ♗d6 8 ♗f4 ♘c6 9 0-0 and although White has some compensation for the pawn it should not be too difficult for Black to improve on Shersher–Natapov, Moscow 1955, which saw 9 ... ♗xf4 10 ♘xf4 ♘d4 11 ♘cd5 ♘xd5 12 ♘xd5 ♘e6 13 ♕b3 and Black is in danger due to his inability to complete his development and get his king into safety.

4	...	♘f6
5	e3	c6
6	♘f3	*(125)*

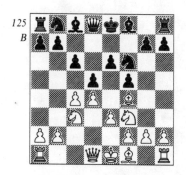

125
B

There is little point for White in deviating from this promising natural development, e.g. 6 ♗d3 ♗e7 7 ♘ge2 0-0 8 h3 (White's plan is to castle queenside and open lines on the other wing by g2–g4) 8 ... ♘e4 9 ♕c2 ♘d7 10 f3 ♘xc3 11 ♘xc3 ♘f6 12 0-0-0 dc (a typical procedure; Black abandons the centre in order to gain time for a pawn storm on the flank) 13 ♗xc4 b5 14 ♗d3 a5 with a double-edged position; Polugayevsky–Ufimtsev, Moscow 1955.

6	...	♗d6

A fundamental positional error. In this position Black gets nothing whatsoever in return for the further weakening of his already sensitive dark squares in contrast to the fianchetto variations where White either has to accept a weakening of his king's position (from the capture sequence ... ♗xf4, gxf4), or loss of time (the Botvinnik ♗a3 variations).

It is, however, difficult for Black to equalize completely even after the correct 6 ... ♗e7, e.g. 7 ♗d3 0-0 8 0-0 (8 ♘e5 helps Black simplify: 8 ... ♘bd7 9 0-0 ♘xe5 10 ♗xe5 ♘g4! 11 ♗f4 g5 12 ♗g3 ♗d6 13 ♗xd6 ♕xd6 14 g3 e5 and Black's opening worries are past; Timman–P. Nikolic, Niksic 1983) 8 ... ♘e4 (that White can gain an advantage by force against this natural move is strong testimony to the inadequacy of this particular Stonewall position; note that the equally normal 8 ... ♘bd7 is also unplayable on account of 9 cd forcing 9 ... cd because of the undefended f-pawn) 9 ♗xe4! de (9 ... fe 10 ♘e5 ♘d7 11 f3 ef 12 ♖xf3 ♗f6 13 e4 is no improvement) 10 ♘e5 ♘d7 (a pawn hunt of the bishop fails tactically: 10 ... g5 11 ♗g3 f4? 12 ef gf 13 ♛g4+ etc. or 10 ... ♚h8 11 f3! g5 12 ♗g3 f4 13 fe! fg 14 ♛h5! and Black cannot survive) 11 f3 ♘xe5 12 ♗xe5 ef 13 ♛xf3 with complete control.

7	♗d3	♛c7
8	g3!	

The question of how the black-squared bishops disappear is a vitally important one; if Black can be forced to capture on f4 then White will recapture with the e-pawn and enjoy pressure against e6 and total domination of e5.

8	...	0-0
9	0-0	♘e4
10	♛b3	

Threatening to take twice on e4 after 11 cd ed (11 ... cd?? 12 ♘b5).

10	...	♚h8
11	♖ac1	♗xf4

Understandable given the various threats generated by the *vis-à-vis* of rook and queen on the c-file, but really anything is preferable to the self-imposed lifelong

structural inferiority brought on by this move.

12	ef	♛f7
13	♘e5	♛e7
14	♗xe4!	

Excellent technique; White liquidates his doubled pawns and enhances his prospects of obtaining a good knight versus bad bishop situation.

14	...	fe
15	f3	ef
16	♖ce1	♛c7
17	♛a3!	

The dark square domination begins; normal development by 17 ... ♘d7 is ruled out because of 18 ♛e7.

17	...	♚g8
18	♖xf3	♘a6
19	b3	♛d8
20	c5	

White has no objections to parrying the indirect threat to his d-pawn by this space-gaining advance.

20	...	♘c7
21	♛b2	♗d7
22	♛c2	♛e7
23	♖ef1	♖ae8
24	g4	♗c8
25	♖h3	

Forcing a further, and ultimately fatal, weakening of the black squares.

25	...	g6
26	b4	

Holding the centre in a vice-like

grip White is free to expand on
the flanks in preparation for a
breakthrough on either side
according to the disposition of
Black's defences.

26	...	♕f6
27	♖hf3	♖e7
28	a4	a6
29	♘d1	

A regrouping to cover f5 and
facilitate immediate occupation of
the weak black squares to be fixed
by g5.

29	...	♖g7
30	♘e3	♕e7
31	g5	♗d7
32	♘3g4	♗e8

Black's wretched position is
utterly passive, like some helpless
creature encoiled by a python and
gradually being squeezed to death.

33	♘h6+	♔h8
34	♕e2	♕d8
35	♘5g4	♗d7
36	♕e5	♘e8
37	♖h3	♕c7

37 ... ♕e7 38 ♕b8 would be an
embarrassing way for the queenside to drop off.

38   ♘f6 *(126)*

The culmination of the first part
of White's strategy, with his pieces
optimally entrenched on the weak
black squares.

| 38 | ... | ♕xe5 |

Forced; 38 ... ♕d8 39 ♘xh7
would win immediately.

| 39 | fe | ♖e7 |

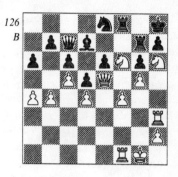

| 40 | ♖hf3 | ♘xf6 |

Again, there is no option
because of the threat to penetrate
to the eighth with mate.

41	♖xf6	♖xf6
42	ef	♖e8
43	♘f7+	♔g8
44	♘e5	

Having acquired a protected
passed pawn on the sixth as a
result of his middlegame pressure,
Schlechter appropriately begins
the final phase with a thematic
re-occupation of e5.

44	...	♖d8
45	♔g2	♔f8
46	h4	♗e8
47	♔f3	♗f7
48	♔f4	

Of course, the king is brought
up as far as possible before commencing the final breakthrough.

| 48 | ... | ♔e8 |
| 49 | ♖b1 | ♔f8 |

Black's helplessness is truly
pitiful.

| 50 | b5 | |

Black resigns. After 50 ... ab 51 ab ♗e8 52 bc ♗xc6 53 ♘xc6 bc 54 ♔e5 White would finally reap material rewards for his masterly display of sustained strategic domination.

Karpov–Spassky
Candidates match 1974

| 1 | d4 | d5 |

The variations with e3 frequently arise via transposition.

| 2 | c4 |

Although White generally develops the QN on c3, as in our featured games and variations, this is not obligatory as the following examples show: 2 ♘f3 c6 3 c4 e6 4 e3 f5 and now:

(a) 5 ♗e2 ♘f6 6 0-0 ♗d6 7 b3 ♕e7 8 ♗b2 ♘bd7 9 ♘e5 0-0 10 ♘d2 g5?! (a risky attempt to complicate; 10 ... ♘e4 11 f3 ♘xd2 12 ♕xd2 ♘xe5 13 de ♗c5 is the solid way to equalize) 11 f4 gf?! (11 ... ♕g7 or 11 ... ♘e4 immediately are both better) 12 ef ♘e4 13 ♘xe4 fe?! (13 ... de was relatively best) 14 ♕d2 ♘f6 15 c5 ♗c7 16 b4 ♗d7 17 a4 ♘e8 (17 ... ♔h8) 18 ♖a3! and White stands better over the entire board; Speelman–Seirawan, candidates match, Saint John 1988.

(b) 5 ♗d3 ♘f6 6 0-0 ♗d6 7 b3 ♕e7 8 a4 0-0 9 ♗a3 ♗xa3 10 ♘xa3 ♘e4 (10 ... ♗d7!? intending

the transfer to h5 via e8 comes strongly into consideration) 11 ♘c2 ♘d7 12 ♕e1 a5 13 ♘d2 b6 14 f3 ♘xd2 15 ♕xd2 ♘f6 16 ♖fd1 ♗a6 with just a tiny edge to White; Korchnoi–Yusupov, Montpellier 1985.

2	...	e6
3	♘c3	c6
4	e3	f5 *(127)*

127
W

| 5 | f4 |

The so-called Double Stonewall in which White creates a fixed, balanced pawn structure in the centre and on the kingside in the hope of being able to make something of his more active c-pawn placement. Practice indicates that Black should have little difficulty in holding the balance.

Nor do other moves hold out much hope for White of achieving an opening advantage, e.g.:

(a) 5 ♘h3 ♘f6 6 ♗d2 ♗d6 7 ♕c2 0-0 8 0-0-0 ♕e7 9 f3 dc 10 e4 fe 11 ♘xe4?! (11 fe is better but also entirely satisfactory for Black after 11 … e5 12 ♗xc4+ ♔h8) 11 … b5 12 ♘xd6 ♕xd6 13 f4 ♘a6 14 ♗e2 c5 and White is in trouble; Bronstein–Botvinnik, World Ch. 1951.

(b) 5 ♗d3 ♘f6 6 ♕c2 ♗e7 7 ♘ge2 0-0 8 f3 ♔h8 9 ♗d2 ♘a6 10 a3 ♘c7 with approximately equal chances as Black is well placed to initiate a pawn storm on the queenside in case White castles there; Burger–Saidy, US Ch. 1965/66.

(c) 5 ♘f3 ♘f6 (the more experimental 5 … ♗d6 6 ♗d3 ♕f6 also comes into consideration as shown by Osnos–Novotelnov, Leningrad 1956, which went 7 b3 ♘e7 8 ♗b2 ♘d7 9 ♕c2 0-0 10 h3 and now, instead of 10 … ♔h8?! as played, 10 … dc 11 ♗xc4 b5 with … e5 to follow would have whipped up promising counter-play) 6 ♗d3 ♗d6 (more active than 6 … ♗e7 while 6 … ♘e4?! invites the sharp retort 7 g4!) 7 b3 0-0 8 ♗b2 ♘e4 9 ♕c2 ♘d7 10 0-0-0 (10 0-0 ♖f6 would be very risky; cf. Maroczy–Tartakower, p. 99) 10 … a5 11 h3 with a sharp battle of opposite wing attacks to come. The game Zak–Holmov, semi-final USSR Ch. 1951, showed that White cannot save a tempo by 11 g4?! because of 11 … ♘xc3! 12 ♗xc3 fg 13 ♘e5 (13 ♗xh7+ ♔h8 14 ♘e5 ♘xe5 15 de ♗a3+ 16 ♔b1 ♕h4 and the f-pawn falls)

13 … ♘xe5 14 de ♗a3+ 15 ♔b1 ♕h4 with advantage.

5	…	♘f6
6	♘f3	♗e7
7	♗e2	0-0
8	0-0	♘e4
9	♕c2	

9 ♘e5 achieved nothing in Tukmakov–Lerner, Cheliabinsk 1980: 9 … ♘d7 10 ♘xe4 fe (10 … de?! 11 g4 brings unpleasant tension to Black's centre) 11 ♘xd7 ♗xd7 12 ♗d2 a5 13 ♖c1 b6 14 ♗g4 ♗d6 Black's queenside counterplay is under way.

| 9 | … | ♘d7 |
| 10 | b3 | (128) |

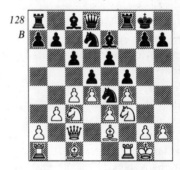

128
B

10 … ♘xc3?!

It certainly looks misguided to exchange the stallion on e4 for the colt on c3. Both 10 … ♖f6 11 a4 b6 (Botvinnik) and 10 … ♘df6 11 ♘e5 ♗d7 intending … ♗e8–h5 (Kotov) are acceptable.

11	♕xc3	♘f6
12	♘e5	♗d7
13	a4	♘e4?!

Seeking the exchange of light-squared bishops by 13 ... ♗e8 14 ♗a3 ♗h5 is a more sensible procedure.

14   ♕d3   ♗f6?!

Yet another inaccuracy which allows White to improve his position; 14 ... ♗e8 was still preferable.

15   ♗a3   ♖e8
16   ♗h5!

Compelling Black to weaken his pawns.

16   ...   g6
17   ♗f3   ♗xe5

Given that Black's game is rapidly going downhill anyway, this otherwise crazy concession of the black squares at least has the merit of gaining the necessary tempo to prevent White opening lines by g2–g4.

18   de!   h5
19   ♗xe4!

Correctly eliminating Black's only good piece. Despite the remaining bishops being of opposite colour, White retains a vast positional advantage due to the superior activity of his position in general and his bishop in particular.

19   ...   fe

Opening a file for the white rooks would be suicidal.

20   ♕d2   ♔f7
21   a5   ♖h8

To try and discourage line-opening on the kingside.

22   ♗d6   ♖h7
23   ♕b4   ♗c8

The qualitative difference between the bishops could not be greater.

24   ♖a2   ♔g8
25   h3   a6

25 ... h4 would enable White to open the g-file with deadly effect.

26   g3   ♗d7!

This offer of a pawn in order to bring the QR into play is Black's best chance.

27   ♕xb7   ♗e8
28   ♕b4   ♖aa7
29   ♖g2   ♖ab7
30   ♕c3   ♖bf7
31   ♗c5   g5

Spassky is doing his best to complicate matters.

32   ♗b6?

An inaccuracy which keeps Black's hopes alive. This was the right moment to play 32 cd! obliging Black to recapture with the c-pawn (32 ... ed? 33 f5! is crushing) thus opening a route of invasion for White's heavy pieces.

32   ...   ♕d7
33   cd   ed

Now Black has f5 under control and this means that White must permit the opening of the h-file in order to make progress.

34   g4   hg
35   hg   gf
36   ef   ♖h4

37	f5	♖fh7
38	e6	♛d6
39	♛g3?	

In mutual time-trouble Karpov chooses the wrong method of parrying the threatened ... ♖h1+ and ... ♛f4+. 39 ♛e3! makes a crucial check on g5 available, e.g. 39 ... ♖h1+ 40 ♔f2 ♖1h3 41 ♛g5+ ♖g7 42 ♛d8! and Black's resources are practically exhausted.

39	...	♖h1+
40	♔f2	♛b4!
41	♛e3	

Here the game was adjourned and analysis established that White should accept the repetition 41 ... ♖1h3 42 ♖g3 ♖h2+ 43 ♖g2 ♖2h3 44 ♖g3 etc. since 42 ♛g5+ ♖g7 43 ♛d8 c5! gives a counterattack at least sufficient to draw. Thus, draw agreed.

Standard Stonewall

The standard Stonewall begins from the following diagrammed position:

1	d4	f5
2	g3	♘f6
3	♗g2	e6
4	♘f3	♗e7
5	0-0	0-0
6	c4	d5

We shall examine White's three major schemes of development in turn:

Petrosian's 7 ♘bd2

Botvinnik's 7 b3

the Classical 7 ♘c3

Petrosian's 7 ♘bd2

Benko–Guimard

Buenos Aires 1960

1 d4 f5 2 c4 e6 3 g3 ♘f6 4 ♗g2 ♗e7 5 ♘f3 0-0 6 0-0 d5

7 ♘bd2 *(129)*

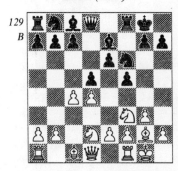

129
B

Introduced and popularized by Petrosian, this flexible variation generally aims to cover e5 by means of the manoeuvre ♘f3–e5–d3 and ♘d2–f3. The knight on d3 is also handy for supporting a space-gaining march by the b-pawn. Black needs to find the right balance between disputing control of e5 (by ... ♘b8–d7, ... ♘f6–e4–d6–f7, and ... ♗e7–f6) and pursuing the traditional kingside attack.

Other seventh moves to note:

(a) 7 cd (this premature release of the central tension improves Black's pawn structure and increases the range of his QB) 7 ... ed 8 ♘c3 c6 9 ♖b1 ♕e8 (9 ... a5!?) 10 ♗f4 ♘bd7 11 b4 a6 12 ♕b3 ♔h8 13 ♘a4 ♘e4 14 ♘c5 ♗f6 15 ♕c2 ♖g8 16 ♘xd7 ♗xd7 17 ♘e5 g5 18 ♗c1 ♘d6 and Black has successfully impeded White's minority attack whilst preparing a kingside attack; Panov–Chistiakov, Moscow Ch. 1938.

(b) 7 ♕c2 (a very flexible move which will normally transpose to the major lines) 7 ... c6 (the experimental 7 ... ♘c6 failed to impress in Lengyel–Spassky, Moscow 1971, which saw 8 a3 a5 9 b3 ♗d7 10 ♘c3 ♗e8 11 cd ♘xd5 12 ♗b2 ♗h5 13 ♘a4 ♕e8 14 ♘c5 ♗xc5 15 dc ♕e7 and now, instead of 16 ♘e5? f4!∓, 16 e4!± would have highlighted the deficiencies of Black's position) 8 ♗f4 ♕e8 (8 ... ♗d7 9 ♘bd2 ♗e8 also comes into consideration) 9 ♘bd2 ♕h5 10 ♖ae1 ♘bd7 11 ♘g5?! (an interesting idea which does not quite come off) 11 ... ♘g4 12 h4 ♕g6 13 f3 e5! with massive complications not unfavourable to Black; Sokolov–Berkovich, USSR 1973.

7   ...   c6

7 ... b6 intending to contest the centre by ... c7–c5 is a totally different plan providing much food for thought, e.g. 8 b3 c5 9 ♗b2 (the black pawns would be full of dynamism after 9 cd ed 10 dc bc) 9 ... ♗b7 10 ♖c1 ♘c6!

(improving on the seminal ... b6 game, Petrosian–Tolush, USSR Ch. 1958, where Black went wrong with 10 ... ♘a6? 11 ♘e5 ♕e8 12 e3 ♖d8 13 ♕e2 ♗d6 14 ♘df3 ♘e4 15 ♘d3 ♕h5 16 ♖fe1±) 11 e3 ♖c8 12 ♕e2 ♘e4 13 ♖fd1 ♕e8 14 dc (14 cd ed 15 ♘e5 has been recommended as a better try) 14 ... bc 15 ♘e5 ♘xe5 16 ♗xe5 ♗f6 17 ♘f3 ♕e7 18 ♕b2 ♖fd8 with healthy prospects; Grefe–R. Byrne, US Ch. 1977.

7 ... ♘c6 has a better chance of being playable here than after 7 ♕c2 (see above), e.g. 8 e3 ♘e4 9 a3 a5! and having prevented the opponent's queenside expansion Black can turn to continuing his development by ... ♗d7–e8.

8   ♕c2   ♕e8 *(130)*

130
W

In addition to this normal move, and 8 ... b6 which was played in the next game, Black has a noteworthy alternative in the multi-purpose prophylactic 8 ... a5!?, e.g. 9 ♘e5 ♘bd7 10 ♘d3 (after 10 ♘df3 Black exchanged his way to equality in Malich–Mariotti, Skopje Ol. 1972, by 10 ... ♘xe5 11 ♘xe5 ♘d7 12 ♗f4 ♘xe5 13 ♗xe5 ♗d6) 10 ... ♘e4 11 ♘f3 ♘d6 12 b3 ♘f7! 13 ♗b2 ♕e8 14 e3 ♔h8 15 ♘fe5 ♘fxe5 16 de b6 17 f3 ♘c5 18 ♘f4 ♗a6 with a fine game; Spassov–Bellin, Albena 1979.

9 ♘e5   ♘bd7

It would be a grave error to ignore the centre and stake everything on a kingside assault, as this first of two instructive examples clearly shows: 9 ... ♕h5 (premature) 10 ♘df3 ♘e4 11 ♘d3 g5 12 ♘fe5 ♘d7 13 f3 ♘d6 14 b3 ♖f6 15 h3 ♘f7 16 ♗b2 ♘dxe5 17 de ♖h6 18 ♖ae1 f4 19 g4 ♕g6 20 ♕c3 ♖h4 21 e3 and by opening the centre White exposes the lack of coordination in the black camp; Doda–Scheparets, Prague 1956.

10 ♘d3

It is generally in the interests of the player with more space to avoid exchanges.

10 ...   ♔h8

The second warning against intemperate attacking: 10 ... g5 11 ♘f3 ♘e4 (Flohr's 11 ... h6 is better) 12 b4! ♕h5 13 ♖b1 ♖f6 14 b5 f4 (14 ... ♖h6 15 h3 brings Black to a grinding halt) 15 gf g4 16 ♘fe5 ♖h6 17 h3 gh 18 ♗f3 h2+ 19 ♔h1 ♕h3 20 ♗e3 and again Black's initiative has dried up leav-

ing White in complete control; Szabo–Duckstein, Bamberg 1968.

10 ... ♘e4 is quite acceptable, however, with a likely return to the column after 11 ♘f3 ♔h8.

11 ♘f3

It is nearly always mistaken for Black to exchange his Stonewall knight for no reason as happened in Petrosian–Cardoso, Leipzig Ol. 1960: 11 b3 ♘xd2?! 12 ♗xd2 ♔h8 13 e3 ♗d6 14 cd ed 15 ♗b4 and with the exchange of black-squared bishops White's queenside minority attack is ready to roll with effect.

11 ...   ♘e4
12 ♖b1   ♘d6

12 ... a5 first comes into consideration.

13 c5   ♘f7
14 ♗f4

Bringing the bishop into play clearly has its attractions but the disadvantage is that Black can attack it with gain of tempo. 14 b4 would be consistent.

14 ...   ♗f6
15 ♕c3

Keeping control of e5.

15 ...   g5
16 ♗c7 (131)

A fertile and mutually difficult middlegame awaits the players. The present game unfolded as follows: 16 ... ♖g8 (16 ... ♕e7 has its points) 17 ♘fe5 ♘dxe5 18 de ♗g7 19 ♕d4? (this innocent cen-

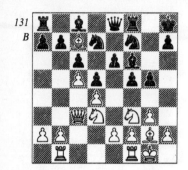

131
B

tralization turns out to be a serious error which Black punishes with great energy and accuracy) 19 ... ♛d7 20 ♝a5 (20 ♝d6? ♞xd6 21 cd ♛xd6!, exploiting White's undefended queen, shows the tactical inadequacy of his nineteenth move) 20 ... b6! 21 cb ab 22 ♝xb6 ♝a6! (capturing on a2 would be premature because of ♖a1 seizing the file, but now that becomes an auxiliary threat to the undermining of the e-pawn) 23 ♞c5 ♛c8 24 f4 gf 25 gf ♝xe2 26 ♖f2 ♝h5 (the QB arrives at its traditional outpost via an unconventional route) 27 a4 (this passed pawn is now White's main asset) 27 ... ♞d6! 28 a5 ♞e4 29 ♞xe4 fe 30 b4 ♝h6 31 f5? (inappropriate aggression based on a flawed conception; 31 ♔h1 was necessary) 31 ... ef 32 e6+ ♝g7 33 ♖xf5 ♝f3! (avoiding the messy complications of capturing the queen in favour of placing yet another threat over White's head) 34 ♖g5 ♛xe6 35

♝xf3 ♝f6! 36 ♖xg8+ ♖xg8 37 ♝g2 ♖xg2+! 38 ♔xg2 ♛g4+ 39 ♔h1 ♛f3+ 40 ♔g1 ♛g4+ 41 ♔h1 ♛f3+ 42 ♔g1 ♝xd4+ 43 ♝xd4+ ♔g8 (the smoke has cleared leaving Black's queen dominating the insecure pieces) 44 ♖e1 ♛d3 45 ♝c5 ♔f7 46 ♖a1 e3 47 a6 ♛g6+! 48 ♔h1 ♛f6 0–1. Material loss is unavoidable, e.g. 49 ♖c1 e2 (threatening 50 ... ♛f1+) 50 ♔g2 ♛g5+.

Portisch–Radulov
Budapest 1969
1 d4 f5 2 g3 ♞f6 3 ♝g2 e6 4 ♞f3 ♝e7 5 0-0 0-0 6 c4

6   ...   c6 (*132*)

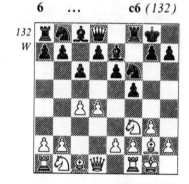

132
W

An important nuance of move order which is mainly aimed at avoiding the trade of black-squared bishops which occurs in Botvinnik's Variation (6 ... d5) 7 b3 etc. The deferring of structural commitment is a generally useful concept which arises quite regularly in the Dutch (cf. Alekhine's

Variation), and this particular application is probably the most successful. Attempts to take advantage of this move order have so far been unconvincing:

(a) 7 c5 b6 8 cb ab (8 ... ♕xb6 also comes into consideration) 9 ♘c3 ♗b7!? intending ... c5 and protecting c6 in readiness to eject a ♘e5 by ... d6 looks promising for Black, and 9 ... ♘a6 aiming to place the QN on d5 via b4 or c7 also seems playable.

(b) 7 b3 a5! 8 ♗a3 (Black is very active on the queenside after 8 c5 b6 9 cb ♕xb6) 8 ... ♗xa3! 9 ♘xa3 ♕e7 10 ♕c1 (10 c5?! b6! is good for Black) 10 ... d6 (the advantage of restraining the d-pawn now becomes apparent) 11 ♕b2 ♘bd7 12 ♘c2 e5 and Black's opening has been a complete success: Kelecevic–Bellin, Eerbeek 1978.

(c) After 7 ♘c3 or 7 ♘bd2 Black may transpose to the Stonewall having circumvented Botvinnik's simplification.

7 ♕c2

This keeps the strategic guessing game going.

7 ... b6

This is playable, but 7 ... a5 is a more resolute continuation, intending to answer 8 b3 by 8 ... ♘a6 with all sorts of intriguing possibilities to come.

8 ♘bd2 d5

Of course, e2–e4 must be prevented.

9 ♘e5 ♗b7
10 ♘d3

The knight is extremely well placed here, looking at both flanks as well as the centre.

10 ... ♘bd7

Declaring himself ready to answer 11 ♘f4 with 11 ... ♔f7, but 10 ... ♗d6 may be preferable.

11 b4

Beginning an energetic pawn advance on the queenside which gains useful space and leads to the opening of a file for the rooks.

11 ... ♖e8

This seems superfluous and should be replaced by an immediate 11 ... ♗d6.

12 a4 ♗d6
13 ♘f3 ♘e4
14 c5 bc

Avoidance of this exchange would entail living with the constant threat of b4–b5.

15 bc ♗c7
16 ♗f4

The now familiar formula of removing Black's best bishop.

16 ... ♗xf4
17 gf!

This effectively puts the centre under lock and key while White furthers his queenside initiative.

17 ... ♕c7
18 ♘fe5 ♘ef6

Not relishing being left with a

bad bishop against a good knight as was on the cards.

| 19 | ♖fb1 | a5?! |

It is understandable that Black should want to activate his bishop but this preparatory move (19 ... ♗a6? 20 ♘b4) seriously weakens b6 and also presents the a-pawn as a target. The best chance was 19 ... ♖eb8 hoping to exchange some pieces and hang on.

| 20 | ♘xd7! |

Portisch instantly sets about removing the defenders of b6.

20	...	♘xd7
21	♘e5	♘xe5
22	fe	♖eb8
23	♖b6	♗a6
24	♖ab1	♖b7
25	♕d2!

Forcing Black into an unpleasant exchange.

| 25 | ... | ♖xb6 |
| 26 | cb! |

The introduction to a decisive infiltration manoeuvre.

| 26 | ... | ♕b7 |
| 27 | ♕xa5 | ♗b5 |

27 ... ♗xe2? would permit an amusing conclusion: 28 ♕xa8+! ♕xa8 29 b7 ♕b8 30 ♗f1! followed by the victorious march of the a-pawn.

| 28 | ♕b4 | ♖xa4 |

28 ... ♗xa4 would lose in more predictable fashion: 29 ♖a1 ♗b5 30 ♖xa8+ ♕xa8 31 ♕e7! ♕a1+ 32 ♗f1 h6 33 b7 ♗xe2 34 ♕xe6+

♔h7 35 ♕xf5+ g6 36 ♕f7+ and mate next move.

| 29 | ♕d6 | ♔f7 (133) |

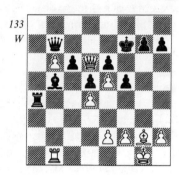

133
W

| 30 | e4!! |

A stunning and very instructive breakthrough. Despite the paucity of pieces, Portisch mounts a ferocious and irresistible assault on the black king.

| 30 | ... | ♕xb6 |

30 ... fe? 31 ♗h3 is instantly decisive, but the most beautiful variation would have occurred after 30 ... de, *viz.* 31 d5! ed 32 ♗h3! g6 33 ♕f6+ ♔g8 34 ♗xf5!! gf 35 ♔h1 ♗e2 36 ♖g1+ ♗g4 37 ♕xf5 etc. The sweep of the attack from the queen's flank through the centre to the kingside is remarkable. After the text move everything is simple and the game ended: 31 ef ♕a7 (31 ... ef 32 e6+ ♔f6 33 e7+ ♔f7 34 ♕d8±±) 32 ♕xe6+ ♔f8 33 ♗xd5 cd 34 ♖xb5 ♖xd4 35 ♕c8+ 1-0.

Botvinnik's 7 b3
Kasparov–T. Petrosian
Niksic 1983
**1 d4 f5 2 g3 e6 3 ♗g2 ♘f6 4 ♘f3
♗e7 5 0-0 0-0 6 c4 d5**

7   b3 *(134)*

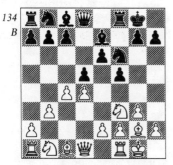

Given Black's general dark square debility in the Stonewall, the primary positional logic behind the intention to exchange black squared bishops by ♗a3 is clearly impeccable. Interestingly though, it turns out that the immediate implementation of this strategically desirable goal detracts from its strength (another vindication of Nimzowitsch's dictum that the threat is stronger than the execution). There is no great mystery here: basically, it is simply that the early exchange simplifies Black's defensive task both conceptually, by removing strategic complexity, and physically, by giving him more space to work in.

Nowadays, therefore, Botvin-

nik's variation is rarely seen in its pure form, and 7 b3 tends to be employed for its general usefulness and concomitant flexibility, waiting to see Black's reaction, and usually transposing elsewhere as it is a common denominator in both ♘bd2 and ♘c3 variations.

7   ...   c6

With this standard response Black declares himself unafraid of the threatened exchange. Alternatively, two contrasting methods of avoiding simplification and promoting strategic complexity are also available:

(a) 7 ... ♘c6 8 ♗b2 (Black can answer 8 ♗a3 by either 8 ... ♗xa3 9 ♘xa3 ♕e7 or 8 ... ♘b4!?, but it could be that the as yet untested 8 ... ♘e4 is even more attractive) 8 ... ♗d7 (8 ... ♘e4 is also worth attention, e.g. 9 ♘c3 ♗f6 10 e3 ♘e7 11 ♕e2 ♗d7 12 ♘e5 ♗xe5 13 de ♗c6 14 ♖fd1 and although White has an edge earlier improvements for Black could well exist; A. Mikhalchishin–Eingorn, USSR Ch. 1985) 9 ♘c3 (Schmidt–Spassky, Buenos Aires Ol. 1978, went 9 ♘e5 ♗e8 10 ♘d3 ♗f7 11 ♘d2 a5 with a. rich middlegame in prospect) 9 ... ♗e8 10 ♘g5 ♗f7 11 e3 ♕d7 12 ♘xf7 ♖xf7 13 ♘a4 b6 14 ♖c1 ♗f8!? (White obtained an unpleasant central spatial superiority after 14 ... ♘d8 15 ♘c3 ♖f8

16 f3 ♘f7 17 e4 in Polugayevsky–Spassky, Tilburg 1983) 15 ♕c2 ♘b4 16 ♕b1 ♘e4 17 ♖fd1 ♖d8 18 a3 ♘c6 19 ♘c3 ♘f6! 20 b4 ♘e7 21 ♕a2 g5 22 a4 ♗h6 and both sides have their chances and problems in a difficult opposite wing attack situation; Law–Bellin, Commonwealth Ch. 1985.

(b) 7 ... b6 8 ♗b2 ♗b7 9 ♘bd2 c5 (contesting the centre with pawns rather than pieces as in the previous example) 10 e3 ♘c6 11 ♕e2 ♖c8 12 ♖ac1 ♘e4 13 ♖fd1 ♕e8 (White will not find it easy to gain an advantage from this complex position; his pieces are generally well placed but he lacks a strong central outpost corresponding to Black's on e4) 14 dc bc 15 ♘e5 ♘xe5 16 ♗xe5 ♗f6 17 ♘f3 ♕e7 18 ♕b2 ♖fd8 19 cd?! ♖xd5 20 ♗xf6 ♕xf6 21 ♕xf6 gf 22 ♖xd5 ♗xd5 and Black stands somewhat better as his pieces are working in concert on the important queen's flank; Grefe–Byrne, US Ch. 1977 (also cited on p. 158; note the transpositional possibility).

8   ♕c2

Not surprisingly, Kasparov rejects simplification in favour of maintaining maximum flexibility. It should be noted that the white queen is usually best placed on c2 from where, amongst other things, it keeps an eye on Black's f-pawn in the hope of being able to induce a favourable cd cd exchange.

Black has tried various methods of reacting to 8 ♗a3 but the following two lines are probably the most satisfactory:

(a) 8 ... ♘bd7 9 ♕c1 (or 9 ♗xe7 ♕xe7 10 ♕c2 ♘e4 11 ♘c3 ♘d6 12 ♘a4 b6 13 cd cd 14 ♖fc1 ♗a6 15 ♕b2 ♖fc8 16 e3 ♕d8=; an example of when the opening of the c-file does not favour White as Black can easily contest its control; Gligoric–Mariotti, Nice Ol. 1974) 9 ... ♘e4 10 ♘bd2 (or 10 ♗xe7 ♕xe7 11 e3 b6=) 10 ... ♗xa3 11 ♕xa3 b6 12 ♖ac1 ♗b7 13 ♖fd1 ♕f6 14 cd ed and Black's strong central position and potential kingside play balance out White's queenside pressure; Szabo–Botvinnik, Budapest 1952.

(b) 8 ... ♗d7 (very solid) 9 ♕c1 (9 ♗xe7 ♕xe7 10 ♕d3 ♗e8 11 ♘bd2 ♘e4 12 ♘e5 ♘xd2 13 ♕xd2 ♘d7 14 ♘d3 ♗h5 15 ♕e3 ♖ae8 gave Black very sound equality in Antunac–Smederevac, Wijk aan Zee II 1970; similarly, 10 ♘bd2 here would gain no advantage after 10 ... ♗e8 11 ♘e5 ♘bd7 12 ♘df3 ♖d8) 9 ... ♗e8 10 ♘g5 (in Uhlmann–Guimard, Buenos Aires 1960, Black obtained the advantage by tactical means, beginning with a typical double attack on White's d- and c-pawns, after 10 ♘c3 ♘bd7 11 ♘g5 ♗f7

12 f3? ♗xa3 13 ♕xa3 dc! 14 bc
♘b6 15 ♕c5 ♘fd7 16 ♘xf7 ♕f6!;
simplification by 10 ♗xe7 ♕xe7
11 ♕a3 ♕xa3 12 ♘xa3 as in
Salov–Short, Barcelona World
Cup 1989, gives White nothing
after 12 ... ♗h5 13 ♖fe1 ♘bd7)
10 ... ♗f7 11 ♘d2 ♘bd7 12 ♘xf7
♖xf7 13 ♗xe7 ♕xe7 14 ♕c3 (thus
far Reshevsky–Gligoric, match
1952) and now 14 ... ♖e8! to prime
a possible advance of the e-pawn,
gives Black completely satisfactory play.

It should be noted that 8 ...
♗xa3 9 ♘xa3 does not leave the
knight offside as might appear to
be the case at first sight, but in
fact helps it on the way to controlling e5 via ♘a3–c2–e1–d3.

8 ... ♗d7 *(135)*

135
W

This move, by which the QB
prepares to thread its way through
to an active position on the kingside, was awarded an exclamation
mark by Kasparov in his notes to
the game.

9 ♗b2

The consistent continuation.
Alternatives look unlikely to
unsettle Black:

(a) 9 ♘e5 ♗e8 10 ♗a3 ♗xa3
11 ♘xa3 ♘bd7 12 ♘d3 g5 with a
typically balanced position; Gerusel–Troger, West Germany 1968.

(b) 9 ♗a3 ♗xa3 10 ♘xa3 ♕e7
11 ♕b2 ♗e8 12 ♘e5 (12 ♘c2 ♗h5
would oblige White to counter the
x-raying of e2) 12 ... g5 13 ♘c2
(P. Nikolic notes 13 f3 ♘bd7 14
e4 fe 15 ♘xd7 ♗xd7 16 fe ♘xe4
as slightly in Black's favour) 13
... ♘bd7 14 cd (this is a further
example of simplification easing
Black's defensive task) 14 ... ed
15 f4 (revealing White's idea–to
solidify the centre and eventually
proceed with a minority attack
on the queenside) 15 ... ♘g4!?
(preferring to maintain the tension
rather than clarify matters by a
line like 15 ... gf 16 gf ♘e4) 16
♕c3 a5 17 ♖ae1 (threatening 18
♘xg4 fg 19 e4) 17 ... gf 18 gf ♘df6
19 ♕h3 ♔h8 20 ♕h4 ♘g8 21 ♕g3
(exchanging queens would give
Black somewhat the better ending)
21 ... ♘8f6 (21 ... h5 would be
one way of playing on) 22 ♕h4 (it
would be an error to weaken the
kingside: 22 h3? ♘h5 23 ♕f3 ♘h6
and Black can follow up with ...
♖g8 and ... ♕h4) 22 ... ♘g8
23 ♕g3 ♘8f6 ½–½, T. Petrosian–P.
Nikolic, Plovdiv 1983.

9   ...   ♗e8
10   ♘e5

The right moment to reposition the knight in order to better control the dark squares and prepare to threaten e4. 10 cd cd would be a mistake not only on account of the exposed position of the queen on the c-file but also because Black would be able to profit from the option of developing his QN on c6.

10   ...   ♘bd7
11   ♘d3

Of course, White has no interest in exchanging this valuable piece.

11   ...   ♗h5 *(136)*

Completing the manoeuvre begun on the eighth move.

12   ♘c3

A natural enough move but Kasparov subsequently thought he ought to have preferred 12 ♘f4 ♗f7 13 ♘d2 intending ♘f3, and claimed a slight edge for White.

12   ...   ♗d6

A typical move to increase the

bishop's scope and improve the cover of e5.

13   f3

This has the positive effect of making e4 a constant threat but markedly deadens the KB.

13   ...   ♗g6!

Not only directly discouraging e2-e4 but also lining up 14 ♖ae1?! f4! ∓.

14   e3   ♖c8
15   ♕e2

The queen is understandably uncomfortable with the double x-raying of c2.

15   ...   ♖e8

And this opposition of rook and queen serves to prevent 16 e4 which would run into problems after 16 ... e5! The immediate 15 ... e5?! would be premature, allowing White to settle down to quiet exploitation of the dark square weaknesses in Black's camp following 16 cd ed (16 ... cd? 17 ♘b5) 17 ed cd 18 ♕d2.

16   ♕f2   a6

Once again activating the possibility of playing ... e5.

17   ♖ac1   ♕e7

Having protected c3, White could meet 17 ... e5?! by 18 cd cd 19 de ♘xe5 20 ♘xe5 ♗xe5 21 f4 with some advantage according to Kasparov.

18   ♖fe1   ♕f8

As with White's fifteenth, Black provokes and then side-steps a queen–rook opposition.

19   ℤcd1 *(137)*

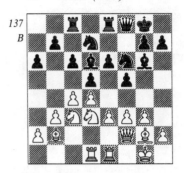

Kasparov points out that the opening of the position by 19 e4?! de 20 fe e5! would be slightly to Black's advantage.

19   ...   dc

After a phase of sophisticated strategic fencing, reflecting credit on both antagonists, it is clear that the tension could not be maintained much longer, and therefore Black decides to force matters with a sequence aimed at exploiting White's relatively weak c-pawn.

20   bc   c5

21   ♗f1

White must protect the pawn indirectly as it would be too dangerous to allow Black to mobilize his queenside pawns by 21 d5?! ed 22 cd b5.

21   ...   ♗f7!

Activating the threat against the c-pawn which could not be taken immediately: 21 ... cd? 22 ed ℤxc4 23 ♘f4 with a double attack on c4

and e6.

22   ♘a4   cd

23   ed   b5

This time the pawn is taboo because of 23 ... ℤxc4? 24 ♘dc5±.

24   cb   ab

25   ♘ac5!

Preferring to offer a pawn rather than permit Black to stifle the game with a blockade on d5 after 25 ♘c3 b4 26 ♘b5 ♘d5 27 ♘e5 ♘7b6.

25   ...   b4!?

Black has it in mind to turn the tables with his own activity-gaining pawn sacrifice. Kasparov analyses 25 ... ♘xc5 26 dc ♗xc5 27 ♘xc5 ♛xc5 28 ♛xc5 ℤxc5 29 ℤe5! as giving at least sufficient compensation for the pawn.

26   ℤc1   ♛e7

Her majesty echoes the opening manoeuvre of her QB.

27   ♗h3   ♛d8!

Avoiding weakening f6 by 27 ... g6? which would be strongly met by 28 ♘xb4.

28   ♘xb4   ♛a5

29   ♘c6

Playing to keep the initiative at all costs. Hanging on to the pawn by 29 ♘xd7 ♘xd7 30 a3 would leave Black in little danger given his well coordinated and active pieces and White's structural weaknesses (obviously Black would not allow 30 ... ♗xb4? 31 ab ♛xb4 32 d5!±).

29	...	♛xa2
30	♘xd7	♘xd7
31	d5!	

Freeing the QB and preventing the blockading and consolidating ... ♛d5.

| 31 | ... | ♛xd5 |
| 32 | ♖ed1 | ♗c5 |

In time trouble, Petrosian has insufficient time to evaluate 32 ... ♖xc6 33 ♖xd5 ♖xc1+ 34 ♗xc1 ed 35 ♗b2 g6! which was probably better, and instead liquidates to a positionally slightly inferior ending, albeit one which should be tenable.

33	♖xd5	♗xf2+
34	♔xf2	ed
35	♗xf5	♘b6

There is no way to hold on to the exchange; 35 ... ♘e5? loses after 36 ♘e7+! ♖xe7 37 ♖xc8+ ♗e8 38 ♗a3.

| 36 | ♗xc8 | ♘xc8 |

The smoke has cleared leaving an indisputable advantage to White. Even so, it is quite astonishing that Petrosian does not manage to hold on to the draw in the final part of this well contested battle: 37 ♗a3 h6 38 ♖b1 ♖e6 39 ♘d4 ♖a6 40 ♗c5 ♘d6 (40 ... ♖a5!) 41 ♖b8+ ♔h7 42 g4 ♖a4! 43 ♔e3 ♘c4+ 44 ♔f4 g5+? (weakening everything; 44 ... ♘d6 45 ♖b6 ♖c4 46 ♖xd6 ♖xc5 47 ♖d7 ♔g8 48 h4 was much better, leaving White in evident control

but a long way from the win) 45 ♔g3 ♖a2 46 ♖b7 ♔g6? (missing the opportunity to counterattack with 46 ... ♘e3! 47 ♗d6! ♔g6 although 48 h4 would preserve White's chances) 47 ♘f5 ♖a6 48 h4! gh 49 ♘xh4+ ♔g7 50 ♘f5+ ♔g6 51 ♗d4 1-0. 51 ... ♘d6, the only way to try to save the bishop, loses to 52 ♘xd6 ♖xd6 53 f4.

The Classical 7 ♘c3
Botvinnik-Smyslov
World Ch. 1958
1 d4 f5 2 g3 ♘f6 3 ♗g2 e6 4 ♘f3 ♗e7 5 0-0 0-0 6 c4 d5

| 7 | ♘c3 | c6 (138) |

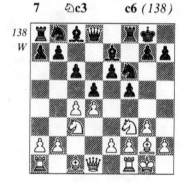

It is not surprising that the natural 7 ♘c3 is White's oldest and most explored continuation. Clearly, the knight is generally more active on c3 although it takes longer for it to be able to control e5, a manoeuvre which is usually accomplished via the route ♘c3-e2-f4-d3.

Whilst the broad strategic outlines naturally remain the same, there are a few opening wrinkles with which Black needs to be familiar in order to be sure of obtaining a playable game.

To conclude these introductory comments, it is interesting to note that the actual move order of the present game was 6 ... c6 7 ♘c3 d5 — to avoid Botvinnik's 7 b3, of course — thus providing the highest possible level of endorsement for the validity of 6 ... c6.

8   ♗g5

There is a vast array of alternatives which need to be mentioned, but the student may take comfort in the fact that the fundamentals underlying Black's response remain much the same in all cases:

(a) 8 ♘e5 ♘bd7 9 ♕b3 (not 9 ♘d3? dc 10 ♘f4 ♘b6 11 e4 e5! 12 de ♕xd1 13 ♖xd1 ♘g4∓) 9 ... ♘e4 10 cd ♘xe5 11 ♘xe4 cd 12 de fe 13 ♗e3 b6 with full equality; Filip–Szabo, Gothenburg IZ 1955.

(b) 8 ♕d3 ♘e4 9 ♘e5 ♘d7 10 ♘xd7 (supporting the knight by 10 f4?! leads to trouble: 10 ... ♘xe5 11 fe b6 12 e4 ♗a6 13 b3 ♘xc3 14 ♕xc3 b5∓ Black has stolen the initiative with his typical QB pressure along the a6–f1 diagonal; Nielsen–Husak, corr. 1960) 10 ... ♗xd7 (10 ... ♕xd7 intending a queenside fianchetto may well be better) 11 f3 ♘xc3 with

roughly even chances; Grünfeld–Tartakower, Teplitz-Schonau 1922.

(c) 8 ♗f4 ♕e8 (8 ... ♘e4 is perfectly playable) 9 ♕d3 (the c-pawn cannot constantly be left unprotected, e.g. 9 ♖b1 ♘bd7 10 b4? dc! 11 ♕c2 a6 12 a4 b5 13 ♘g5 ♘b6∓) 9 ... ♕h5 10 ♘e5 ♘bd7 11 f3 g5 12 ♘xd7 ♗xd7 13 ♗e5 (thus far Budo–Chistiakov, USSR 1950) 13 ... ♗e8 and the arrival of the bishop on g6 will prevent White lightly advancing in the centre, whilst the kingside counterplay ensures a mutually difficult game.

(d) 8 ♕b3 ♔h8 (a precautionary measure, but Black could well choose either 8 ... ♘e4 or 8 ... b6) 9 ♘e5 (9 ♗f4 is best met by 9 ... b6) 9 ... ♘bd7 10 ♘xd7 (or 10 cd ed 11 ♘xd7 ♘xd7!) 10 ... ♘xd7! 11 ♖d1 ♘b6 12 cd (12 c5?! ♘d7 would leave Black free to counter with ... e5 or ... b6) 12 ... ed 13 ♘a4 ♘c4 14 ♘c5 (thus far Capablanca–Botvinnik, Moscow 1936) and now Black should forgo the structurally weakening ... b6 in favour of 14 ... ♕b6 with a fine game.

(e) 8 ♖b1 (with the clear intention of a queenside pawn storm) 8 ... ♔h8 (perhaps the simplest way of meeting White's plan is 8 ... ♘e4 9 ♕c2 ♘d6!?, with the ideas 10 c5 ♘f7 preparing the ... e5 counterpunch immediately, and 10 cd ed when the knight on d6 is excellently placed, particularly with regard to the potential white square weaknesses on White's queenside) 9 cd (forfeits any hope of an opening advantage, but nor do the alternatives promise much: 9 c5 ♘e4 10 ♕c2 ♘d7 intending ... ♗f6 and ... e5=; 9 ♕c2 ♘e4 10 b4 ♘d7 11 c5 ♗f6= etc.) 9 ... cd! 10 ♗f4 ♘c6 11 ♘e5 (not 11 ♘b5 ♘h5∓) 11 ... ♗d7 12 ♖c1 ♖c8 (Black has a very easy game) 13 ♕d3 ♘h5 14 ♗d2 ♗d6 15 ♘xc6 ♗xc6 16 ♕f3 ♕e8! and although White's position is solid there is little for him to undertake whereas Black is free to operate on either flank; Keres–Botvinnik, Moscow 1948.

8   ...   ♘bd7
(139)

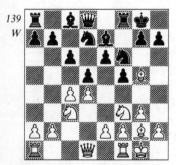

139
W

9   e3

White's intentions are clear: to exchange first QB for knight, thus reducing Black's attacking poten-

tial, and then central pawns (cd ed) in order to stabilize the position for a minority attack on the queenside (opening the c-file would be asking for trouble as Black is in no position to contest its control). This is a fundamentally sound plan which must be countered with a well judged blend of defence and aggression if Black is to obtain a playable game.

Other examples:

(a) 9 cd ed 10 ♖b1 (or 10 e3 when both 10 ... h6!? and 10 ... ♘e4 come into consideration) 10 ... a5! and Black's game is perfectly satisfactory.

(b) 9 ♕c2 ♘b6 (apart from the interesting text move, Black has the solid 9 ... ♘e4 and the challenging — risky! — 9 ... h6!?, e.g. 10 ♗xf6 ♘xf6 11 ♘e5 ♗d6!? 12 ♘g6 ♖f7 13 f3?! ♔h7 14 ♘e5 ♗xe5 15 de ♘d7 16 f4 ♕b6+ 17 ♔h1 ♘c5 with an obscure position) 10 c5 ♘bd7 11 b4 ♘e4 12 ♗xe7 ♕xe7 13 e3 e5 with approximately equal chances; Nei–Bronstein, USSR Ch. 1963.

(c) 9 ♕d3 ♘e4 (9 ... h6!?) 10 ♗xe7 ♕xe7 11 ♕e3! (the queen is well placed here after the exchange of bishops) 11 ... b6 (it could be that Black should seek an alternative here) 12 ♘xe4 fe 13 ♘d2 ♗a6 14 cd cd 15 f3 with a slight pull for White; Donner–Larsen, Leiden 1970.

9   ...   ♛e8

Botvinnik prefers 9 ... ♞e4. A game Eingorn–Abramovic, Bor 1986, saw yet another approach: 9 ... h6 10 ♗xf6 ♗xf6 11 cd ed 12 ♞e2 a5 13 ♞f4 ♛e8 14 ♛c2 g6 15 ♞d3 ♛e7 and although White enjoys some initiative Black may have confidence in his bishop pair and generally solid position.

10   ♛c2   ♚h8
11   ♞e2

The knight begins its journey to control e5 from d3. Of course, 11 cd ed 12 ♛xf5?? ♞e4 is not possible.

11   ...   h6
12   ♗xf6   ♗xf6
13   cd

Not obligatory, as the opening of the position after 13 ♞f4 dc 14 ♛xc4 e5 15 de ♞xe5 16 ♞xe5 ♗xe5 17 ♛b4! ♚h7 18 ♖ad1 would be to White's advantage thanks to his active pieces.

13   ...   ed
14   ♞f4   g5
15   ♞d3 *(140)*

The knight has arrived, and the battle lines for the coming middle-game are clearly drawn: White will operate in the centre and on the queen's flank while Black will seek attacking chances on the king's wing. Theoretical assess-ments of this (type of) position tend to give White a slight edge,

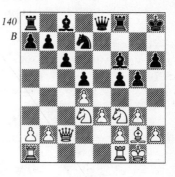

but even should this be true the further course of our model game shows that Black is always liable to pounce at the least slip: 15 ... ♖g8 16 ♛c3 ♗e7 17 ♞fe5 ♞f6 (Black's last two moves make one wonder about Black's twelfth) 18 f3 ♗e6 19 ♞c5 (19 b4, with a4 and b5 in mind, seems more promising) 19 ... ♗xc5 20 ♛xc5 (permitting a further simplification after which most of Black's problems are behind him and he can start to think about his counterattack; 20 dc± was better) 20 ... ♞d7 21 ♞xd7 ♛xd7 22 ♖ae1 ♖g7 23 ♖f2 b6 24 ♛c3 ♛d6 25 ♖c2 ♗d7 26 b4 (White begins to go wrong; there is no longer much to be achieved on the queenside and it would have been better to distract Black with play in the centre by 26 e4) 26 ... h5! (the attack finally begins!; this is in fact an excellent example of a late middlegame pawn storm, typically following a period of drawing the sting of

White's early initiative) 27 ♔h1 (again, 27 e4 was better) 27 ... h4 28 gh (28 f4 ♖h7!) 28 ... gh (28 ... ♖h7 29 e4 ♕f4 also came strongly into consideration) 29 f4 ♖ag8 30 ♗f3 ♗e8 31 ♕d2 ♕h6 32 ♕e2 h3 33 ♖cc1 ♖g2! 34 ♗xg2 ♖xg2 35 ♕f3 (the decisive mistake; 35 ♕f1 would probably have been sufficient to hang on, e.g. 35 ... ♗h5 36 ♖c3! ♗g4 — 37 e4 was threatened — 37 e4! fe 38 ♖ee3 ♗f3 39 ♖xf3 ef 40 ♖xf3 ♕h5 41 ♖xh3 ♕xh3 42 ♕xg2 ♕d3 with a very likely draw) 35 ... ♕h4! 36 b5 ♗h5 37 ♕xg2 (37 ♕f1 ♖f2) 37 ... hg+ 38 ♔g1 c5 0–1. A consistently executed and characteristic attack on the light squares.

Flohr–Botvinnik
Match 1933
1 d4 f5 2 g3 e6 3 ♗g2 ♘f6 4 ♘f3 ♗e7 5 0-0 0-0 6 c4 d5 7 ♘c3 c6

8   b3 *(141)*

With the knight already developed this move has little purpose beyond simply preparing to complete development by fianchettoing the QB. In his notes Botvinnik remarked, somewhat severely perhaps, that the move has a serious defect in that it weakens f4. As we shall see, however, that certainly turns out to be the case in this game.

8   ...   ♕e8
Black commences the traditional transference of the queen to the kingside, a procedure which lacks in subtlety compared to today's positional interpretations of the Stonewall. Nevertheless, when White fails to find the correct response this plan can be crushing as the present game is intended to show.

Nowadays, both of the following continuations are considered superior to the text move:

(a) 8 ... a5 (this position frequently arises through use of 6 ... c6) 9 ♗b2 ♘e4 10 e3 ♘d7 11 ♕c2 ♘d6 12 ♘e2 ♖e8 13 ♘f4 ♗f8 14 ♘d3 ♘f7 (a radically different approach to the old-fashioned kingside hacking!; Black has harmoniously protected his one weakness and retains the flexibility to operate over the entire board) 15 ♖fd1 b6 and with the imminent development of his QB Black can look forward to a rich middlegame with balanced chances; Ungureanu–Bellin, Moscow 1977.

(b) 8 ... ♘e4 9 ♗b2 ♘d7 10
♕c2 (10 ♘e1 ♗f6 11 f3 ♘xc3 12
♗xc3 dc! 13 bc e5! is excellent
for Black) 10 ... ♗f6 and in the
absence of practical examples
there is a theoretical consensus
that this position offers approximately equal chances.

9   ♗b2   ♘bd7
10   ♕d3

Botvinnik considers this to be
slightly less exact a placement for
the queen than c2. His suggestion
that White should aim to equalize
matters by playing 10 ♘g5 ♗d6
11 f4, however, tends to leave
Black with rather the better of it
after 11 ... ♘g4 12 ♕d2 ♘df6
13 h3 ♘h6 (Biryanis–Tal, USSR
1951) as his pieces are more effectively placed to take action on the
kingside.

10   ...   ♕h5

The queen takes up her com-
mand post from where she will
direct kingside operations. Note
also the f-pawn is protected so
that cd can be answered by ... ed.

11   cd

White wants to move his KN
but dare not do so immediately
because of the sequence (11 ♘d2
or ♘e1) ... e5! 12 cd e4. This
line strongly supports Botvinnik's
contention that the bishop is misplaced on b2, and that the queen
should be on c2.

11   ...   ed

The exchange of pawns in the
centre has helped Black by opening up the path of his QB.

12   ♘d2

White's position is already
beginning to look a little uncomfortable – he appears to be
doing nothing while Black is
gradually building up his attack.

12   ...   ♘e4
13   f3

The attempt to gum things up
by 13 f4 intending ♘d2–f3–e5
would come unstuck after 13 ...
♘xd2 14 ♕xd2 ♘f6, and whereas
the black knight is surveying e4
its white counterpart is very far
from being able to occupy e5.

13   ...   ♘xc3
14   ♗xc3   f4! *(142)*

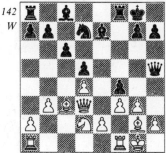

142
W

The 'Dutch' pawn itself delivers
a thematic attacking blow which
instantly puts White's king's position under severe pressure. Consider White's predicament: the
pawn cannot be captured because
the arrival of a black rook on the

h-file would be terminal, while advancing the g-pawn would create grave dark square weaknesses and invite ... h5. There remains only the passive holding operation chosen in the game.

15	♖fe1	♗d6
16	♘f1	♖f7!

This little move is of the utmost importance to the successful prosecution of Black's attack. It is born of the fact that the natural 16 ... ♘f6 is not good since White could reply with 17 ♗d2! attacking the f-pawn, and if 17 ... fg 18 hg and the bishop would cover important squares on the c1–h6 diagonal. Now if White marks time Black has the option of bringing his knight to the kingside via f8, all the time keeping control of f4.

| 17 | e3 | |

If 17 e4 then 17 ... de! 18 ♕xe4 (18 fe?? f3) 18 ... ♘f6 is very strong.

| 17 | ... | fg |

Now that White has weakened f3 and blocked the c1–h6 diagonal this exchange is the best continuation.

| 18 | ♘xg3 | |

After 18 hg Black would have the pleasant choice between 18 ... ♖xf3!, 18 ... ♕g5 and 18 ... ♘f6, all roads leading to Rome.

18	...	♕h4
19	♘f1	♘f6
20	♖e2	♗d7

21	♗e1	♕g5
22	♗g3	♗xg3
23	♘xg3	

Or 23 hg ♘h5 and White would have to advance with 24 g4, laying himself open to the can-opening ... h5 after the retreat of the knight, as 24 ♔h2 fails against 24 ... ♘xg3.

| 23 | ... | h5! |

The final phase of the attack commences; White is hard pressed to meet the threatened march of the h-pawn, winning a piece.

| 24 | f4 | ♕g4 |
| 25 | ♖f2 | |

This allows Black to administer a rapid and pleasing *coup de grâce*; 25 ♖f1 would have held out longer.

| 25 | ... | h4 |
| 26 | ♗f3 | |

26 h3 ♕e6 (not 26 ... ♕xg3 27 ♖f3) 27 ♘f1 ♘e4 is also hopeless for White.

| 26 | ... | hg |

Gaining a decisive material advantage.

| 27 | ♗xg4 | gf+ |
| 28 | ♔g2 | |

28 ♔xf2 ♘xg4+ would enable Black to attack and win the e-pawn.

28	...	♘xg4
29	h3	♘f6
30	♔xf2	♘e4+

0–1

31 ♔g2 ♗xh3+ and the

bishop is immune on account of the knight fork.

Smejkal–Larsen
Leningrad IZ 1973
1 d4 f5 2 g3 e6 3 &g2 &f6 4 &f3 &e7 5 0-0 0-0 6 c4 d5 7 &c3 c6

8   ♕c2 *(143)*

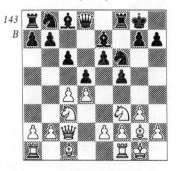

A natural and elastic follow-up to 7 &c3, placing the queen on its best square, from where it observes Black's f-pawn, thus preventing 8 ... &bd7 because of 9 cd cd 10 &f4 with a marked advantage.

8   ...   &e4!

8 ... ♕e8 must reckon with Chekhover's 9 &g5 after which Black can easily find himself in an inferior Botvinnik–Smyslov type of position (see above) if he tries to do better than the direct transposition by 9 ... &h8 10 e3 &bd7 etc.

The text move is natural and good.

9   &e5

A game Bolbochan–Najdorf,

Mar del Plata 1945, went 9 &e3 &bd7 10 ♖ad1 ♕e8 (10 ... &d6!?) 11 &e5, and now, as is often the case when the possibility exists, Black should have captured the knight on e5, with level chances.

9   ...   &d7
10   &xe4   fe

In his notes, Larsen gave 10 ... &xe5 11 &d2 &f7 12 &f3 b6 as an equality-securing variation deserving attention.

11   &f4   &f6

This looks right, but 11 ... &g5 might also be worth consideration.

12   ♖ad1

White would have done better to play 12 &xd7 ♕xd7 13 ♖ad1 ± according to Larsen, rather than permit an alteration of pawn structure which helps Black to equalize.

12   ...   &xe5
13   &xe5   &xe5
14   de   ♕e7
15   ♕c3   &d7
16   f3   ef
17   ef   ♕c5+
18   ♖d4?!

This self-pin and the active black queen are the source of White's later troubles, and therefore 18 ♕d4 was better, although the ending after 18 ... ♕xd4+ 19 ♖xd4 c5 20 ♖d2 d4 would be fine for Black.

18   ...   a5
19   f4   ♕a7
20   f5?!

This assault on Black's pawn centre turns out to be much too optimistic and only succeeds in weakening White's own e-pawn.

20 ...   ♖ae8!

Seeing through the incredible trap 20 ... c5 21 ♖xd5!! ed 22 ♗xd5+ ♔h8 23 e6 with f6 to follow.

21   cd

If White escapes the pin by 21 ♔h1, then 21 ... c5 becomes playable since 22 ♖xd5? now fails because of 22 ... ed 23 ♗xd5+ ♔h8 24 e6 ♗xe6! etc.

21	...	cd
22	♔h1	♖c8
23	♕d2	♖c2!

How White must have regretted his 18th move!

24	♕xc2	♕xd4
25	♕c3	♕xc3
26	bc	♖c8

The ending is very much in Black's favour due to the opponent's split queenside pawns.

27   ♖d1   ♖c5

Naturally, Black has no interest in 27 ... ♖xc3? 28 fe ♗xe6 29 ♗xd5 ♔f7 30 ♗xb7 ♗xa2 31 ♗d5+ with a drawn ending.

28	fe	♗xe6
29	♔g1	♔f7
30	♖d3	♖b5!
31	♖d2	a4
32	a3	

In time trouble White is understandably alarmed at the prospect of ... a3 and ... ♖b2, but his only chance was to rush the king to the centre by ♔f2–e3 when there would still be some slight hope of salvation. As it is, Larsen seizes the opportunity to obtain a passed a-pawn and makes no mistake in shepherding it home: 32 ... ♖b3 33 ♗xd5 ♖xa3 34 c4 ♖b3 35 ♔f2 a3 36 ♔e2 ♖b2 37 ♖xb2 ab 38 ♗e4 ♗xc4+ 39 ♔d2 ♗a2 0–1. An excellent example of the pawn structures arising after captures on both e5 and e4 and the technical type of game following multiple minor piece exchanges.

16 Stonewall with ... ♗d6

From the mid-eighties onwards there has been an explosion of interest in playing the Stonewall with ... ♗d6 instead of ... ♗e7. The advantages are obvious: the bishop is more actively placed on the b8–h2 diagonal, covering e5 and looking towards the white king, and the queen can usefully take up the vacated e7 square. The disadvantages are rather less apparent, especially since the logical attempt to profit from the exchange of black-squared bishops with ♗f4 (cf. Schlechter–John in Chapter 15) has been shown to be much less dangerous for Black than was once thought.

The starting position for the variation arises after the following moves:

1	d4	f5
2	g3	e6
3	♗g2	♘f6
4	♘f3	

With this particular move-order White may consider deferring ♘f3 in favour of c4 if he is particularly

concerned to avoid the ... ♗d6 variations. A recent example: 4 c4 d5 (Black has the option of playing the Dutch Indian instead) 5 ♘h3 ♗e7 (persevering with 5 ... ♗d6?! would enable White to exchange the black-squared bishops by 6 ♗f4 without incurring any structural weakness) 6 0-0 c6 7 ♕c2 0-0 8 ♘d2 ♗d7 9 ♘f3 ♘e4 10 ♘e5 ♗f6 11 b3 (thus far P. Nikolic–Short, Belgrade 1987) and now Nikolic gives 11 ... c5! 12 e3 ♘c6 as best, with an unclear position.

It is because of such possibilities that the ... ♗d6 variations frequently arise via transposition, with White already having committed himself to ♘f3.

4	...	d5
5	c4	c6
6	0-0	♗d6 *(144)*

As in the standard Stonewall, White has a large choice at this juncture. Apart from the moves covered in our featured games, the following also merit noting:

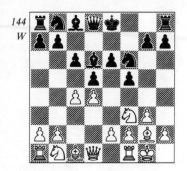

144
W

(a) 7 ♘c3 ♘bd7 8 ♕c2 ♘e4 9 ♖b1 (thus far Dubinin–Novotelnov, USSR 1948) 9 ... a5 with a typically rich middlegame in the offing with chances for both sides.

(b) 7 ♕c2 ♘e4 8 ♘e1?! (a misguided attempt to take advantage of the early advance of Black's knight; 8 ♘c3 ♘d7 would transpose above, and on 8 b3 Black could try 8 ... ♕f6 9 ♗b2 ♘bd7) 8 ... ♘d7 9 ♘d3 (9 f3?! ♘xg3! 10 hg ♗xg3 with 11 ... ♕h4 to follow would give Black a very dangerous attack — a good illustration of the advantages of having the bishop on d6!) 9 ... ♕f6! (forcing White to lock in his QB in order to protect the d-pawn) 10 e3 h5! (utilizing the fact that he has postponed castling; Black is now assured of a strong attack no matter how White responds) 11 f3 ♘xg3! 12 hg ♗xg3 13 ♘f2? (13 f4 ♕h4 14 ♖f3! ♕h2+ 15 ♔f1 h4 16 ♖xg3 was the best hope) 13 ... g5! with a fierce attack which

Black brought to an energetic and beautiful conclusion in Gofstein–Kupreichik, USSR 1979: 14 e4 de 15 fe g4 16 ef ♕h4 17 ♖e1 0-0 18 ♖xe6 ♘f6 19 ♖e2 ♘e8!! 20 f6! ♖xf6!! 21 ♖xe8+ ♔f7 22 ♖e2 ♗f5 23 ♕d2 ♖e8! 24 ♖xe8 ♕h2+! 25 ♔f1 ♗d3+! 0-1. An inspired game which provides much food for thought.

(c) 7 c5 is probably best met by 7 ... ♗e7 intending to challenge the advanced pawn with ... b6 and also ... a5 in case White supports it with b4.

Kotov–Bondarevsky
Moscow 1936

7   ♘bd2 *(145)*

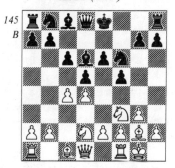

145
B

The main idea behind this move is to increase the control of e5 by transferring the QN to f3 after shifting the KN to d3 via e1.

7   ...   0-0

Of course, it is also possible to play 7 ... ♘bd7 8 ♕c2 ♘e4 before castling.

8 b3

Black had no problems whatever after 8 ♕c2 ♘bd7 9 cd cd 10 b3 ♕e7 11 ♗b2 b6 12 e3 ♗a6 13 ♖fc1 ♘e4 in Gheorghiu–Yusupov, Luzern 1985.

8 ... ♕e8

9 ♘e1

After the straightforward 9 ♗b2 Black should be careful about rushing to h5 with the queen: 9 ... ♘bd7 10 ♘e5 ♕h5 (10 ... ♘e4!) 11 e3 ♕h6 12 ♕e2 ♘e4 13 ♘xe4 fe 14 ♘g4 ♕g5 15 f3 and White succeeds in opening up the position before Black is quite ready; Fine–Bondarevsky, Moscow 1937.

9 ... ♘bd7

10 ♘d3 ♘e4

11 ♘f3 ♕h5

12 ♘f4

Gaining a tempo which must shortly be returned. Similarly, Black would answer 12 ♗f4 with 12 ... ♗e7 and then hit the enemy bishop with ... g5.

12 ... ♕f7

13 ♕c2 g5

14 ♘d3 ♕h5

15 ♘fe5 ♖f6

16 f3 ♖h6!

17 h4

Unhappy that he would be obliged to return the piece after 17 fe de White tries a remedy which turns out to be more dangerous than the disease.

17 ... ♘xg3

18 hg

White appears blissfully unaware that he is walking the edge of a precipice; 18 ♗xg5, keeping the approaches to the king closed as long as possible, was essential.

18 ... ♕h2+

19 ♔f2 ♖h4

20 ♖g1 ♖xd4

An uncommonly sprightly rook!

21 ♗b2 ♕h4!

22 ♗xd4 ♘e4+

23 ♔e3

After 23 ♔f1 ♗xe5 24 ♗xe5 ♘xe5 25 fe ♘g4 White is faced with mate and loss of his queen.

If White was still hoping to show that the black attack had been too extravagant he is soon disabused of that illusion. There now follows a stunningly beautiful mate in five.

23 ... f4+!

24 ♘xf4 ♕f2+

25 ♔d3 ♕xd4+!!

26 ♔xd4 ♗c5+

27 ♔d3 ♘xe5mate!

(146)

The final tableau seems the work of a magician.

Belyavsky–Bareev
USSR Ch. 1987
1 d4 f5 2 g3 e6 3 ♗g2 ♘f6 4 ♘f3 d5 5 c4 c6 6 0-0 ♗d6

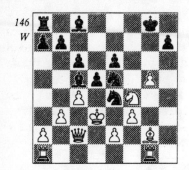

146
W

7   ♗f4   (147)

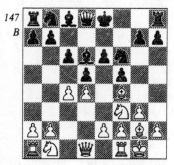

147
B

Clearly the most direct challenge to Black's set-up.

7   ...   0-0?!

An error, although it takes Belyavsky's copybook play to show exactly why.

Black's best continuation is 7 ... ♗xf4 8 gf 0-0 with good chances of equalizing, thanks to the damage inflicted on White's king's position, as the following examples show:

(a) 9 ♕c2 ♘bd7 10 e3 ♕e7 11 ♘bd2 ♘e4 12 a3 ♖f6 13 ♖fd1 ♖h6 14 ♘f1 ♘df6 15 ♘e5 ♗d7

16 f3 ♘d6 17 ♖d2?! ♘xc4 18 ♘xc4 dc 19 ♕xc4 ♘d5 and the powerful knight plus attacking chances assure Black the better game; Zamikhovsky–Panov, ½-final USSR Ch. 1952. This is a good illustration of how Black can proceed if White is slow in playing positively.

(b) 9 ♘e5 ♘bd7 10 e3 ♘xe5 11 fe ♘g4 12 ♘d2 ♗d7 13 h3 ♘h6 14 f4 ♗e8 15 ♔h2 ♔h8 16 ♕e2 g5 17 fg ♕xg5 18 ♕f2 ♗h5= Black's 'bad' bishop is every bit as good as White's; Belyavsky–Salov, match, Vilnius 1987.

(c) 9 ♘bd2 ♘bd7 (9 ... ♗d7 intending the transfer to h5 is possible) 10 ♖c1 ♘e4 11 e3 ♕e7 (11 ... ♘df6 12 ♘e5 ♗d7 13 f3 gave White an edge in Groszpeter–Smagin, Zenica 1987) 12 ♘xe4 de! 13 ♘d2 c5! 14 ♘b3 b6 15 dc (15 f3 is a better try) 15 ... ♘xc5 16 ♘xc5 bc 17 ♕a4 ♖b8! 18 b3 ♖b6! 19 ♕a3 e5∓ Black's QR is ready to switch to the king's flank; Kalinichev–Glek, USSR 1987.

8   ♗xd6   ♕xd6
9   ♕c2   b6

With this, Black's idea behind not exchanging on f4 becomes clear: he is trying to treat the position as a kind of Botvinnik Variation in the standard Stonewall, where the queenside fianchetto often procures equality for

Black after the exchange of black-squared bishops.

10 &a3!

Priming a possible foray to b5, an essential element in White's fight for an opening advantage. Black would have little difficulty after quieter methods, e.g. 10 &bd2 &b7 11 &acl &bd7 12 &fdl &ac8 13 &a4 &b8, and with ... c5 in the air the game is quite level.

10 ... &a6

Black sees the need to protect c7: 10 ... &b7 11 cd cd 12 &b5 &d7 13 &c7! &c8 14 &xd7 &bxd7 15 &d6 &c7 16 &fcl &c6 .17 &c2 and Black's position is very uncomfortable indeed.

11	&acl	&b7
12	cd	cd
13	&b5	&e7
14	&a4	

Note how useful it is for White not to have played b3 as in Botvinnik's variation.

14 ... &e8

Deciding to remove the powerful knight on b5 which is exerting troublesome pressure on the queenside, especially a7.

15	&c3	&ec7
16	&xc7	&xc7
17	h3!!	

A truly profound conception. Instead of doubling rooks and continuing with his play on the queen's wing White discerns the possibility of commencing action on the opposite flank, and the seed of this tiny pawn move is destined to grow into a flourishing attack.

17 ... &fc8

Interestingly, Black's best course lay in the reciprocal 17 ... a6 aiming to bring the knight to d6 via b5.

18 g4 g6

It is understandable that Black does not want to accept the structural weakness arising from 18 ... &e8 19 gf ef 20 &xc8 &xc8 21 &e5 &f6, but that might have been the lesser evil.

19	gf	gf
20	&e5	&e8
21	&g3+	&h8
22	&h2	&f6
23	&g1	&c7

Bringing extra protection to f7 in order to be able to play his next move and chase the enemy queen away. After 23 ... a6 White would transfer the queen to the kingside with gain of tempo: 24 &b3 b5 25 &e3, with a strong attack.

24	&f3	&c6

Not 24 ... &e4 25 &xe4 de 26 &xa7!

25	&b3	&g8
26	&h5!	

The final assault begins.

26	...	&f8

Forced.

27	&xg8+	&xg8

28   ♕g3

Her majesty arrives to lead the troops to victory.

28   ...   ♗b5

28 ... ♗e8 would lose to the prosaic 29 ♗xe8 ♕xe8 30 ♘g6+ winning the exchange.

29   ♕h4   ♘f6

There is nothing to be done, e.g. 29 ... ♖g7 30 ♖xg7 ♔xg7 31 ♕g5+, or 29 ... ♗e8 30 ♗xe8 ♕xe8 31 ♘g6+ ♔g7 32 ♘e7+.

30   ♗f7!

1-0

An elegant final blow: the knight is *en prise* and ♘g6+ forking king and queen is threatened; Black must therefore protect the knight with a queen move, but after 30 ... ♕e7 comes 31 ♕xf6+! ♕xf6 32 ♖g8 mate.

Belyavsky–Yusupov
USSR Ch. 1987
1 d4 f5 2 g3 e6 3 ♗g2 ♘f6 4 ♘f3 d5 5 c4 c6 6 0-0 ♗d6

7   b3 *(148)*

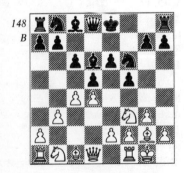

As with Botvinnik's variation in the standard Stonewall, this move aims to exchange the dark-squared bishops, whilst avoiding the structural weakening following 7 ♗f4 ♗xf4. It is currently the most popular continuation.

7   ...   ♕e7

The natural way of preventing ♗a3.

8   ♗b2

The best move at this juncture has yet to be determined. There are many candidates:

(a) 8 c5 ♗c7 9 ♗f4 ♗xf4 10 gf b6 (Polovodin suggests 10 ... ♘bd7 as a preliminary to playing for ... g5 by ... h6 and ... ♖g8) 11 ♕c2 bc 12 ♕xc5! ♕xc5 13 dc ♘a6 14 ♖c1 ♘e4 15 ♘e5 ♘exc5 16 ♘xc6 ♗d7 17 ♘e5 and White has some advantage due to his queenside pawn majority and potential occupation of the blockading squares e5 and d4; Polovodin–Glek, USSR 1986.

(b) 8 a4 (insisting on the exchange of bishops at the cost of slightly compromising the queenside pawns) 8 ... a5! 9 ♗a3 b6 10 ♘e5 ♗b7 11 ♗xd6 ♕xd6 12 ♘d2 0-0 13 cd cd 14 ♖c1 ♘bd7 with a completely satisfactory position for Black; Joksic–Klinger, Zurich 1987.

(c) 8 ♘e5 0-0 9 ♗b2 (9 ♘d3 b6 10 ♗b2 ♘bd7 11 ♘d2 a5 12 ♖c1 ♗b7= Flear–Short, Wijk aan

Zee 1987) 9 ... ♗d7! 10 ♕c1 ♗e8 11 ♗a3 ♘bd7 12 ♘d3 (12 ♘xd7 eases Black's task: 12 ... ♕xd7 13 ♘d2 ♗xa3 14 ♕xa3 ♗h5 15 ♖fe1 ♘e4 16 ♕b2 ♖ad8= F. Portisch–Knaak, Balatonbereny 1987) 12 ... ♗h5! 13 ♖e1 ♖ae8 and Black's forces are very compactly and harmoniously grouped (=); Dizdar–Knaak, Halle 1987.

(d) 8 ♘bd2 b6!? 9 ♘e5 ♗b7 10 ♗b2 0-0 11 ♖c1 a5! 12 e3 ♘a6 with a typically complex and balanced position; Petursson–Short, Reykjavik 1987.

(e) 8 ♘c3 0-0 9 ♗f4 ♗xf4 10 gf ♗d7! 11 ♘e5 ♗e8 12 ♕c2 ♘bd7 (12 ... ♘e4 is an excellent alternative) 13 cd ed 14 ♕xf5 ♘e4 15 ♕h3 ♘xc3 16 ♕xc3 ♖xf4 gives roughly equal chances.

(f) 8 ♗f4 ♗xf4 9 gf 0-0 10 ♘e5 ♗d7! 11 ♘d2 ♗e8 12 ♖c1 ♗h5 13 ♖c3 ♘bd7 14 ♗f3 ♗xf3 15 ♘xd7 ♕xd7 16 ♘xf3 ♘e4 and here, as is frequently the case in similar situations, Black has excellent prospects since his attacking possibilities against White's weakened kingside are far more important than White's absolute control of e5 and queenside play; Kouatly–Smagin, Trnava 1987.

8 ... 0-0

Two examples which indicate that the queenside fianchetto is a good alternative: 8 ... b6 9 ♕c1 0-0 (the alternative is to keep the king in the centre in readiness for an ending: 9 ... ♗b7 10 ♗a3 ♘bd7 11 ♗xd6 ♕xd6 12 ♕a3 ♕xa3 13 ♘xa3 ♔e7 14 ♖ac1 ♘e4 15 ♖fd1 ♖fc8 16 ♘e1 c5= Alburt–Short, Subotica 1987) 10 ♗a3 ♗b7 11 ♗xd6 ♕xd6 12 ♕a3 c5 13 dc bc 14 ♘c3 ♘bd7 15 ♖fd1? (15 e3) 15 ... f4! (the 'Dutch' pawn strikes!; now the white kingside finds itself under restraint, awaiting attack) 16 ♖ac1 a6 17 ♗h3? (a poor idea which exacerbates White's difficulties) 17 ... ♖ae8 18 ♖c2 h6 19 ♘a4 ♘e4 20 cd ed 21 ♗xd7? ♕xd7 22 ♘xc5 ♘xc5 23 ♖xc5 ♖xe2 24 ♘d4 fg! 25 fg (25 ♘xe2 gf+ mates) 25 ... ♕f7 0-1 H. Olafsson–S. Agdestein, Reykjavik 1987. After 26 ♘xe2 ♕f2+ 27 ♔h1 d4+ the 'bad' bishop comes good!

9 ♘c3

Alternatively:

(a) 9 ♕c2 ♗d7 10 ♘e5 ♗e8 11 ♘d2 ♘bd7 12 f4 (as a rule, Black is instantly OK after this) 12 ... ♗h5 13 cd?! cd 14 ♕d3 ♖ac8 15 ♖fc1?! ♗a3! and it is Black who takes charge of the open c-file (∓); Ree–Pieterse, Amsterdam Open 1986.

(b) 9 ♘bd2 b6!? (9 ... ♗d7 heading for h5 is perfectly playable here too) 10 ♘e5 ♗b7 11 e3 a5 12 a3?! (12 ♖c1=) 12 ... ♘bd7 13 a4 ♖ac8 14 ♕e2 ♗a6 15 ♖fc1 ♖fd8 16 ♕e1 (it was necessary to

seek to keep the balance by playing 16 f4) 16 ... ♗xe5! (an instructive capture; in the closed position
White's bishops are more of a
handicap than an advantage) 17
de ♘e4∓ Renet–Yusupov, Dubai
Ol. 1986.

9	...	♗d7
10	♘e5	♗e8
11	♘d3	

Criticized by Yusupov who prefers 11 e3.

11	...	♘bd7
12	e3	g5!

Yusupov is of the opinion that
Black now stands somewhat
better. It is true that Black's minor
pieces are more purposefully pos-
itioned.

13	a4	

With ideas of exchanging bishops by ♕c1 and ♗a3.

13	...	♗g6

13 ... ♗h5 14 ♕c1 ♘e4 would
be a good alternative, but Yusupov decides to provoke the centre-
deadening f4 first.

14	f4	

Naturally not 14 ♕c1? f4.

14	...	♗h5
15	♕c1	♘e4
16	fg	

It is remarkably difficult for
White to find a meaningful plan
and he therefore decides on this
capture in the hope of obtaining
f4 for the use of his knight.

16	...	♘xc3!

Very precise. 16 ... ♕xg5 17
♘xe4 followed by ♘f4 would
improve White's prospects.

17	♕xc3	♗e2
18	♖fe1	♗xd3
19	♕xd3	♕xg5

Black's clever series of
exchanges have left him in possession of the last remaining
knight, a real advantage in a closed
position where White's bishops
languish with nothing to do.
Black's bishop is also well posted
for supporting an attack on
White's king and so Belyavsky
decides to exchange that as well.

20	♗a3	♗xa3
21	♖xa3	♘f6
22	♕f1	h5!

Placing the threat of a future ...
h4 over White's head.

23	♕f4	

White judges that his best
chances of salvation are to be
found in the endgame.

23	...	♕xf4
24	gf	

24 ef would make Black's e-
pawn backward and vulnerable
but also weaken the white d-pawn
and leave Black the break with ...
h4.

24	...	♔f7
25	♖a2	♖g8
26	♔h1	

According to Yusupov, 26 a5
should have been played.

26	...	♖g7
27	♗f3	♖ag8
28	♖g2	♖xg2
29	♗xg2	a5

With the fixing of White's queenside pawns and the fact that e3 needs to be guarded there is nothing left for the first player to do but sit and wait.

30 ♔g1

Avoiding 30 ♗f3?! h4 31 ♖g1? ♖xg1+ 32 ♔xg1 ♘g4 winning the e-pawn because the ending after 33 ♗xg4 would be completely lost.

30	...	h4
31	♔f1	♘g4
32	h3	♘f6
33	♔f2	♖g3

The rook gratefully takes up residence on the weakness created by the knight. Black has made real progress, but he is still a long way from winning.

34 c5

34 ♖b1 aiming for b4 at a suitable moment was probably the best chance.

| 34 | ... | ♘e4+! |
| 35 | ♗xe4 | fe (149) |

A fascinating rook ending has begun where Black displays great mastery in extracting the full point from his positional advantage: 36

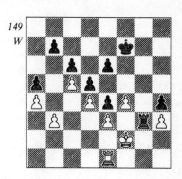

149
W

♖h1 ♔e8 37 ♖g1 (seizing the opportunity to activate his rook; if White remains passive then the king will go to the queen's wing and prepare ... b6) 37 ... ♖xh3 38 ♖g7 ♖h2+ 39 ♔f1 (not 39 ♖g2 ♖h1 40 ♖g1 ♖xg1 41 ♔xg1 b6! 42 cb ♔d7 followed by ... c5 decisively creating a second passed pawn) 39 ... ♖h3 40 ♔f2 ♖h2+ 41 ♔f1 ♖b2 (after a repetition in time trouble Black once more picks up the thread) 42 ♖xb7 ♔d8! 43 ♔g1 ♖e2 44 b4 ab 45 a5 ♖xe3 46 a6 ♔c8 47 ♖xb4 ♖a3 48 ♖b6 e3! 49 ♖xc6+ ♔d7 50 ♖d6+ ♔e7 51 f5 ef 52 ♖xd5 ♖xa6! 53 c6 (after 53 ♖xf5 ♖g6+ 54 ♔f1 ♖f6! the split pawns win the king and pawn ending) 53 ... ♖xc6 54 ♖xf5 ♖g6+ 0–1. Black magic!